REA

ACPL ITEM
DISCARDED

YO-ABZ-057

DO NOT REMOVE
CARDS FROM POCKET

Thanks, Mr. President

Thanks, Mr. President

The Trail-Blazing Second Term of George Washington

North Callahan

Cornwall Books
New York • London • Toronto

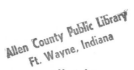
© 1991 by North Callahan

Cornwall Books
440 Forsgate Drive
Cranbury, NJ 08512

Cornwall Books
25 Sicilian Avenue
London WC1A 2QH, England

Cornwall Books
P.O. Box 39, Clarkson Pstl. Stn.
Mississauga, Ontario,
L5J 3X9 Canada

The paper used in this publication meets the requirements of the American National Standard for Permanence of Paper for Printed Library Materials Z39.48-1984.

Library of Congress Cataloging-in-Publication Data

Callahan, North.
  Thanks, Mr. President : the trail-blazing second term of George Washington / North Callahan.
    p.   cm.
  Includes bibliographical references and index.
  ISBN 0-8453-4835-3 (alk. paper)
  1. Washington, George, 1732–1799.   2. United States—Politics and government—1789–1797.   I. Title.   II. Title: Thanks, Mister President.
E312.C35   1991
973.4'3'092—dc20
[B]
                                                      90-84706
                                                      CIP

PRINTED IN THE UNITED STATES OF AMERICA

To Dr. Joseph A. Jackson

Contents

President George Washington. Lansdowne Portrait by Gilbert Stuart, by courtesy of the Pennsylvania Academy of Fine Arts, the bequest of William Bingham.

Introduction

The bicentennial of the establishment of the American presidency in 1989 is an appropriate occasion for reconsidering this remarkable institution created by the Framers of the Constitution. Feared by Antifederalists as the harbinger of an American monarchy and hailed by Federalists as the linchpin of the new system of government created at Philadelphia in 1787, the presidency assumed its basic character during the two administrations of George Washington. The office was described in the Constitution in only the barest terms: "The executive power shall be vested in a President . . .," but just what that office meant, in fact, had to evolve from the practices of those who occupied it.

George Washington never formulated a systematic theory of presidential administration. It was not his style to theorize. As he remarked in 1797, "With me, it has always been a maxim rather to let my designs appear from my works than by my expressions." His presidency illustrated this maxim perfectly. During his two terms as chief executive, Washington gave the office the "energy" contemplated by the Framers without exacerbating popular fears of concentration of power. More, Washington's actions produced precedents which have impressed themselves upon the office almost permanently. Recognizing the importance of his actions, he sought to establish those precedents "on true principles." Some of these precedents were set during Washington's first administration: the simple title accorded the chief executive—"Mr. President"; the use of the principal executive officers as a "Cabinet"; the practice of seeking the Senate's "advice and consent" in treaty-making, an effort that turned out differently from the way Washington envisioned it. But more vital were precedents set in the second administration, and these are the focus of the book which North Callahan has written.

Dr. Callahan is well equipped to write about George Washington. He has already produced a very readable account of Washington's Revolutionary War career; he has written biographies of two of Washington's contemporaries, one of whom, Henry Knox, served as an indispensable member of Washington's

Thomas Jefferson.

Alexander Hamilton.

Henry Knox.

Edmund Randolph.

President Washington's first (and our greatest) cabinet. The above four portraits are used with the kind permission of the Print Collection, Miriam and Ira Wallach Division of Art, Prints, and Photographs, The New York Public Library, Astor, Lenox, and Tilden Foundations.

Cabinet; he is the author of numerous other works covering the early years of our history. Dr. Callahan is an unabashed admirer of George Washington, and in the present volume he finds ample support for his approbation. Apart from Washington's virtues as an administrative leader, Dr. Callahan finds much in the first President's personal life to commend: his high sense of morals, his basic religiosity, his devotion to his wife and family, his concern for his friends. But, more substantively, Dr. Callahan reveals how important Washington's official actions were in shaping the nature of the presidency.

While domestic affairs occupied most of Washington's attention during his first administration, foreign affairs dominated much of the activity of his second term. Here Washington showed a capacity for both coolness and sagacity, maintaining the country's neutrality in the Anglo-French war arising from the French Revolution; handling the impetuous and imperious minister from France, Edmund Genet, correctly and impartially; procuring peace with England and Spain through the Jay and Pinckney Treaties; and establishing a precedential three-mile limit to the nation's off-shore sovereignty. On the domestic side, Washington's energy in suppressing the Whiskey rebels affirmed the Framers' hope that the presidency would be an office of power as well as of prestige. Washington may have overdone this exhibition of presidential authority, but he was determined that "neither the Military nor the Civil government shall be trampled upon with impunity." At the same time, however, Washington exhibited his skill as a conciliationist, keeping both Hamilton and Jefferson in his Cabinet, maintaining harmony among his advisers, and securing the collective advice of his executive officers much as he had done by his councils of war during the Revolution.

Washington sought to be a President above parties during his second administration, but the bitter political divisions that developed in the wake of the Jay Treaty made this a forlorn hope. Washington and his supporters were astonished by the vitriolic attacks levelled against him by political enemies in the highly partisan press of the 1790s. Nevertheless, Washington continued throughout his second administration to act the part that a later chief executive, Franklin D. Roosevelt, insisted was the ultimate role the most successful holders of that office should play: to make the presidency "preeminently a place of moral leadership." It is this quality that Dr. Callahan illuminates so markedly in his well-researched and informative account of Washington's second administration. No one reading this narrative can fail to be impressed with the ideals of integrity, competence, and impartiality which Washington imparted to the new office of the presidency, an experiment conceived by the Framers with anxiety but optimism. It is fortunate that this first holder of that office was a man of such character and ability. He well merits the attention that so many historians have accorded him and that North Callahan devotes to him in the present volume.

MILTON M. KLEIN

University of Tennessee, Knoxville

Preface

Writing a new book about George Washington may seem like building an unnecessary extension to the Washington Monument or the proverbial carrying of coals to Newcastle. On the other hand, a subject as momentous and far-reaching as our founding President and his lasting influence has ample potentiality for endless development. Especially is this true in the last decade of the twentieth century when the bicentennial of our Executive Branch of Government is being observed.

According to Samuel Eliot Morison, "Washington's services in time of peace have never been adequately appreciated." This inadequacy can be particularly applied to his second administration when he set so many vital precedents for executive prerogative, the relations of the President with Congress, foreign relations and personal conduct in the leadership of our nation. "Few people who are not philisophical spectators," Washington said, "can realize the difficult and delicate part which a man in my situation had to act. I walk on untrodden ground. There is scarcely any part of my conduct which may not hereafter be drawn into precedent."

My book is an effort for the *general reader* to bring into focus a new viewpoint on the significant events of 1793–97 when President Washington was at the epogee of his high office and thus made an indelible imprint on American history. True, he received set-backs and in the crucial period was vilified and depressed by his political enemies. His magnanimous character, however, always shone through and surmounted the political storms until even his critics had to admit that here was a man who towered above mundane conflicts and solidified his image of being "First in Peace." Herein I also answer some of the pusillanimous trash recently published in rapacious attempts to smear Washington—and in so doing, I have researched and presented in what is believed to be extraordinary depth, his devoutly religious side.

As for source material on Washington, it is of course, mountainous. In the New York Public Library, for example, an examination of the voluminous Dictionary Catalog, revealed that 167 pages, 11x14 inches in size, and containing an average of 21 titles on each page are devoted to books about George Washington. Where then does the researcher stop in his interminable quest? The answer has to be, as any successful historian knows, to contain the search to the specific interest and include as much as feasible of general, appropriate background. In my case, I have had the accrued advantage of the research for my previous books on Washington, Henry Knox, Daniel Morgan, and the Tories of the American Revolution, plus the teaching of early American History for many years. This does not mean that I was fully equipped to write authoritatively about the second term of Washington as President. But it has given me valuable background in addition to the original material which was included in my previous volumes. Footnotes in this book indicate more fully.

The foregoing does not embody the current research in the Washington, Hamilton, Jefferson, Knox, and Randolph Papers, some of which has been utilized here. Every original stone unturned gives at least a slightly new aspect to one's subject. Historian Robert Partin has stated that such new discoveries contribute to "the changing image of George Washington from Weems to Freeman." But, as I endeavor to establish, while the outward features of this eminent American may appear different to some well-meaning but skeptical individuals, the solid granite character of George Washington remains the same. Samuel Flagg Bemis of Yale put it neatly: "Detractors may try to tear him down but he still stands like Pike's Peak, towering above the lower mountains."

The first term of President Washington was an experiment, an exploration. He had no helpful precedents to guide him in setting up the new Federal Government. "As President, every step he took was without precedent." The English system held some examples worthy to be followed—but Washington had led the American rebellion *against* that country! He could have become a monarch or an executive for life, but that would be going in the same old-world direction. The raging French Revolution at first beguiled many Americans into believing it to be a democratic path to follow. Washington, although grateful to France for its help in winning our own Revolution, was more cautious, then justifiably condemnatory of its bloody violence. So what did the President rely on? The new U.S. Constitution and its added Bill of Rights.

Washington appointed the first cabinet with care and the results showed it. The imposing array of Alexander Hamilton, Thomas Jefferson, Henry Knox and Edmund Randolph proved to be, in my estimation, the greatest Presidential cabinet in the history of our country. Like his general staff in the Continental Army, this coterie of able men advised the Chief Executive in the early vital issues of the government, and after they left office, early in the second term of Washington, the importance and vitality of the cabinet diminished. This led to some of Washington's biggest problems.

In the first term, the driving force of Hamilton was felt in the establishment of the Bank of the United States which Jefferson opposed as unconstitutional. But the Secretary of the Treasury was undaunted and pushed through Congress Federal assumption of state's debts by a Northern-Southern compromise on the location of the nation's capital in its present site. Also passed was the Presidential Succession Act, which Washington favored and adhered to. Secretary Henry Knox instigated the Militia Act which enabled the President to call out state troops in emergencies. Jefferson continued to oppose Hamilton on matters relating to the national government versus states rights, industry opposed to agrarianism and Federalism as contrasted to the rising Republican (now Democratic) faction, Hamilton of course being the conservative. This schism was to cause Washington great concern and later led to the formation of our two political parties.

My book is concentrated on the second administration of George Washington because that is when the most vital aspects of the new Federal government came to fruition. That was when the character and leadership of Washington were mainly tested; and that was when he was impelled to set precedents which underpin our national government and sustain its progression.

Just a month after Washington took his second oath of office he was confronted with one of the most dificult diplomatic problems ever to confront our Chief Executive. On April 8, 1793, Edmund Charles Genet, Minister of the French Republic landed in Charleston, South Carolina and caused as much furor of its kind as a military invasion. Gilbert Chinard has said, "The full story of Genet and Washington has never been told." How much my chapter on Genet has added in this respect it is hard to say; but new research into his papers and those of Washington, as much as this space allows, does, I believe, increase the general impression of the Frenchman's image, particularly the later phase of his personal life in America after he married the comely daughter of Governor George Clinton of New York.

Citizen Genet, as he was called, was a handsome, dashing young man who was determined to make a big splash in this new world—and he did. He was under instructions from the Girondist regime to win U.S. amity and negotiate a new treaty of commerce. But he did not stop at this. Even before he presented his credentials, Genet commissioned four war vessels and sent them to prey on British ships along our coast. He also organized expeditions on American soil against the Spanish and British territories. En route to the nation's capital in Philadelphia, the young Frenchman was warmly received by many who favored the cause of France. This reception was cooled, however, when Genet was received by President Washington who informed him that his military and naval actions infringed on U.S. sovereignty. Instead of heeding this warning, Genet continued to try such subversive activities. Even Jefferson who had favored him turned against Genet and Washington demanded his recall. By now the Jacobins had succeeded the Girondists in France, and Genet's successor requested that the former be sent back there, probably to be guillotined. Washington mercifully refused and Genet remained here, courted and won Cornelia Clinton and for years, they lived happily on her estates along the Hudson River, a romantic episode well worth recounting.

In the summer of 1793, there occurred what has been called, "the most appalling collective disaster that has ever overtaken an American city." It was the yellow fever epidemic in Philadelphia and at the time, little was known about its treatment and cure. In this damp, low-lying community of 55,000 with no water system and one sewer, the plague struck like one of the calamities of old. Characteristics were high fever, nausea, yellow skin and death. It spread until almost every family in the nation's capital was afflicted. Thousands died and many bodies were piled in the street awaiting burial. The doctors did not know then how to treat the malady; that it was caused by a female mosquito. A hero of sorts was Dr. Benjamin Rush who though he did not correctly treat the disease, strove mightily to combat its ravage until he was ill and exhausted himself. Other doctors disagreed with Rush but all courageously banded together and did their best—which was not enough. Pertinent to this study is the fact that our highest national government officials were in the city and exposed to the plague. Washington left at the behest of his wife and went to Mount Vernon. Jefferson fled early but Alexander and Mrs. Hamilton came down with the fever and he almost died. Henry Knox was the last of the cabinet to leave, Washington having asked him to act as caretaker, so for a time, Knox was acting President. A considerable amount has been written about this horrible epidemic. My research and writing on Knox has provided some new aspects of the event.

The Neutrality Act of 1794 which forbade U.S. citizens to enlist in the service of a foreign power and armed vessels from fitting out in our ports somewhat eased the tension between this country and Britain for the time. Then came the Whiskey Rebellion as a result of protests by Western Pennsylvania farmers against Hamilton's excise tax which impaired their sale of corn liquor that was easier transported across the mountains than the heavy corn itself. Led by some radical figures, the farmers rejected the tax and threatened a rebellion. Some of the tax collectors were harassed, attacked and tarred and feathered, their houses burned. Hamilton was so alarmed that he persuaded Washington to call out the militia from four states to suppress the uprising. Such action was opposed by the Jeffersonian Democratic Societies, but the President, under the Militia Act, felt empowered to launch the expedition. He led it himself, seconded vigorously by Hamilton who always wanted to be a general. The Whiskey Rebels soon capitulated and the 12,000-man army was taken over by General Daniel Morgan whose biography I have written and thereby have included some fresh details about this colorful insurrection.

A continuing source of American grievance against England was the British refusal to evacuate the Northwestern military posts. That government gave as reasons unpaid pre-Revolutionary debts owed British merchants and Tory property confiscated by the states. English Orders in Council resulted in the seizure of American ships and the impressment of American seamen. The two nations were close to war. In order to avert this, Washington sent Chief Justice John Jay to London as a special envoy to negotiate the main differences. After several months and mounting suspense, Jay's Treaty was brought to Philadelphia and was a disappointment. About the only concession it made was agreement to remove British troops from the Northwest by 1796. Nonetheless, President Washington breathed a sigh of relief—for at least, war had been prevented. Congress was not in session at the time, so he decided to keep the terms secret until the treaty could be submitted to the Senate. When the contents became known, Jefferson and his followers howled in protest that this was too much of a concession to England. The Federalists mainly supported the agreement, and the controversy became so vehement that it culminated in the most serious political crisis in Washington's administration. Opposition newspapers screamed in criticism and even personal abuse of the President and his advisers, until he described the outcry as "like that of a mad dog." This discord brought Washington unwillingly into the center of American politics and party strife. Jay's Treaty was barely approved by the Senate and when it reached the House for the needed appropriations, the Antifederalists tried to nullify it by withholding the money. The President was asked by the House to forward all papers relating to the treaty for its consideration. He refused and thus set another precedent. After a great debate, the treaty was finally approved. My volumes on the Tories of the American Revolution are a helpful source for additional aspects of this important episode in which our two political parties materialized.

In the 1920s, W. E. Woodward and Rupert Hughes wrote books attempting to "debunk" George Washington. But their bilious mouthings were dashed against the eminence of his character like waves against the Rock of Gibraltar. The same pusillanimous efforts have been tried in more recent times—hopefully, with the same disastrous results to their perpetrators. For as *The New York Times* has commented, "By the standards of the present no less than his own age, Washington's greatness cannot be debunked."

Even so, such attempts continue. As recently as the spring of 1990, a syndicated columnist wrote that the young Washington proposed to eleven "aristocratic ladies who turned him down." After I challenged his absurd statement and asked for his source, the columnist admitted it was copied from a small Mid-Western newspaper, and retracted the statement in the many dailies using his column.

President George Washington had posterity in mind when he wrote his Farewell Address, a lasting legacy of a yet unequalled implementation of our Constitution. After decades of research and writing on the subject, Douglas Southall Freeman concluded: "The more I study George Washington, the more I am convinced that the great reputation he enjoyed with his contemporaries and with men of the next generation, was entirely justified."

During the numerous years of my own work on the life of this great man and his associates, in myriad sources from crumbling manuscripts to printed pages, I have been fortunate in having invaluable assistance. A great many institutions and individuals I would like to mention. I shall name only a few in connection with this book: Thomas Yoseloff, president of Cornwall Books; Dr. Joseph Jackson, Ray Hall and William Prince of the Lupton Library, University of Tennessee at Chattanooga; James H, Hutson, Chief, Manuscript Division, Library of Congress; Dorothy Twohig, The Papers of George Washington, University of Virginia; Eugene F. Sheridan, The Papers of Thomas Jefferson; Bernard R. Crystal, Columbia University Library; John P. Riley, Mount Vernon Ladies Association; Dr. Milton M. Klein, University of Tennessee Historian; Elizabeth Evans and James E. Lewis, Jr., researchers; and especially my wife, Helen, for her editorial assistance and patience.

Thanks, Mr. President

1

A Grim Awakening

It was with mixed feelings that President George Washington faced the day of 4 March 1793. This was to be his second inauguration as President of the still-small United States and he was torn between cherished memories of the past and now some forebodings for the future. So far, he had found the office of Chief Executive reasonably manageable, more so than he had imagined when reluctantly first taking the office after tearing himself away from his beloved Mount Vernon.

Three years in this damp and bustling Philadelphia, the nation's largest city and once the second largest in the British Empire, had been hard but satisfying to his soul. His memories of the city during the Revolution were clothed in military uniform. Dreary Valley Forge and the American loss at suburban Germantown were somewhat balanced by his leadership of the Continental Army through the streets en route to ultimate victory at Yorktown. Now the nation's capital, Philadelphia, marked a long step southward from where it had been for a year in New York; until within a few years, under Washington's leadership, the dome of the new country's apex was to rise in a city which was to be named after him, whom historian James Bryce was to call "the purest character in American history."

What strengthened Washington most was the tribute that had been paid him by his people. This had made his leadership easier than in the tormenting days of the difficult war when at times he almost gave up. Here too in this place which had been somewhat misnamed "the City of Brotherly Love," he had presided in a hot summer over the Constitutional Convention, albeit silently. Now his almost equally silent collaborator in that great enterprise, Benjamin Franklin, had been gone for three years—and was indeed missed. Still, Washington had tested the waters and found them navigable. Fresh in his memory was that triumphant journey from Mount Vernon to New York for his first inauguration where in the heart of Alexander Hamilton's Wall Street, he had received a tumultous outpouring of popular affection. He had at last "captured" New York City—something he intensely wanted during the war but was unable to do. At least, he had personally maintained a dignified military manner—to the chagrin of some of his less elite followers. Washington had also set the important precedents of establishing a cabinet—he always called general-staff meetings for important decisions during the war, so this was simply following suit. It worked well until Hamilton and Thomas Jefferson clashed. Also, the President set the precedent of only two terms in office, and that has been followed ever since with the exception of the perpetuating Franklin D. Roosevelt during the extenuating circumstances of World War II.

George Washington was well conscious he was setting precedents. He had written to James Madison, "As the first of everything, *in our situation will serve to establish a precedent,* it is devoutly wished on my part, that these precedents may be fixed on true principles."[1]

Propitious too was the celebration of Washington's sixty-first birthday, just ten days before his second inauguration. He certainly felt joy when cannon shots and ringing bells greeted the dawn of this day. In typical acknowledgement, he stepped to the window and graciously returned the military salute, a gesture which alarmed some who had felt he might establish a monarchy. But his conscience was clear on this score, for long before, at the end of the Revolution, he had angrily turned down such a suggestion and harshly criticized those who had put forth the idea of his becoming king. Now, across the land, gala balls were held, the diplomatic corps turned out in their best dress and the local socialites held what was perhaps their grandest ball, with the President and his stout little wife by his side.

Outside, an Englishman visiting Philadelphia, was said to have expressed a wish to see President Washington. As they were talking, the American who was asked, looked across the street and exclaimed,

"There he goes now!"
"That is General Washington?" the Englishman asked.
"Yes, it certainly is."
"Then where is his bodyguard?" asked the visitor.
"Here" replied the American, striking his own breast.[2]

It was good that there were cheer and celebration in these preliminaries; for sobering events were soon to come to the Chief Executive which would make him long for such diverting relief.

At this juncture, Washington was more in tune with the mood and condition of the common people than he had been at the premier inauguration in New York where strict formality was fastidiously observed until some thought him pompous. Now he asked his cabinet their opinions on how far he should go in public ceremonials. Jefferson felt there should be a modicum of formality and he expected Hamilton to recommend a great fanfare. But that canny individual, probably suspecting Jefferson's attitude, instead filed a written opinion stating that he thought Washington should take the oath at his own home and only in the presence of the department heads. On the other hand, the amiable Henry Knox and the Attorney General Edmund Randolph hit the ceiling in protest. Knox, as ever the adoring disciple, wanted his chief to be in the limelight and as conspicuous as his high position deserved. The Secretary of War also looked unashamedly on Washington as the shining symbol of the new nation's progress thus far. The result of the impasse was a compromise. It was decided that the swearing-in was to be held in the small Senate chamber, it of course being quite unlike that of today since at this time, there were only fifteen states with two Senators each.

President Washington acquiesced in the arrangements. He chose to ride alone in his coach from his residence to the Senate chamber. The weather on that 4 March was fair enough for the streets to be lined with people. For George Washington to walk, as a few others have since done, was uncharacteristic; it is quite possible that safety was also considered, in view of the known hostility of some of the radicals present. Doubtless he took advantage of this solitary moment to reflect upon the gravity of what he had reluctantly agreed to undertake for "the second time around" and then only at the desperate urgings of Hamilton, Jefferson, Knox, and other associates. On the other hand, he was buoyed for the time at least by the friendly cries of adulation of the crowds which lined the cobbled streets. Arriving at the Senate room, Washington stepped down from his carriage into a welcoming crowd and could not help but notice the large "assemblage of ladies" present, something which always cheered him greatly.[3]

Ushers with white wands made way for the President as he

ascended the steps in his stately manner. Inside, he found an elegantly furnished chamber. This setting was new to him because he had hardly addressed the Senate personally since that regrettable time in 1789 when in following the "advice and consent" provision of the Constitution, he appeared before the Senate to advise him on an appropriate negotiation strategy regarding a border dispute between the Southern Indians. Accompanying the President was Secretary of War Henry Knox. Would the Senate, Washington asked, give him its "advice and consent" to a series of eleven questions? At this moment, a Senator arose and asked that because of the noise of passing carriages, the questions be read again. Then, Senator William Maclay of Pennsylvania, the "self-appointed guardian of grassroots republicanism" began a series of motions with the purpose of delaying the proceedings and insisting on a full written disclosure of the President's plans. At this, Washington became angry and responded that such would "defeat every purpose of my coming here." After a second session the Senate finally agreed but the President realized that his idea of a King-and-Council procedure would not work. Many scholars of the Constitution regard this event as an important precedent in establishing the separation of powers. For since that time, no President has formally asked for the collective advice of the Senate before the fact. Nor has any President similarly appeared before the Senate for a personal exchange of ideas, although of course the Chief Executive confers in other ways with the upper chamber and must obtain its consent in certain matters such as treaties and vital appointments.[4]

So this was not the former's favorite place.

The President took his chair, the one usually occupied by Vice President John Adams, President of the Senate, who now was seated on the right. On the left was Justice William Cushing who was to administer the oath of office. (This was a precedent, the first time a U.S. Supreme Court Justice administered the Presidential oath, the initial one being administered in New York by Robert R. Livingston, chancellor of the state of New York.) It was not a secret ceremony. The doors of the chamber were wide open and every space inside and outside near the entrance was filled with state and municipal officers, foreign diplomats and others of prominent nature.[5]

There was a brief pause. The crowd became silent. Then Vice President Adams arose and announced that a Supreme Court judge would administer the oath. President Washington stood erect in a military manner and read his short simple address:

> Fellow Citizens: I am again called upon by the voice of my country to execute the functions of its Chief Magistrate. When the occasion proper for it shall arrive, I shall endeavor to express the high sense I entertain of this distinguished honor, and of the confidence which has been reposed in me by the people of the United States.

> Previous to the execution of any official act of the President, the Constitution requires an oath of office. The oath I am now about to take and in your presence, that if it shall be found during my administration of the government I have in any instance violated willingly or knowingly the injunction thereof, I may (besides incurring Constitutional punishment) be subject to the upbraidings of all those who are now witnesses of the present solemn ceremony.[6]

Speaking at a normal pace, this address is about one minute long, perhaps the shortest such one in our Presidential history. This is half the time it required for Abraham Lincoln to deliver his Gettysburg Address, though of course the comparison is otherwise fanciful. Certainly the two are rare examples of intelligent brevity.

The simple ceremony ordinarily would have been a routine matter except that this was our first President and a first succession in office. That was the way Washington wanted it and his brief participation set the stage for those who followed although later chief executives were to elaborate on the occasion more. As Washington left the scene, the spectators were at first quiet then burst into a cheering chorus.

The festive quality of the inauguration held something of the proverbial calm before the storm, however. As Washington Irving who was ten years old at the time observed some sixty years later, "It was under gloomy auspices, a divided cabinet, an increasing exasperation of parties, a suspicion of monarchical tendencies and a threatened abatement of popularity that Washington entered upon his second term of presidency. It was also a portentous period in the history of the world."[7]

The dire description was all too true. On 17 March 1793, word came to the President that King Louis XVI had been guillotined. Less than two weeks into his second term, Washington was thus thrust into the world crisis which followed. The decisions he was now called on to make were to be the most important concerning foreign relations in his entire time in office. For the French Revolution and its consequences affected world affairs that included America, even until this day.

Our part went back to 1778 and beyond, when the struggling United States had called upon France to help Washington's army defeat the British. Louis XVI and his ministers were glad to comply, mainly because they regarded England as a deadly enemy. This was a chance to avenge the defeat of the French in the Seven Years War of 1756–63. Washington had looked upon the King of France as a friend. Now the former was so shocked and disturbed in his reaction that he could not write down anything about it. Instead, he authorized Secretary of State Thomas Jefferson to write a letter in which the American policy was expressed as conceding to every nation the right to govern itself in whatever form it pleased—something which is actively debatable today. In the same letter, Jefferson offered to pay the new French republic the money which was currently due as installment on our Revolutionary War debts, this being a unanimous cabinet decision.[8]

Added to Washington's worries was his concern for the safety of the Marquis de Lafayette whom he loved as a son and who was at the time a prisoner in Austria. (Some wag had remarked that with no natural children of his own, it was ironical that Washington was called "The Father of his Country.") It was Lafayette's singular and risky position that in France he had tried to steer a moderate course and move that Revolution in the direction of the American one to which he had been so devoted. This of course did not work, so Lafayette was forced by the radicals to flee to Austria where he was soon imprisoned by the elite there. His frantic wife wrote a letter to Washington begging him to use his wide influence to secure the release of her husband. Personally, the President would have come quickly to the rescue. But now he was in a delicate, official position. He requested that Jefferson answer her letter with the message that he would convey "all the consolation I can with propriety give her, consistent with my public character and the national policy."[9]

Jefferson's letter explained that although the President could not under the circumstances comply with her request, he would not be "inactive" regarding the deplorable situation. He directed Jefferson to instruct Gouverneur Morris, the American minister to France, "to neglect no favorable opportunity to express informally the sentiments and wishes of the United States toward Lafayette."[10]

To add to the embarrassing situation, Comte de Noailles, the brother-in-law of Lafayette, arrived in Philadelphia. He had been a soldier with Washington during the American Revolution and became a personal friend. In ordinary circumstances, Washington would have been eager to see him. But the count had come to this country as head of a delegation of persons who had been forced to leave France and now were reportedly seeking to present a petition to the President. He therefore felt compelled to handle the matter impersonally so he asked Hamilton to convey to Noailles the word that in order to preserve the impartiality of the government, it was not possible to show his old friend any favors. Local opposition newspapers, learning of the rebuff, published a spurious report that Washington and the Frenchman had secretly met and conferred for hours over some mysterious documents. Another Frenchman, Charles Talleyrand, a revolutionary leader, arrived and sought to see Washington, only to meet the same official refusal. The former later became the French Minister of Foreign Affairs and never forgot the "insult."[11]

These diplomatic incidents, while significant, were small in comparison to the news which began to filter in from Europe. For three months, no regular mail boat from England or France had arrived in New York Harbor. What this could mean increasingly aroused speculation. The answer was that war seemed imminent between England and France. Now was Washington placed in what was probably his greatest international quandary. How he would deal with it he could not know. But his final stand on the position of America in the foreign conflict was to stamp him unmistakably with the greatness that most people already realized and was to set a precedent for future Presidents, that in the main has been a lasting, guiding light.

Meantime, as the news only trickled in through the slow overseas channels of the day, Washington decided to attend to a domestic problem that was near to his heart. He decided to visit Mount Vernon. It was no idle whim. Word had come that his plantation manager was ill and that Washington was needed there to straighten out some difficulties which those temporarily in charge did not feel they could handle. And after all, his new administration for the moment was functioning well domestically. He would make sure he was kept informed of the European activity en route and while he was at home. So he instructed his young secretary, Tobias Lear, to send him frequent dispatches and accordingly left for Mount Vernon.

The first message he received at Alexandria on 29 March 1793 was a pleasant surprise. It was from a young girl of Elkton,

Maryland, Mary Endress, who wished "long life and uninterrupted happiness to our country's father." He must have smiled with relief at this affectionate expression in such contrast to official matters. At Baltimore, Washington was handed a letter which Lear had posted the day before saying that the war news had not been confirmed but that Philadelphia shipowners were under "great apprehension." Arriving at the site of the new Federal City which was to bear his name, the President talked with Andrew Ellicott, the official surveyor, and asked him to improve his relationship with the commissioners of the momentous project.[12]

As the sun set over the Virginia countryside, George Washington arrived on 2 April at his cherished haven. He was glad to find that the health of his manager, Andrew Whiting, had improved. But Washington himself was too tired to take over much of the farm supervision of the Mount Vernon estate. Instead, he was faced with official duties conveyed to him by letters from Lear: Secretary of War Henry Knox, usually unstoppable, was ill; Jefferson was trying to play down the war rumors from Europe; officials appointed to repair to their posts in the Northwest Territory had not yet departed. As one biographer has noted, "His very presence on the Potomac brought him solace but it could not bring him rest."[13]

Even the solace was broken by a letter from Hamilton saying that late news left no doubt that Europe was in a general conflagration. Prime Minister William Pitt had ordered the French minister to leave London; Queen Marie Antoinette had also died by the guillotine; and France had declared war against England, Spain, and Holland. The people of Philadelphia were excitedly speculating over the war rumors and what they might mean to the United States, most expressing the hope "that we may not be drawn into it. But the general and commanding sentiment of the people was complete confidence in their President."[14]

Enough was enough. The President wrote to Jefferson on 12 April that "it behooves the government of this country to use every means in its power to prevent the citizens . . . from embroiling us with either England or France, by endeavoring to maintain a strict neutrality." In a letter to Hamilton, Washington stressed his desire for "immediate precautionary measures." He would start for Philadelphia the next morning by the shortest practicable route and hope to reach the capital in ten days. When he arrived, he devoted himself at once to the tempestuous affairs at hand, his "long anticipated vacation curtailed and his much-needed rest ruined."[15]

If ever a President of the United States was on the proverbial horns of a dilemma, it was George Washington, caught between respect for his ancestral England and warm regard for France which had helped us win the American Revolution. He was neither an Anglophile nor a Francophile and fortunately neither a Hamiltonian or Jeffersonian, although later he did come to lean more to Hamilton. Washington, no intellectual, believed that the battle of ideologies in Europe did not greatly involve the United States which had enough problems of its own. In a letter to a former aide, David Humphreys, Washington summed up his attitude:

> If it can be esteemed a happiness to live in an age productive of great and interesting events, we of the present age are very highly favored. The rapidity of national revolutions appear no less astonishing than their magnitude. In what they will terminate, is known only to the Great Ruler of events, and confiding in his wisdom and goodness, we may safely trust the issue to him. . . . If we are permitted to improve without interruption, the great advantage which nature and circumstances have placed in our reach, many years will not revolve before we may be ranked not only among the most respectable, but among the happiest people on this globe.[16]

As has been pointed out, the uniqueness of Washington's position was that he had no precedent to guide him and fortunately, no United Nations Security Council to argue and delay a decision. The Presidents who were to follow have had the good fortune to be able to observe those of Washington—and those who have followed him. Like our Supreme Court, they can rely endlessly on legal and political antecedents. Whether Washington would have consulted the Senate on this international crisis is a moot point, for the Senate was not in session at the time, and quick action was called for. He could act fast when necessary. "It is happy for us," said Chief Justice John Jay, "that we have a President who will do nothing rashly and who regards his own interests as inseparable from the public good."

As was his custom, Washington soon called upon his cabinet to offer their opinions regarding the crisis. He sent notices to the members asking their comments on "a general plan of conduct for the Executive." On 10 April the cabinet gathered in Washington's office and opened a spirited discussion on whether a proclamation should be issued containing a declaration of neutrality. Hamilton felt one should be issued immediately. Jefferson took exception on two counts. He felt that such a proclamation of neutrality would mean there should be no war; holding back such a pronouncement might give the United States a bargaining point with both warring nations. As with Hamilton, Knox and Randolph believed a proclamation was imperative, and it was so decided, the document to exclude the word "neutrality." So the Proclamation of Neutrality was duly issued by the President "forbidding the citizens of the United States to take part in any hostilities on the seas and warning them against carrying to the belligerents any articles deemed contraband by the modern usage of nations and forbidding all acts and proceedings inconsistent with the duties of a friendly nation toward those at war."

Washington asked Randolph to formulate the language of the proclamation. Jefferson, the penman, might well have been the logical one to draft the document but he did not wish to write it, partly because it did not favor France. There then was a question of whether a minister of the French Republic should be received. Over the objections of Hamilton (who favored Britain), it was decided that such an official would be received. Little did the Cabinet members realize what they were in for. France was to send them a surprise in the impulsive person of its envoy.

By issuing this proclamation and trying to enforce it, Washington and his aides set more important precedents. The very issuance of the proclamation asserted the initiative of the executive branch of the government in its conduct of foreign relations and implanted the principle, from an American standpoint, for what was to become a vital point in international law, namely, the law of neutrality. (Although we often ignore international law today.) A further precedent was established in the efforts to restrain, as we shall see, the French agents who were operating in the United States and their American supporters. No United States Navy yet existed—it was to be initiated by Secretary of War Henry Knox—and the small national army was busy fighting Indians in the West. So the Washington administration had as its only law inforcement arms, treasury agents and state governments. The former individuals were not sufficient to do the job required and as a consequence, the state governors were often requested to use their law officers and state militia to enforce Federal law.[17]

Washington felt relieved after the cabinet had unanimously, albeit after some argument, concurred in the issuance of the

Proclamation of Neutrality. He had given emphatic instructions to his department heads:

> Let me impress the following maxim upon the executive officers. In all important matters, deliberate maturely, but execute promptly and vigorously and do not put things off until tomorrow which can be done and require to be done today. Without an adherence to these rules, business will never be done in an easy manner, but will always be in arrears, with one thing treading upon the heels of another.[18]

Enforcing the laws was one thing but guiding the public sentiment was another, Washington found. As has been noted, throughout the land, gratitude to France for its help in the American Revolution was widespread. The people had yet to learn the ugly aspects of the terror that gripped the French. As a recent historian has pointed out, Vicomtesse de Fars-Fausselandry said, "The American cause seemed our own; we were proud of their victories, we cried at their defeats, we tore down bulletins and read them in all our houses. None of us reflected on the danger that the New World could give to the old." Another Frenchman, the Comte de Segur, commented, "In the rueful altermath of the American Revolution, we stepped out gaily on a carpet of flowers, little imagining the abyss beneath."[19]

When the Proclamation of Neutrality was published, cries of anger and disappointment arose in all parts of the United States. The republican press vociferated that "the executive had finally betrayed its true predilections by unfurling the flag of monarchy." These attacks worried, discouraged and angered Washington, but Jefferson's feelings were mixed. He exulted to Senator James Monroe, "All the old spirit of '76 is rekindling. The newspapers from Boston to Charleston are obliged to publish the most furious philippics against England."[20]

Public criticism for a time was muted because of the general reverence for Washington and his leadership. It was not easy to go against the only man who had even been seriously considered for President. But as the clamor increased against England, fed by Jefferson, and the sympathy for France heightened, the passions of many of the people grew into serious proportions. Washington's popularity could not withstand all of the torrent of abuse and condemnation. His Proclamation was stigmatized as the edict of a royal ruler, an unjust assumption of executive authority and an open demonstration of partiality for England and hostility to France. On 21 May 1793, Philip Freneau, the mouthpiece of Thomas Jefferson, published in his *National Gazette* that President Washington had signed the Proclamation of Neutrality only because the Anglophiles had threatened that if he did not, they would cut off his head. As ridiculous as this was, it made Washington very angry. (One wonders if he suspected that his Secretary of State was at least indirectly behind much of the verbal abuse.) In reply, the President told Jefferson that "he despised all their attacks on him personally, but that there had never been an act of government, not meaning in the executive line only but in any line, that the *National Gazette* had not abused." By this time, Washington saw France in its light of Terror. "The affairs of France," he commented, "seem to me to be in the highest paroxysm of disorder, not so much from the pressure of foreign enemies . . . but because those in whose hands the government is entrusted are ready to tear each other to pieces and will more than probably prove the worse foes the country has."[21]

The President himself emphasized that he did not wish to take sides. That the European conflict, in accordance with the policy of no "foreign entanglements" appeared to him not to be vitally relevant in the shaping of American policy toward other nations. Caught between a Scylla and Charybdis tension in his own cabinet—and the conflict between Hamilton and Jefferson seemed to be growing—he was weary at heart. Now on top of all this, word had come from France that the Republic was sending over an envoy, Edmund Charles Genet, who from his reputation boded nothing like "havens ahead." Only George Washington was equipped to deal with what was to come.

2
Washington—and Genet's Fiasco

As Citizen Genet neared the Carolina coast in the forty-gun French frigate *Embuscade* he did not realize how appropriately named was his ship. For he was heading into an ambuscade far more shattering to his future than would have been random cannon shot. Anyway, Charleston, South Carolina on this balmy 8 April 1793 though scenically appealing was not the place he was supposed to land.

After sailing from France, Genet's warship though sturdy enough for an eighteenth-century sailing vessel, had struck a storm and instead of landing at Philadelphia, its destination, swerved southward and came to anchor just outside the harbor of the city named for an English king. The rough voyage had taken twenty-eight days. Undaunted, the cocky, thirty-year-old French minister to the new United States, strode ashore and was greeted by a huge, cheering crowd. Bells rang and the roofs were crowded with people yelling loud welcomes. Such was to be typical of his initial reception on our shores. But it was not to last. He became known as "more like a busy man than a man of business."

This Edmund Charles Genet whom the people saw was rather handsome. Somewhat stocky, he had a ruddy face with a prominent nose that sloped backward to a high forehead. Reddish hair curled down his cheeks in flowing sideburns. His preserved profile looks ironically much like that of George Washington. But that was where the similarity stopped. Here from France had come a moppish smart-aleck masquerading under the title of an official minister. His mission: to bring the United States (which had really come into being a decade before with French help in the American Revolution) onto the side of France which was now in a state of chaotic fluidity—its anniversary of revolution to be feverishly celebrated in 1989.

From the standpoint of his country at that time, Genet was a perfect choice. His family had been in the royal circles, a sister having been close to Marie Antoinette as her lady-in-waiting, his father head of the bureau of information office and Genet himself a favorite, youthful linguist at Versailles. To cap it off, he had dined with that universal character, Benjamin Franklin who gave accelerating advice to this young, ambitious man who aimed to reach a high mark in life.

The enthusiastic reception at Charleston was sincere. What Genet's thoughts were as he passed Fort Sumpter in the harbor, a military post in both our Revolutionary and Civil Wars, one can only conjecture. But the people who greeted him ardently wished that the results of the French Revolution would be as benevolent as the American ones. Though Charleston was not his choice for landing, Genet was not to be disappointed. Not only did the public turn out in warm welcome but the officials of the town and state proved equally hospitable as soon as they recovered from their surprise at having a foreign dignitary pop up in their midst. There were a few Federalists who wanted no part of the French Revolution, but they were not typical. Some of the planters jumped at the chance to benefit themselves materially. It could hardly be said that they were good examples of Liberté, Egalité, and Fraternité, for they were substantial slave owners. For example, William Clay Snipes owned 87 slaves, Isaac Huger 200, and Alexander Moultrie 300. These plantation owners, after they learned that Genet planned to "liberate" Louisiana and Florida saw an opportunity to get in on the spoils and enrich themselves by increased acreage and more slaves.[1]

Among these would-be speculators were friends of Thomas Paine, two of the most prominent being James O'Fallon and Alexander Gillon who had invested in the fraudulent Yazoo Land Company of South Carolina. Not only were they financially interested but they were among the first to accept military commissions which Genet had brought over in abundance and was indiscriminately handing them out like a vote-seeking politician at a picnic. It was said that he was ready to bestow enough commissions for privateers to have swept the British navy from American seas. Such were Citizen Genet's grandiose ambitions which he felt would be successful, judging from the favorable reception he was receiving. Thus, this arriving diplomat thrust himself into a vital foreign crisis of the second administration of George Washington. "It still stands as one of the most fascinating episodes in the diplomatic history of the United States." And one historian has labelled it "the most lamentable episode in the history of relations between France and the United States."[2]

Meanwhile the Washington administration was aware of the

situation and was making preparations to deal with it. Even while Genet was at Charleston, the President issued a Neutrality Proclamation on April 22, 1793 which, although the word "neutrality" was purposely omitted in deference to Jefferson who was pro-French, declared that the United States was at peace with Great Britain *and* France, and warned citizens to abstain from acts of hostility against *any* belligerent power. The pro-British Hamilton was overjoyed and wished to go further and repeal the treaties made with France in 1778.[3]

Governor William Moultrie of South Carolina, an important and respected Revolutionary War general, seemed to find a kindred soul in Genet, admiring his personality and promising to do all in his power to cooperate. He allowed Genet to arm privateers, helping in the process. The governor was pleased that the French had proposed to free Louisiana from Spanish rule for such would lessen Indian attacks on the white settlers and open up the Mississippi River to local traffic, a goal eagerly sought by the Americans in the West.[4]

At length, Citizen Genet, flushed with the success of his Charleston sojourn, convinced that the American people were with him all the way in his designs and with their cheers sounding in his ears, set out for Philadelphia. Although it rained much of the way, he could hear wet flags flapping in the wind, the barking of dogs and the happy yells of children seeing him off. The roads were rough as his carriage bumped along but he found them improved when he reached Virginia. Primitive thoroughfares, however, did not prevent more cheering. Crowds gathered, huzzas continued, rum flowed and prominent residents stood by the roadside with hats in hand to greet this gallant gentleman from across the sea. As he moved on, people came running after his carriage shouting for France and condemning the Neutrality Proclamation. What Genet did not then realize was that it just happened he was passing through the republican South which was the most anti-Federalist, anti-British part of the country. Had he traversed New England instead, the passage would have been a different story.

By the time he reached Richmond, Genet began to weary of the adulation. Farmers near there crowded in to see him and offerd him grain and flour and wanted to receive him "with open arms under their modest roofs . . . true Americans at their height of joy." Baltimore proved to be quieter because there resided many Federalist merchants whose sentiments were in a different direction. At Chester, 500 carriages came out to meet him with the inevitable bells, so many ringing that he felt he never wanted to hear another. But Genet observed that he had "collected without intermediary the fraternal sentiments of the American people for the French people." He was greatly buoyed by this outpouring of pro-French feelings and "sustained by its imposing voice."

Even in puritanic Boston there was a civic feast in French style. A procession of citizens eight deep escorted a roasted ox labelled "A Peace Offering to Liberty and Equality, together with 1600 loaves of bread and two hogsheads of punch, to a spot renamed Liberty Square. As the punch fell lower in the hogsheads, the spirits of the citizens rose, and what was said and sung was not complimentary to John Bull."[5]

One thing the people liked about Genet was his ability to respond to their comments in English, especially on the formal occasions. From his youth, he had been an able linguist which now stood him in good stead. Especially was this true at the large public reception given for him in mid-May at Philadelphia just after he arrived. Outside the hall, the streets were abuzz with shouting spectators and of course there were the ever-present bells welcoming the French Minister Plenipotentiary to the United States. The festive reception was given to Genet to impress upon President Washington the great general affection for France although this was strictly a Republican partisan event. Even so, prominent Philadelphians headed the reception committee, among them David Rittenhouse, president of the American Philosophical Society, Alexander Dallas, Secretary of State of Pennsylvania, noted attorney Jonathan Sergeant, and Charles Biddle, member of one of the most eminent families of the city.

The committee led, according to Jefferson, "a vast concourse" of citizens to where Genet was staying at the City Hotel. According to the political leanings of the estimators, the crowd varied from 500 to 6,000. It was certainly a sizeable gathering. The chairman presented an address which acknowledged this nation's obligations to France, "our first and best ally." Genet replied modestly and graciously and dwelled on how appreciative he was for the favorable sentiment he had aroused in the people; he emphasized that France did not expect the United States to enter the war; but he reminded his listeners that his country "had combatted for your liberties—and if necessary, and she had the power, would enlist again in your cause."[6]

Genet had chosen to travel to Philadelphia by private carriage, later changing to a public one to impress the crowds, but his vessel, the *Embuscade*, had sailed up the coast and was now at

Philadelphia. Not to be outdone, officers of the French warship entertained a large group of Americans on board including Governor Thomas Mifflin of Pennsylvania and Secretary of War Henry Knox, under whose jurisdiction, at this time, was the United States Navy. At a later party, an artillery battery fired fifteen rounds, each resounding at the conclusion of as many elaborate toasts—which must have taxed the drinking capacities of those taking part. Notwithstanding, for the last toast, the host managed to declaim: "May the clarion of freedom sounded by France awaken the people of the world to their own happiness, and the tyrants of the earth be prostrated by its triumphant sounds." In response, Genet sang the "Marseillaise" in French and his host then repeated it in English. Philip Freneau composed a poem especially for the occasion, to be sung to the tune of "God Save the King." The last stanza:

> Rejoice ye patriot sons,
> With festive mirth and glee
> Let all join hands around the cap of liberty
> And in full chorus join the song
> May France ne'er want a WASHINGTON![7]

Genet did not accept all invitations. Nor could he, they were so numerous. But one he purposely declined was a dinner given by the conservative Society of the Cincinnati at which Vicomte de Noailles would be present. He had served in the Continental Army under General Washington. Genet wrongly suspected that Noailles was a spy for the French royalists who were seeking American support.

On 22 May, Genet presented to Secretary Jefferson a request for repayment by the United States of the balance of its debt to France, money borrowed for expenses of the American Revolution. The request struck Alexander Hamilton as abominable, pitting him as usual against Jefferson who favored the petition. Washington seemed to take a neutral course but in the end agreed with Hamilton.

There was one appointment which the French envoy could not ignore, one which he viewed with some trepidation. That was with the President. Neither did Washington relish the prospect. He had already heard from Gouverneur Morris in Paris that Genet had "more genius than ability," and despite the beneficent impression which Jefferson had of Genet, Washington surmised that he would face a formidable adversary. For his part, the envoy on his way north had already formed a strong prejudice against the President and his advisers, particularly Hamilton and Knox. The impression of Genet was that "a very distinct party had arisen against Washington: his political enemies were especially numerous in the rural districts; men are to be found there more sincere, more energetic, less commercially attached to the interests of England and ready to testify without hesitation as to what they like and what they hate."[8]

Hamilton had fierily stated that as far as the comparison of the French and American revolutions was concerned, "Would to heaven we could discern in the mirror of French affairs, the same humanity, the same decorum, the same gravity, the same order, the same dignity, the same solemnity which distinguished the American cause." He went on to decry the bloodiness, the passion and tumult, violence and atheism of the French upheaval. At the same time, Jefferson was extolling the virtues of that conflict—and herein between him and Hamilton was widened for the first time, the crucial chasm between the Republicans and the Federalists, a ringing precursor of the formation of two major political parties in this country—something which was to disturb and sadden Washington into a different person from what he had been so long.

For Paris had its mobs; now Philadelphia did also. Years later John Adams was to write of this time when "ten thousand people in the streets of Philadelphia, day after day, threatened to drag Washington out of his house and effect a revolution in the government, or compel it to declare war in favor of the French Revolution and against England."[9]

It was within such an atmosphere that on the afternoon of 18 May 1793 that President Washington received Citizen Genet in his office. Also present was Secretary of State Thomas Jefferson, the official most directly concerned with the Frenchman and his diplomatic mission. Genet could probably not conceal his surprise at the cold manner of the stately chief executive, though the envoy did not expect a red carpet welcome. What he faced was a frigid contrast to his own exuberance which was soon brought to bear. The head of the new nation simply sat and stared at his visitor and gave little indication of what was on his mind. He allowed the man from France to say his piece which he did with his usual eloquent show of confidence. He presumed that this infant nation which France had helped to establish, had an obligation to help its benefactor in her hour of need, specifically in regard to the current status of the French West Indies, the promotion of mutual commerce; in return, France would lend its assistance to the needs of the United States. At the end of his address, Genet actually seemed pleased with his performance.

He undoubtedly was not very perceptive. The great stone face which looked down upon him still gave no hint of what was his reaction. This was a classic example of Olympian dignity being assailed by a Lilliputian challenger who tried not to see the gathering storm which he had helped to create. Finally, Washington spoke but in vague generalities, mentioning the desire that his country had to live in peace with all the powers of the world. It was not until later that Genet realized he had been given a lofty brush-off by a master of self-control. But the meeting was not without significance. During the meeting, Genet presented to Washington a letter from the President of the French National Convention hinting that American help might be *demanded* at some future time. "The day is not far off," the latter stated, "when political sanity will establish the bases of commerce. It depends on the courage of the United States to accelerate this happy moment and the French Republic will hasten to cooperate in every such effort." Washington still was not impressed. Later Genet wrote his Minister of Foreign Affairs that "Everything has succeeded beyond my hopes: the true Republicans triumph, but old Washington, *le vieux Washington*, a man very different from the character emblazoned in history, cannot forgive me for my successes and the eagerness with which the whole city rushed to my house, while a mere handful of English merchants went to congratulate him on his proclamation."[10]

It has been stated that Genet was only doing his duty as an officially designated representative of France; that he was naturally more interested in the welfare and advancement of his own country than that he was visiting. But if so, his was one of the most glaring examples in diplomatic history of an envoy misjudging the leadership of a nation and bungling his approach to the solution of his problems. True, the Frenchman was subjected to a reversal of American sentiment when, after being so warmly received, he came up against the cold rejection of Washington. During that interview, Genet was more provoked when he spotted in the President's office a bust of Louis XVI and declared that its presence there was an insult to France. He was also taken aback when he learned that relatives of Lafayette were friends of Washington, though why he should is difficult to understand. On the other hand, Genet was heartened by the entertainment given him by the Republicans including one at which a "tree of Liberty" was on the table and a red cap representing Liberty was placed on his head. At a dinner given by Governor Mifflin, a roasted pig received the name of the murdered French king, its severed head being carried around to each of the guests. The envoy was also treated to the sight of a display in a Philadelphia tavern of the mutilated and blood-stained imitation corpse of Queen Marie Antoinette.

In the midst of such occurrences, Jefferson was informed that Washington was not feeling well. A fever which he had contracted had affected even his appearance. This was no wonder, considering what he had been going through. More and more he chaffed at the bitterness of the stinging attacks made upon him by the press. Said Jefferson, "He feels those things more than any person I ever met with. . . . It is the more unfortunate that these attacks are planted on popular ground, on the love of the people for France and its cause, which is universal."[11]

Secretary Jefferson was becoming tired of his office and it would not be long before he would resign it. More and more he differed with Washington and as the foregoing statement indicates, criticized him as well. Particularly galling to Jefferson was the increasing favoritism which Washington showed to Hamilton and Knox. Of course such friction greatly disturbed Washington, and time was to show that this, as well as public criticism and the growth of the two political factions, hastened the exit from office of the Chief Executive himself.

Genet sensed this friction and soon determined to use it to his own advantage. He was not only an ardent admirer of Jefferson but reasonably felt that the secretary of state in his official capacity was the logical one to handle the French problems. Hamilton, however, sensing a challenge to his own influence and always eager to increase it, thrust himself into the tense situation and made trade with Britain a pretext with which he assumed a participating position. Genet tried to ignore Hamilton. This was like spitting into the wind. At first Jefferson was quite taken with Genet. Having spent five years in France, the former naturally understood the Gallic nature better than his associates. The useful talents of the young envoy and his warm personality appealed to the artistic side of Jefferson. He wrote to Madison about Genet: "It is impossible for anything to be more affectionate, more magnanimous than the purport of his mission. . . . In short, he offers everything and asks nothing."[12]

How premature could the secretary be?

The closest observer in the cabinet of the personal side of

Washington was his faithful Henry Knox. Concerned mainly with the military aspects of the Franco-American situation, the Secretary of War (as his voluminous papers show) was also involved in the general decisions about Genet. Now he saw and was quite solicitous about the declining health of his chief. On 5 August 1793, Knox wrote to Washington that "The sober and prudent part of the community regard, as in the case of a storm, the mind and countenance of the chief pilot. While he remains confident and composed, happiness is diffused around; but when he doubts, then anxiety and fear have their full effect."[13]

Regardless of anyone's health, that Citizen Genet would give up on his official mission was as distant from the truth as he was from George Washington. One of the first things that the envoy had done at Charleston was to outfit four privateers to prey upon English shipping along the coast. Even Jefferson saw the folly of this and asked Genet to desist from it. This he did not and continued to fit out eleven other such vessels. In early August, the President called his cabinet to meet and form a definite policy for such contingencies. The result was a set of "Rules Governing Belligerents" which forbade such equipping of privateers in American ports. Not just France but England also was barred. Enforcement of this rule and others relating to the neutrality of the United States was assigned to Hamilton in his capacity as Secretary of the Treasury through the customs officials under his control. Jefferson was offended and felt that his department should have had the assignment—and that Hamilton was again interfering in foreign relations. Jefferson again saw his influence slipping and offered to resign—which was not accepted."[14]

In the cabinet meeting, it was agreed that full information about decisions on Genet be sent to the French government along with a request for his recall. Henry Knox urged that the minister be immediately expelled. This motion got no takers. Genet would be allowed to continue in office until his government acted. Hamilton and Knox then proposed that the American public be informed of the cabinet's action, the former holding forth eloquently for forty-five minutes in this behalf. Jefferson scoffed at the idea, saying it would be "unkind". Inpassioned by the anguish Genet had caused Washington, Knox then, according to Jefferson who did not like him, made a "foolish and incoherent sort of speech." He pulled out a current newspaper article entitled "The Funeral Dirge of George Washington and James Wilson" which described Washington being guillotined for his "crimes." The President was usually partial to Knox but this time he was not. He lost his temper. According to Jefferson, the President became "much inflamed, got into one of those passions when he cannot command himself, ran on much on the personal abuse which had been bestowed on him, defied any man on earth to produce one single act of his since he had been in the government which was not done in the purest motives . . . that he had never repented but once having slipped the moment of resigning his office, and that was every moment since, and that by God he had rather be in his grave than in his present situation; that he would rather be on his farm than emperor of the world, and yet they were charging him with wanting to be king; that that rascal Freneau sent him three of his newspapers every day, as if he thought he would become the distributor of his papers, and that he could see in this nothing but an impudent design to insult him." Jefferson said later that the President's mind had so long been used to unlimited applause that it could not brook contradiction or even advice offered unasked.

Word came via the slow Atlantic route that the dire events in France were darkening. Royalists had arisen in the province of Vendée but were crushed by the radicals, many thousands of the king's followers cut to pieces, some of them drowned. French armies had been driven out of Belgium and Holland, and Dumouriez, their commander, had deserted and taken refuge with the opposing allies. Although the American people wanted no part of such extreme measures, the Republicans here still tried to put a good face on the matter. The worsening situations drove Genet to desperate measures. Jefferson wrote to a friend, Harry Innes: "This summer is of immense importance to the future of mankind all over the earth, and not a little so to ours. For though the issue should not be marked by a direct change in our constitution, it will influence the tone and principle of its administration." Indeed it did. Herein was a struggle in which the stakes were monarchy or republicanism.[15]

By this time, Genet was becoming disillusioned with Jefferson. At first, he had almost idolized the Secretary of State who in turn had encouraged and aided the envoy in his headlong foray. But the latter was finally seeing that Jefferson told him one thing, Washington and the cabinet another. Genet had felt that with Jefferson as his champion, he would need no other; that the Secretary, enamored of France and a prime leader in the United States government could pave the way to French success in this infant nation which owed its very existence to the help of France.

If Jefferson could not do it, thought Genet, then Congress could. But he was wrong; here he found no barbarous Robespierre, Danton, or Marat, but a paragon of humane and democratic virtues, George Washington.

Citizen Genet did not understand American government.

Now "drunk with enthusiasm and popular support and at best not the soul of discretion," he publicly threatened to defy the rules by appealing over Washington's head to the people. That ruined him."[16]

Of all the stupid things that the Frenchman did in his first few hectic months on our shores, this was the most ridiculous. How could he for a moment think that he could accomplish anything by appealing to people who had, through their elected representatives, unanimously elected twice the "Father of His Country" who was to be aptly described by Henry Lee as "First in Peace" as well as in other respects? Yes, Washington had for the time reached a low ebb of popularity; he was facing not only foreign entanglements but bitter division within his appointed cabinet, the birth of American political parties and the imposed duty of the priceless setting of precedents. But he was not so far down that he was out; and in his forthcoming, longed-for retirement, the people would again rise and call him blessed.

Jefferson, Madison, and Aaron Burr now recognized that Genet was harming the republican cause. Jefferson reacted by portraying the envoy as "all imagination, no judgement, passionate, disrespectful, and even indecent toward the President." A prominent journal stated that unless Genet was stopped short in his career, it seemed entirely possible that he would raise the tricolor and proclaim himself proconsul.[17]

The audacious Frenchman actually demanded that the President call Congress into special session so that the elected representatives of the people could judge between the Chief Executive of the United States and the minister of the French Republic. Genet announced that in case Washington refused to summon Congress, he would take his request directly to the people. It is indicative of how far Genet was gone in his folly that he confidently expected the public to repudiate Washington and throw in their lot with France.[18]

But now it was not Washington whom Genet resented most. At least the President had been frankly unfavorable. It was Thomas Jefferson who had so warmly befriended Genet who received the most of the latter's animosity. After the affair was all over, he wrote to Jefferson accusing him of being "skillful in the art of deception, you continued to see me . . . for I told you everything. I consulted you about everything." Alexander Hamilton added fuel to the flames by writing caustic articles which appeared in the press. For example, he stated in one of these that "Self-preservation is the first duty of a nation. Good faith does not require that the United States should put in jeopardy their essential interests, perhaps their very existence, in one of the most unequal contests in which a nation could be engaged, to secure to France—what? Her West India islands and other less important possessions in America." After several such articles appeared, Jefferson became enraged at the extent of their public influence. Wrote he to James Madison, "For God's sake, my dear sir, take up your pen, select the most striking heresies and cut him to pieces in the face of the public. There is nobody who can and will enter the lists against him."[19]

Generally there was peace in the land; but in the cabinet a tug of war existed. Also an aroused and involved section of the public was manifesting its feelings in various new ways. Ordinary workmen were reading the speeches of Mirabeau, the French orator and revolutionary leader; even the women read Joel Barlow's anti-royalist *Conspiracy of Kings;* commoners were walking the streets and jostling the more prominent personages; a medallion with a bas-relief of George III wearing his crown, on the front of a church was torn down. "Occasionally the lower element, drinking itself drunk, staggered out of the beer houses to shout imprecations on a government that would not war with England."[20]

"There are in this as well as in all countries," Washington wrote, "discontented characters, and these characters are actuated by different views, some good, some diabolical. . . . In what will this abuse terminate?"[21]

One thing in which it had terminated was his demand for the recall of Minister Genet. At last, Washington had had enough. The situation was serious enough that Hamilton told George Hammond, British minister to the United States, that if France should refuse such a recall request there was danger of war between the two countries. Secretary Knox was in agreement. So it was that in December of 1793, President Washington laid before Congress the correspondence of Citizen Genet, commenting to the lawmakers that the French envoy's conduct "showed nothing of the friendly spirit of the nation which sent him." Maintaining his attitude of fairness despite the objections of Hamilton, Washington also included in his message a description of the depredations committed by the British as well as the French upon commerce. This comment was justified by the fact that vessels of both countries had appeared armed for offensive action in American ports.

For all the fuss about it, Washington's request for the recall of Genet turned out to be mainly academic. During the absence of the envoy from France, his Girondist party was swept out of office and a more violent faction, the Jacobins, came into power. Soon afterward, Genet was declared to be a public enemy, his acts were disavowed by the new French government as "criminal maneuvers," and that master of human carnage, Maximilian Robespierre, ordered him home to face trial for his crimes. The predicament of Citizen Genet is remindful of a recent popular song, "Who Can I Turn To When Nobody Needs Me?"

The harassed Frenchman, however, was in for a big surprise. President George Washington, out of concern for the envoy's life, refused to extradite him!

And just who were these Jacobins? A satirical answer was set forth by a New England journal:

THE JACOBIN'S CREED

I believe there is no God but nature; no religion but revolution.
No just government but anarchy; and no civil liberty where the
guillotine is not erected.
I believe that Robespierre is the great apostle of liberty and that he
would emancipate the world from the shackles of law.
I believe that Genet is a prodigal of wisdom and that his *ipse dixit* is
better authority that Pufendorf, Montesquieu and Vattel, those
musty, antiquated aristocrats.
I believe that war is better than peace, confusion than order, terror
than mildness, and the guillotine than all the courts of justice.
I believe that the United States of America ought to be under the
direction of my brothers in France, and that George Washington,
commonly called President Washington, is an impertinent
jacknapes for countering our noble designs.
I believe that terrorists are a band of consummate statesmen,
genuine patriots, great benefactors and virtuous representatives.
I believe that no person who dissents from our fraternity ought to be
permitted to speak, write or communicate his sentiments.[22]

Under the existing conditions in the French government, it was no surprise that Robespierre quickly had accepted Washington's request that Genet be recalled. In fact, he wanted him back. The guillotine was poised and ready to descend upon this noxious Girondist now out of favor who had so stirred up Washington that little could be expected of him in the way of help.

The French could also play hard ball. In retalitation, Robespierre demanded that the American Minister to France, Gouverneur Morris be sent home. This was not as serious as it might appear, for the irrepressible Morris had stirred up as much mischief in France as Genet had in America. Now relations between the two countries were at a new low.

Citizen Genet may have become *persona non grata* but his influence was still being felt. By the time of his aborted recall, a number of so-called "Democratic Societies," mainly instigated by the Frenchman, had sprung up in the United States. This apparently was the first time a descriptive title referred to these partisans using a capital "D" and suggests the modern Democratic Party. At any rate, eleven such organizations were formed across the country in 1793 and twenty-four more the next year. These societies were said to have made an important contribution toward the nationalization of American politics. At a later date, Washington was to place some blame upon them for stirring up the Whiskey Rebellion in western Pennsylvania. He condemned the societies in general because he felt they were trying to undermine the government by destroying public confidence in it. Reaction to the societies was varied and in some instances extreme. One in Wilmington, Delaware, refused to drink a toast to the President because the members felt "he had gone over to the Tories."[23]

The Federalist press, spurred on by Hamilton, excoriated the societies. One of these, *The New London Bee*, accused the members of "lying, cheating, whoredom, adultery, gaming, peculation, bribery, bankruptcy, fraud and atheism." These conservatives used their hero, George Washington, to the hilt in discountenancing the liberal groups. Instead of emphasizing Independence Day they suggested that two other holidays be nationally observed, the discovery of America by Columbus and the birthday of Washington. *The Federal Orrey*, a Boston newspaper, compared him with Moses: "By night your pillar and your cloud by day." One toast began, "To Washington, loved as a father, as a god adored." Songs about him were composed to the tune of "God Save the King" and poems compared the Republican mobs to the "lice of Egypt."[24]

A political leader, Elbridge Gerry, observed that Washington did not have the broad basis of support that he once did; that his support now came mostly from banks, Societies of the Cincinnati and monarchical interests. Prominent democrats such as Benjamin Bache, William Duane, James T. Callender, and Thomas Paine critized the loftiness of Washington, while in Joel Barlow's notebook (among his papers at Harvard) there is found the following:

> Take from the mine the coldest, hardest stone
> It needs no fashion, it is Washington.
> But if you chisel let your strokes be rude,
> And on his breast engrave INGRATITUDE!

Historian Perry Link has commented, "It would be interesting to try to discover why Genet was kept in America after his recall, and his friend, Thomas Paine was held by imprisonment in France, even though both wanted to return home. Washington would not intercede to free Paine for return to America."[25]

The largest of the Democratic Societies was in Philadelphia with some two hundred members including such leaders as David Rittenhouse, Charles Biddle, Peter S. Duponceau, George Logan, and Alexander Dallas. But Genet was more involved with the Philadelphia French Society composed of local Frenchman. He was its president and helped draft the constitution which pledged the members to support government dedicated to preservation of the rights of man.

By this time, however, Genet had nearly lost his usefulness in the City of Brotherly Love. He made his way to New York where he found strong support from Governor George Clinton, a former Revolutionary general and now an active anti-Federalist. (This connection was to become extremely important for Genet later.) The long-time governor (1777–95) was unusually powerful in politics and did not hesitate to use dubious methods to gain his ends. Hostile to strong national government, he had opposed attempts to strengthen the Articles of Confederation. Although a great landowner, Governor Clinton lived rather simply. He extended to the ex-envoy a sincerely warm welcome which was much appreciated by Genet in his time of turmoil and disturbing circumstances. A welcoming committee met him at Paulus Hook, he was ferried to the Battery, was saluted by artillery and escorted to his New York hotel by an enthusiastic crowd wearing tricolored, cockaded hats, the French flag flying in the breeze on top of the Tontine Coffee House where an address to him was read which warmed his heart.

On the evening of 7 August, Governor Clinton gave a colorful reception for Genet. This was politically an important occasion but for the fabulous young Frenchman it was an even more memorable evening, one of the most meaningful of his life. For here he met the captivating daughter of the governor, twenty-year-old Cornelia Tappan Clinton and "fell passionately in love with her." With the dashing pursuance of a Parisian boulevardier, Genet courted Cornelia until her affection equalled that of his own. Such a mutual attraction was not only romantic but practically logical because she was an ardent republican and warmly admired the French Revolution. It was reported that Cornelia was "half in love with Genet before he arrived in New York. She envisaged him as a paragon of republican virtue, a dedicated patriot and defender of the rights of man, and her encounter with the attractive and witty Frenchman simply confirmed her infatuation. She made no secret of her emotions." When a friend asked if she might tell Genet that she looked forward to seeing him again, she nodded and murmured, "Mention my love as well."

On 5 January 1794, Cornelia wrote to Genet from Government House in New York City that

> My prayers on New Year's Day were for your happiness and for the liberty of your country. You claim the greatest share of our conversation every day. Our friends speak of you to please me; if I am with your enemies, they abuse you in order to hurt my feelings—which I assure you is frequently the case but I have too much spirit to let them see that anything they may say can hurt or give me pain, and I generally treat them with silent contempt. . . . I take my leave of such hostile company that I am determined not to be seen with again, for your enemies I consider as mine. . . . My father has expressed to me his opinion of you in the warmest and most affectionate manner.[26]

Cornelia Clinton had for that day a good education and unlike most eighteenth-century maidens was allowed to be outspoken in her convictions. Five years before her meeting with Genet, Cornelia had known the perceptive and candid Abigail Adams who described her young friend "as smart and sensible a girl as I ever knew and a high anti-Federalist." Genet found Cornelia to be not only lovely but unlike the convent-bred *jeune-fille* of his country, one of open intellect and interest in public affairs at an early age.

Even before Genet had left France, he was instructed to stir up unrest in Louisiana and Florida. To some extent, he was also to do this for Canada. The French consul in Charleston had been given the Florida phase of the operations but for lack of funds little was done there. The Louisiana action took an earlier and more definite form. According to Frederick Jackson Turner, this was "a critical period in American history. To one who appreciates the importance of the possession of the Mississippi Valley," (as historian Turner did) "its approaches in the history and destiny of the United States, these years are alive with interest."[27]

One of the most salient features of the mission of Genet was the desire of the French Republic to make contact with settlers of the American frontier in order to occupy Louisiana, Florida and Canada. With his hands full at Charleston, Genet had done nothing about the proposed expedition against Louisiana until he reached Philadelphia. Awaiting him there was a letter from the veteran Revolutionary War general, George Rogers Clark who offered to raise a force of 1,500 men to march against the Spanish garrison in New Orleans. Clark and his land-speculator brother-in-law, James O'Fallon had in mind increasing their holdings. What Genet did not know was that Clark had fallen on bad times and had become a heavy drinker. The general had become disillusioned because Virginia and the United States had paid little attention to his claims for land as a reward for his war service. Now he saw a chance to remedy this neglect and he had furthermore received much encouragement from many farmers on the western frontier who were anxious for the Mississippi River to be opened so that their produce could go through for ocean shipping. They were also weary of the Indian raids on their settlements. If Spain did not agree to open the river within a reasonable length of time, they were ready to fight their way through and open it by force.

When Secretary of State Jefferson learned of the plans for such military action, he warned Genet that "enticing officers and soliders from Kentucky to go against Spain was really putting a halter around their necks, for they would assuredly be hung if they commenced hostilities against a nation at peace with the United States."[28]

Jefferson thereupon asked Governor Isaac Shelby of Kentucky to investigate the matter and let him know about it, adding that Shelby must prevent American citizens from taking part in an invasion of Louisiana because this would be an invasion of neutrality. The governor replied that he would cooperate but that he had not seen any recruiting for such an expedition. Secretary of War Henry Knox also wrote Shelby and Arthur St. Clair, governor of the Northwest Territory, asking them to intervene by force if necessary to prevent any expedition southward. But Shelby was not an easy person to convince. He felt that he was being pushed around by the national government unnecessarily. As a former Revolutionary colonel and able leader of the American militia which clobbered the British at the key battle of King's Mountain, he had a mind of his own. A frontiersman, yes, but he knew something about law. At length he replied to Jefferson that while he realized the danger of military violations of neutrality, he had read the statutes and found none which specifically prohibited the recruiting of men for such a purpose as was under discussion; that if the national government wanted such a law, let it pass one and then he would obey it. The recall order of Genet, however, made such an issue moot.[29]

At the end of February, 1794, Edmund Charles Genet wound up his affairs at the French legation and stole quietly out of Philadelphia to the farm of a friend near Bristol, Pennsylvania. His public career, as suddenly as it started in the United States, now came to an end. He was thirty-one years of age but had been involved in European and American governmental activities longer than most men at normal retirement. Genet was to live for forty years more but never again would he hold public office. He was through with such and must have experienced a big sigh of relief. He doubtless could have taken part in the official life of that day somewhere, somehow, for he was undeniably capable and had committed no criminal act—at least in the eyes of most Americans. Genet still had good connections but he was disillusioned by those whom he had trusted both in France and here. Now he only wished to live as a private citizen and pursue his personal interests of a rural nature. He told Cornelia Clinton that his "sole desire was to settle in a country where virtue and liberty were respected; where a man who obeyed the law had nothing to fear from despots, aristocrats or ambitious men."[30]

Some enemies of Genet had meanwhile spread rumors that in France he had a wife and children. This of course was disrupting until Governor Clinton found out that the rumor was false. The way was now cleared for Cornelia and Edmund to get married. The wedding took place at the ornate residence of the governor in New York City—a colorful event. Genet it seems still moved in elegant settings. Some wag remarked that "Genet went not to the guillotine but hand in hand to the altar." Afterward the joyful couple took up residence on a large farm near Jamaica, Long

Island, New York. It was purchased with money saved from the husband's salary and from the wife's dowry. The estate formerly belonged to De Witt Clinton, the governor's nephew and political successor. It became known as "Cornelia's Farm," as indeed the buying of it largely indicated. But if the farm was named after her, their first child, a son, was named after Genet. Later the family moved to a larger estate named "Prospect Hill," three miles from Albany, which overlooked the "Lordly Hudson River" as it was affectionately termed by Washington Irving who lived at some distance downstream and who, half a century later, would write about Genet in his lengthy biography of George Washington.

Although the French expatriate could be deemed a loser in his official capacity, he was a winner in love. The courtship of Genet and Cornelia which had been glowingly romantic from the beginning retained its mutual happiness during all of their married years. As evidence, six years later Cornelia wrote a letter to her husband who was away at the time in which she said, "If I had a thousand hearts, I would beg you to accept them but as I have but one and that has been offered to you six years ago, all I can do is to beg you to love it and cherish the girl who owned it before she gave it to you as much as she adores you."[31]

Her husband despite his desire to be a farmer, by the time he had experienced two years of agrarian living, felt again the call of France. The Jacobins were out of office, the Directory had replaced them and was encouraging republican exiles to come home. Some of Genet's relatives and former associates were holding important positions in the government and urged him to return. The republican party in the United States, however, was criticizing Genet publicly, some of its leaders blaming him for misleading the French government during his period as envoy into feeling that the United States was friendly to France when as a matter of fact, President Washington and most of his cabinet definitely were not. Finally, Genet offered to return to France if he could be guaranteed his former official status, the restoration of his French property and an important diplomatic post—he even suggested that he again become minister to the United States. But assurances came too late and the situation was uncertain because Napoleon was in power so Genet at length decided to remain and become a naturalized American citizen, which he did in 1804 at an Albany ceremony at which Alexander Hamilton was present only a few weeks before he was killed in a duel.

Edmund Genet never returned to France. Although he kept in

touch with his French relatives, he realized that he had a good thing here. After all, he was married into one of the most prominent families in this country, his estate brought an income which enabled him to live in the *grande maniere* of the manorial aristocrats along the Hudson River, and his lovely wife as well as his own wit and charm made him a welcome guest at the festive country parties and gala social events in New York City.

The business adventures of Genet were not so successful.

He proposed a metallic balloon to prevent ships from sinking, a protective fender for steamboats, and advocated exploring artic regions by air. He invested or rather speculated in turnpike companies, wool processing, and plaster manufacturing, all of which were financial failures. His business sense was so deficient that Governor Clinton became disturbed about it. But these reverses were small compared to Genet's personal loss. On 23 March 1810, his dear Cornelia succumbed to lingering tuberculosis. Her untimely death so affected her husband that it was said the only thing which sustained him was his care of their six children, the youngest being only two years of age.

Within a few years, however, Genet had recovered and was again in the social whirl of town and country. Eventually he realized that he was an eligible widower and told his sister that he knew at least twenty-four girls in whom he could be interested for another marriage. He settled on one, Martha Osgood, daugher of the postmaster general who served under President Washington, and married her in 1814. As was his first, his second marrige proved to be a happy one.

In his later years, Edmund Charles Genet spent a good deal of his time writing for the press articles furthering the career of George Clinton. Genet also indulged in some scientific studies in which he had long been interested. These resulted in a book, *Memorial on the Upward Forces of Fluids* in which he contended that fluids and gases are subject to a force of levity which compels them to move upward. The volume received mostly derision from scientists, although it was the first American book published dealing with aeronautics. Genet died on 14 July 1834, ironically on the anniversary of the storming of the Bastille.

L'Affaire Genet was a compelling whirlwind in the early weathering of American government. It was involved in the birth of our political parties and the vital establishment of precedents by President Washington and his administration. Genet was the most undiplomatic diplomat in early American history. Yet he left an unmistakable impact on the formation of lasting Presidential prerogatives. Like the consummate person so well described by his countryman, Hector St. Jean de Crevecœur, who ceased to look behind him but pressed his course ahead, Genet personified the "American who is a new man, who acts upon new principles and must therefore entertain new ideas and form new opinions."

3

Diversion and Devotion

George Washington has been described as being as cold and stolid as his face appears on Mount Rushmore. This is only partly true. In his moments of relaxation, which were all too few, he enjoyed popular diversions as much as any of his associates, often more. When he was in Philadelphia, he attended public events such as the circus, which at that time was in an early stage in America. There had been several troops of players in America since the early 1750s. A company of tumblers and rope dancers came to Boston in 1792. Their visit had an unfortuante effect upon the children who watched them, then tried to emulate their feats by walking on fences—attempts that usually did not work. They were described as "wounding themselves in every quarter."

Exhibits of animals appeared early in America. The first lion was imported in 1716 and the first elephant in 1796. Some of these were trained to perform tricks but most were just exhibited as curiosities. One of the first circus amusements after the war was a large menagerie of birds, reptiles, and the like. In 1792, John Bell Ricketts opened a riding school in Philadelphia and in the next few years, he presented what he called "equestrian exercises" in key cities along the Eastern seaboard. Ricketts had served his time as an apprentice in the riding school of Charles Hughes in London and became known as "the first rider of eminence" at the equestrian amphitheater in White Chapel. In 1790 he came from Scotland to America and his portrait painted by Gilbert Stuart shows a handsome young man with curly hair, gazing from the portrait at the new world which he was about to enter.

In New York in 1793, Ricketts leaped from his knees on horseback over an obstacle twelve feet high, and from the horse he threw a somersault at full speed to land on his feet. This was just one example of his expertness. At this time, the people of the United States were ready to resume more of a normal life after the Revolution. So the New World welcomed the circus. George

Washington saw this circus in Philadelphia and sold Ricketts one of his horses. In other stunts, Ricketts could pick up four handerchiefs from the ground at full speed, and ride blindfold in a sack. His horse was named "Corn Planter." His was a combination of horsemanship, acrobatics, rope dancing, and clowning, all of which received warm receptions. The first building housing the circus was called "Ricketts' Amphitheater" and in 1795 resembed a huge, circular tent though made of wood, ninety-six feet in diameter with white walls eighteen feet high slanting upward to a conical roof fifty feet high. The building had a stage and a seating capacity of 700 people.

Later Ricketts was to have an even larger building in New York on the southern tip of Manhattan. At its height, the Ricketts show grew from four to seventeen artists, two painters, several carpenters and an orchestra. In his Philadelphia appearance which Washington attended not only did Ricketts ride with his knees on the saddle, his horse at full speed, he threw four oranges up in the air, at the same time playing with them while the horse was running. An advertisement in a Philadelphia newspaper in 1793 stated that "the whole performance of Mr. Ricketts and his people resembled two flying Mercuries, one poised on one foot on Mr. Ricketts' shoulder while he stood in the same manner with one foot on the saddle while the horse ran at full speed."[1]

There was one act entitled *The Independence of America of the Ever-Memorable Fourth of July, 1776.* Of course Washington was usually accompanied to these festive occasions by Martha who apparently enjoyed them as much as her busy husband. About one of the popular pastimes, President Timothy Dwight of Yale said "The principal amusements of the inhabitants are visiting, dancing, music, conversation, walking, riding, sailing, shooting at a mark, draughts, and chess. In some of the larger towns, card games and dramatic exhibitions flourished. Considerable amusement was also furnished in many places by the examination and exhibitions of the superior schools; and a more considerable one by the public exhibitions of quoits. Our countrymen also fish and hunt."[2]

Although President Washington had little time for outside amusements, he took part when he could to a considerable extent. Strolling actors passed through Philadelphia and acted out comic scenes, sang sailor's songs and the like for all those who would pay three shillings to hear them. Hundreds of people attended those outdoor amusements. Also played was the game which consisted of a bat and a ball and rapid running, often resulting in bruised shins. Kites were flown and even a primitive type of football was played both by young people and adults. Being a Virginian, Washington was of course very familiar with the sport of horseracing. Long before the Revolution, such sport had become popular in the colonies and Virginia was its center. English horses were imported, many being descendants of the Arabian breed. After the war—which of course had interrupted the sport—racing was resumed on a large scale and there was much rivalry between the states of New York and Virginia. In the cities, more emphasis was placed on social balls, sleigh rides, picnics, parlor games, and theater parties. In Philadelphia at this time, a principal sport was the playing of cricket but in most cities the most popular recreation was dancing and new dance steps spread rapidly. Washington had always enjoyed dancing with his wife but also with other ladies, and at one time during the war was said to have danced three consecutive hours with the wife of General Nathanael Greene.[3]

Plays were often advertised as "moral lectures" and such plays as *Richard III* were called *The state of Tyranny*, Hamlet was labeled "Filial Piety" and *She Stoops to Conquer* named "Improper Education." One reason why some people did not like the early theater was that most of the actors were British, and therefore were regarded with hostility as "foreign minions, lately the enemy." Some people wished to avoid crowds and also the rowdiness of many theater-goers who sometimes shouted profanities and threw various kinds of garbage at the actors. For that day, theaters were rather expensive, one charging two dollars per box and one dollar for the gallery. American playwrights, to whose products Washington was exposed, were Royall Tyler and William Dunlap, the latter being a Boston lawyer who wrote a popular play called *The Contrast*, the first comedy written by a native American, which dwells on Americanism versus foreign affectations. Dunlap helped to organize and stabilize the theater. He was also a painter who studied with Benjamin West in London. His play entitled *The Father of an Only Child* marked the beginning of a theatrical career which lasted forty years. He also adapted a large number of French and German plays for American production and wrote a famous one entitled *Andre* which dealt with the capture and execution of the young Revolutionary, British spy. Dunlap helped to found the National Academy of Design and dared to experiment in producing, acting, staging, and management of theaters but later unfortunately went into bankruptcy. Royall Tyler had been an officer in the militia forces which suppressed Shays Rebellion in 1786. Later he was chief justice of the Supreme Court of Vermont and a professor at that state's university.

Landscape painting got off to a slow start in early America but in due time artists found that this country was a paradise of visual beauty. Sculpture, which had not been popular in England—was called by the Puritans, "graven images." It began to attract the interest of American artists in the 1790s. The idea was that Greece and Rome had their sculpture, why not the United States? The most famous American sculptors of our early period were influenced by the Italian, Antonio Canova. He sculptured a figure of George Washington clad in Roman robes—some said, "without a shirt"—and this figure caused great controversy because of the obvious undress and such an undignified conception of our President. It was probably based upon Canova's statue of Napoleon. This sculptor also did a statue of Washington as a semi-nude emperor, which was fortunately destroyed in a fire in 1831.[4]

The statue of Washington by Horatio Greenough was huge and presented him as an old Roman stripped to his waist with a toga draped over his knees, a sword held in his hands as he sat in a Roman chair. This statue was not unveiled until 1841 in the capital rotunda. Said Architect Charles Bulfinch, "Our people will hardly be satisfied with looking on well-developed muscles when they wish to see the great man as their imagination has painted him. I fear that this statue will give the idea of Washington's entering or leaving a bath. If I should give my advice, it would be to send the statue to Athens to be placed in the Parthenon with other naked Greek men." Although it was not sent to Athens, the statue was eventually placed in the basement of the Smithsonian Institution.

The early American was treated to a breakfast which if not to his liking, held variety and abundance. On the main lines of travel, fresh meat and vegetables were served, but Indian corn was the principal staple and it was eaten three times a day along with salt pork. Only the rich could afford fresh meat, and ice chests were little known. Hogs cost very little to keep and also to kill and preserve in salt. Therefore the ordinary rural American was brought up on salt pork and corn. The probable effect of this narrow diet showed in dyspepsia, arthritis, and diabetes. Of course the wayside inns were centers of dissemination of news among the people. The few newspapers had very limited content. People who stopped at the inns tried to make up for this discrepancy by conversing with each other in order to learn what was going on in their various communities, especially those in distant parts of the land.

President Washington, of course, had to be careful in his public exposure not only because of people who crowded in to see him but because of his own safety, as there were many outlaws on the roads, especially robbers. Philadelphians were particularly fortunate in having a valuable library which had been founded by the foresighted Benjamin Franklin in 1732. From this model, numerous small subscription libraries were formed throughout the country. All the then-public libraries in the United States could hardly have shown a total of 50,000 volumes including duplicates, and one-third of these books were on theological subjects.

Noah Webster, who before beginning his famous dictionary, was a newspaper editor, wrote on many subjects, and constantly complained of the ignorance of his countrymen. He stated that "Our learning is superficial to a shameful degree. Our colleges are disgracefully destitute of books and of philosophical apparatus. I am doubtful that any branch of science can be fully investigated in America, for want of books, especially original works."

President Dwight of Yale struck out at the refusal of local legislatures to build turnpikes. The principal reason, it was said, was that turnpikes, like the establishment of religious worship, had their origin in Great Britain, the government of which was a monarchy and the inhabitants, slaves; that the people of Massachusetts were obliged by law to support ministers, to pay the fare of turnpikes and were therefore slaves also. But if they chose to be slaves, they undoubtedly had a right to their choice.

The people of Philadelphia and presumably George Washington, could look out upon the Schuylkill River and see for that time a strange sight. It was a ferryboat powered by an engine and paddles, invented by John Fitch a mechanic without education or wealth. His boat moved rapidly and steadily against the current with as much efficiency as could be expected in an early experiment. Yet Fitch's company failed because he could not raise money, and the public would not use his boat enough for him to build a better one; and as a result, the inventor's heart was broken. He moved to Kentucky, tried there and again failed and took to drinking. Then with twelve opium pills which he obtained with a physician's prescription, he was found one morning dead.

Although he enjoyed diversion, President Washington stressed the idea of the educational responsibilities of the new nation. He had had comparatively little formal education himself but he realized the increasing need for an educated population. It would be many decades before an organized educational system could come about, and indeed, our country is still in the throes of establishing an effective system today.[5]

Washington had been touched and pleased to receive a letter from a young boy, Charles Lee Coles of Charlestown, Massachusetts. It stated:

To the President of the United States

How Oft, Great Sir, has thy Sacred Name been Sounded in Our Infant Ears, By Our honored Father, and how oft Our Tender Mother taught us to Love, Honour and Obey, the Name of Washington, and, How Great Should be Our gratitude to the supreme Ruler of the Universe, For preserving us through our helpless Years, in war, to behold thy face in peace, and to Lisp forth the Immortal praise, of the savior of his Country.

I am in behalf of my Eight Brothers and Sisters, the President's Young Servant.

Charles Lee Coles, Aged 12 years.[6]

The President enjoyed horseback riding but he also regularly took walks. These exercises helped to keep him in good physical condition because he needed such strength for his arduous trips to Mount Vernon and return, sometimes traveling by horseback and at other times by carriage. During his second term, he returned home nine times, the visits ranging from a few days to a few weeks. It is certain that for him, the longer the better. Washington had much to do in supervising his broad acres, his overseers, farmers, and slaves, but he managed to squeeze in some moments of recreation. He indulged in some fishing, visiting with relatives and friends but he did not like hunting and he refused access to others who were anxious to hunt on his thousands of acres. Washington had a herd of English deer and when he learned that someone had killed one of his bucks, "his fury knew no bounds."[7]

How much the Chief Executive enjoyed his visits at Mount Vernon, one may gather from a letter he wrote to his young friend, the Marquis de Lafayette:

At length my Dear Marquis, I am like a private citizen on the banks of the Potomac, and under the shadow of my own vine and fig tree, free from the bustle and busy scenes of public life. I am solacing myself with those tranquil enjoyments of which the soldier who is ever in pursuit of fame—the stateman whose watchful days and sleepless nights are spent in devising schemes to promote the welfare of his own—perhaps the ruin of other countries, as if this globe was insufficient for us all. . . . I shall be able to view the solitary walk and tread the paths of life with heartfelt satisfaction. Envious of none, I am determined to be pleased with all; and this my dear friend, being the order for my march, I will move gently down the stream of life, until I sleep with my Fathers.[8]

Many encomiums were showered on Washington as he entered both terms of the highest office of our land. One of the first of these, widely publicized, hailed him with an appellation which has been repeated down to the present day. It is as follows:

THE GOOD AND GREAT

Call'd from the bosom of his calm retreat,
At once the Hero's and the Sage's seat;
See Washington! assumes the helm of state
And watches hindly for *Columbia's* fate.
Not only great in war, alike in peace,
He lulls our fears and makes all discord cease;
Aw'd by his virtues, enemies admire,
And wish to emulate his noble fire.
Hail, happy Man, crown'd with immortal rays
Of royal pageantry! whilst ev'ry voice,
Hail thee their leader! and their only choice!
Long may this happy land enjoy thy name,
And distant nations spread thy rising fame;
While freedom's sons presided o'er by thee,
Shall rise in arms and arts, and *still be free.*
Pleas'd with the Guardian of their country's cause,
Confederated States shall shout applause;
On each *new Year* our triumphs we'll repeat
And sing of WASHINGTON, the *good* and *great!*

Broadside for the *Baltimore Maryland Gazette,* 1 January 1790.[9]

There has been considerable impression that George Washington and his family being of the Virginia aristocracy, lived in elegance. That this was not generally true has been evinced by a number of accounts of visitors to the Washington home, one of whom was a Frenchman, J. P. Brissot de Warville. Noted he,

Everything has an air of simplicity in his house. His table is good but not ostentatious; and no deviation is seen from regularity and domestic economy. Mrs. Washington superintends the whole and adds to the qualities of an excellent housewife that simple dignity which aught to characterize a woman whose husband has acted the greatest part of the theater of human affairs. . . . The General informed me . . . that his countrymen are less given to intoxication. It is no longer fashionable for a man to force his guests to drink and make it an honor to send them home drunk. You no longer hear the taverns resounding with the noisy parties once so common. The sessions of the courts of justice are no longer the theaters of gambling, inebriation and bloodshed."[10]

The distance between rural neighbors was of course considerable. At Mount Vernon, Washington was mostly surrounded by his family and employees. But in his native Virginia there was the landed gentry such as the families of Thomas Jefferson, James Madison, James Monroe, Henry Lee, and later Patrick Henry. As in the old world, social distinctions were part of the society. Still men of talent could rise above low station. John Adams was the son of a yeoman farmer and Benjamin Franklin began life as a printer's apprentice. It was therefore all the more remarkable that the patrician, George Washington, could wholly associate with these men in official partnership and personal friendship.

Nor by any means was all of our early American leadership of patriot hue. For example, the father of Attorney General Edmund Randolph was a Tory who along with many others of his leaning fled to England at the outbreak of the American Revolution. It seems remarkable in some ways that George Washington, instead of leading the American cause in war as well as in peace did not adhere to the land of his English ancestry. There were many individuals in the middle of the military and social conflicts who later embraced one side or the other. Among these were conservatives like John Dickinson, John Jay, and Robert Morris who opposed independence but later supported the American cause. Royal governors remained loyal to the Crown and most of the Anglican clergy (to whose church Washington belonged) were Tories.

Washington was not very tolerant of the Tories and issued stern warnings against them. As a result, an estimated 100,000 American Tories left the country, most of them never to return. To say this resulted in a huge gap in American society is an understatement. The exiles settled in Canada, England, and the West Indies.

Their property was seized by the patriot government and this great loss became a problem in the attempt made by John Jay to include recompense for them in the Jay's Treaty. Tory estates of great size were confiscated, among them those of the Philipse and Johnson families of New York, the Wentworth estate in New Hampshire, the Pepperell property in Maine, and the Fairfax estate in Virginia all passed into the hands of the American government. There resulted from this loss of aristocracy a leveling influence which affected Washington in both his personal life in which he was in constant danger during the war and in his official capacity later as President.[11]

The food which Washington had was ample but not exceptional. But he certainly enjoyed a more varied diet than did the average American, at least in the eyes of foreign visitors. One, Constantin Volney, declared

I will venture to say that if a prize were proposed for the scheme of a regime most calculated to injure the stomach, the teeth and the health in general, no better could be invented than that of the Americans. In the morning at breakfast, they deluge their stomach with a quart of hot water, impregnated with tea, or so slightly with coffee that it is mere colored water; and they swallow, almost without chewing, hot bread, half baked, toast soaked in butter, cheese of the fattest kind, slices of salt or hung beef all of which are nearly insoluble. At dinner they have boiled pastes under the name of puddings and the fattest are esteemed the most delicious . . . the whole day passes in heaping indigestions on one another; and to give tone to the poorer, relaxed and wearied stomach, they drink Maderia, rum, French brandy, gin or malt spirits which complete the ruin of the nervous system.

Another visitor gave a perhaps unreliable account, stating that his "dinner consisted of a large piece of salt bacon, a dish of hominy and a tureen of squirrel broth". . . . The American "drank nothing but whiskey which soon made him more than two-thirds drunk. . . . No people on earth lived with less regard to regimen. They eat salt meat three times a day, seldom or never have any vegetables and drink ardent spirits from morning until night."[12]

Some modern accounts have over-emphasized George Washington's slaves. For many years beforehand his ancestors had used slaves in both England and Virginia. In those days it seemed the regular thing to do. The father of George who had died when the boy was eleven, did not own a large estate but he did leave the son ten slaves. At the age of twenty-two, when Washington began the management of Mount Vernon, eighteen slaves were there. His marriage to Martha Curtis saw a large increase in the number, and by 1786 he owned two hundred and sixteen slaves.[13]

During the Revolution, one of Washington's bright young aides was John Laurens, from a wealthy South Carolina family, who had lived in France and there grew to detest the practice of slavery—quite a contrast to the plantation owners in his native state. Laurens wrote his father asking that he send Negroes to fight in the American army and be freed at the end of the war. Asked by the father what Washington's opinion was, the reply:

> The policy of our arming slaves is in my opinion a moot point unless the enemy set the example. . . . Besides, I am not clear that a discrimination will not render slavery more irksome to those who remain in it. Most of the good and evil things of this life are judged of by comparison; and I fear comparison in this case will be productive of much discontent in those who are held in servitude.[14]

Washington had often shared with Lafayette his thoughts and plans and was always glad to have the opinions of the young Frenchman. After Lafayette had returned to France following his part in our Revolution, he wrote Washington and proposed purchasing a small estate in which to experiment with freed Negroes as tenants. Should this succeed, Lafayette added he would be glad to extend the operation to the West Indies. Washington thought this was a good idea and complimented Lafayette on his benevolence but deferred the matter and never found it practicable.

Before he assumed the presidency, Washington was called upon by two British evangelists, Thomas Coke and Francis Asbury, sent by John Wesley to organize the Methodist Church here. These ministers preached the emancipation of slaves and circulated petitions in this behalf. Washington received them politely but did not feel it proper to sign the petition. Evidently Lafayette had not been discouraged by the lack of his success in freeing American slaves. He bought an estate in French Guiana and put freed blacks upon it. Washington thought this was "a generous and noble proof of your humanity. Would to God a like spirit might defuse itself generally into the minds of the people of this country. But I despair of seeing it."[15]

Washington complained to Robert Morris that the Quaker Society was going beyond the law in trying to free Negroes. He told

Morris that "no man living wishes more sincerely than I do to see the abolition but legally by slow, sure and inperceptible degrees." Washington desired "to lay a foundation to prepare the rising generation for destiny different from that in which they were born, this afforded some satisfaction to my mind and could not, I hope, be displeasing to the justice of the Creator."[16]

It has been observed that when Washington lived in Philadelphia he was uneasy lest the few slaves who lived there in his family be freed because they were in a Northern state. So he urged his secretary to return the blacks to Mount Vernon and requested that this movement be kept secret so as not to involve more problems. It goes without saying that had he freed his slaves it would have been a great monetary loss since they were his valuable property aside from his land. He had in mind also that the slaves if freed would not be prepared for a new life, given their dependence on their master and lack of knowledge and responsibility. As it was to be, he left provisions in his will for the ultimate freedom of his slaves.

This benevolent attitude regarding slavery was in keeping with the religious beliefs of George Washington. He was a devout man. Yet in his principal biographies, there appears to be no full discussion of his personal religion. One biographer has called him a deist. This is incorrect because, according to Webster, "deism is a natural religion, emphasizing morality, and in the eighteenth century denying the interference of the Creator with the laws of the universe." On the contrary, throughout his recorded career, references frequently abound, quoting Washington as giving credit to God for virtually every favorable major occurrence in his life. He was an active member of the Anglican Church from his early days and at one time was a vestryman of that denomination in Virginia. His religious beliefs were not as orthodox as those of John Wesley, for example, but they were consistent and lasting. During the early part of the Revolution, he had published a General Order forbidding the use of profanity by his troops nor did he permit the use of it in his presence.

In the New York Public Library within the Gordon Lester Ford Collection and presented by his sons, Worthington Chauncey Ford and Paul Leicester Ford, highly regarded early biographers of Washington, is an interesting tract. It is entitled the *Religious Character of Washington* written by Rev. Henry Harbaugh, D.D., pastor of the Second German Reformed Church of Lebanon, Pennsylvania. The Fords apparently regarded this booklet highly. In it the author states about Washington, "His life was a beautiful, harmonious whole, every part of which was pervaded by the holy light of the pure and good. In one word, *Washington was a Christian*. . . . He was a believer in that religion which centers in Christ; which manifests itself in general uniform habits of piety, running through all the feelings of the heart and the acts of life, giving to them consistency, harmony, beauty and attractiveness."[17]

Aside from such glowing language, this clergyman was convinced of Washington's sincere devotion. Harbaugh quoted Chief Justice John Marshall as saying about Washington, "He was a sincere believer in the Christian faith, and a truly devout man." Biographer Jared Sparks is cited as saying,

> After a long and minute examination of the writings of Washington, public and private, in print and in manuscript, I can affirm, that I have never seen a single hint, or expression from which it could be inferred, that he had any doubt of the Christian revelation, or that he thought with indifference or unconcern of that subject. On the contrary, whenever he approaches it, and indeed when he alludes in any manner to religion, it is done with seriousness and reverence.[18]

According to the Reverend Harbaugh, Washington appealed to the Synod of his Reformed Church, "You gentlemen, act the part of pious Christians and good citizens by your prayers and exertions to preserve harmony and good will towards men, which must be the basis of every political establishment."[19]

As early as 1756, Washington had written to Governor Robert Dinwiddie of Virginia about intemperance and profanity. Washington stated that he had "endeavord" to discountenance gambling, drinking, swearing and irregularities of every other kind; while I have on the other hand practiced every artifice to inspire a laudable emulation in the officers for the services of their country." In the same year Washington noted that the men of his regiment were very profane. He expressed his great displeasure and said that any soldier heard doing this would receive twenty five lashes on his back.[20]

At a vestry meeting in the Truno Parish of Falls Church, Virginia in 1765, Washington was present when there was an argument about where to erect a new church building. Washington settled it by suggesting a proper site, having drawn from his pocket an accurate survey of the whole parish. The pastor of this church, the Reverend Lee Massey stated: "I never knew so constant an attendant at church as Washington. And his behavior in the house of God was ever so deeply reverential that it produced the happiest effects on my congregation and greatly assisted me in my pulpit labors."[21]

Before the expedition to Quebec on 14 September 1775, Washington wrote to Colonel Benedict Arnold saying

> I give it in charge to you to avoid all disrespect of the religion of the country and its ceremonies. Prudence, policy, and a true Christian spirit will lead us to liquid compassion upon their errors without insulting them. While we are contending for our own liberty, we should be very cautious not to violate the rights of conscience in others, ever considering that God alone is the judge of the hearts of men.

On 6 March 1776 General Washington issued at Cambridge, Massachusetts the following order imploring "the Lord and Giver of all victory to pardon our manifold sins in wickedness and that it would please Him to bless the Continental arms with His divine favor and protection." While Washington prayed for his army he deliberately omitted prayers for the king of England.[22]

While the American army was encamped at Morristown, New Jersey in the winter of 1776–77, General Washington visited the house of the local Presbyterian minister, Dr. Timothy Jones and told him that he understood the Lord's Supper was to be celebrated there soon. Washington wondered if it was appropriate for one of another denomination to participate in it. The General was told that he was welcome and thereupon took part in the Holy Communion. The communion was held outside under an apple tree. At Valley Forge the general directed that on 17 December 1777 the army remain at its quarters where chaplains would perform divine service.

It has been charged that at the battle of Monmouth 28 June 1778, Washington swore "till the leaves shook on the trees." Aside from the exaggerated figure of speech, General Joseph G. Swift of Geneva, New York later testified that this was not true. Swift was nearby and heard Washington criticizing General Charles Lee for ordering a retreat but, said Swift, "Washington's manner and language were austere but not profane."[23]

Dr. James Thacher recorded in his military journal that a religious service was held in an open field on Sunday, 23 July 1780, and a sermon was preached by a Chaplain Blair of the artillery while troops were stationed for the purpose. Present were Generals Washington, Greene, Knox, and other officers. After the victory at Yorktown on 20 October 1781, Washington ordered that a divine service be performed. The order stated "that the troops not on duty should universally attend with that seriousness of deportment and gratitude at heart which the recognition of such reiterated and astonishing interposition of Providence demands of us." At the Newburgh, New York encampment on 15 February 1783, Washington directed that divine service should be performed there every Sunday.[24]

When General Washington resigned his commission at Annapolis on 23 December 1783, he closed his service by stating "I consider it an indispensable duty to close this last solemn act of my official life by commending the interest of our dearest country to the protection of Almighty God and those who have the superintendence of them to His holy keeping." The Washington family had prayers daily when he was at home and each Sunday morning when the weather and roads permitted a ride of ten miles, they went to church. After leaving the army he wrote General Knox that he then placed his life in the hands of "the all-powerful Guide and Dispenser of human events." As is well known, when President Washington was first inaugurated, he placed his hand on the Bible, a precedent which every president since has followed.[25]

Soon after taking office President Washington sent formal addresses to various religious societies including the Methodists, Baptists, Presbyterians, United Brethren, and to the Protestant Episcopal Church, thanking them for their felicitations on his assuming the Presidency. He issued the proclamation for our first national thanksgiving day on 3 October 1789, starting it with the words, "It is the duty of all nations to acknowledge the Providence of Almighty God, to obey his will, to be grateful for his benefits and humbly to implore his protection and favor." In his diary, Washington, when he had time, went into some detail but usually the entry was brief and nearly always included mention of his weekly attendance at church. Washington regularly prayed at home and read the Bible with Mrs. Washington. Chief Justice John Marshall who was a personal friend and frequent associate said in his authorized biography of Washington, "He was a sincere believer in the Christian faith and a truly devout man."[26]

When in New York and Philadelphia, Washington attended morning church services regularly. In 1793 during the yellow fever epidemic in Philadelphia, President Washington and his family lived in nearby Germantown for six weeks. They boarded with the family of the Reverend Doctor F. L. Herman, pastor of the German Reformed Church, which the Washington family regularly attended. At Mount Vernon, Washington was a member of the Consistory of the congregations of Pohick and Fairfax. He held a pew in each church. According to his nephew, Bushrod Washington, "The Sabbath was never violated at Mount Vernon during the life of its truly Christian owner." In a letter to General John Armstrong, Washington stated, "I am sure there never was a people who had more reason to acknowledge a divine interposition in their affairs, than those of the United States."[27]

The story of young George Washington and the cherry tree has been held up to cynical disbelief. Whether it is true, it was characteristic of the veracity of Washington. Skeptics have also scoffed at the story of Washington praying at Valley Forge. However John F. Watson in his *Annals of Philadelphia* relates that

> The late Isaac Potts, well known for his good sense, hospitality and urbanity, who resided at Valley Forge near Schuylkill River, a preacher to friends, and with whom my informant spent a few days in March 1788, informed him that at the time our army was encamped there, he one day took a walk up Valley Creek, and not far from the dam he heard a solemn voice, and walked quietly towards it; he observed General Washington's horse tied to a small sapling, and in a thicket he saw the General on his knees, praying most fervently. He halted, as he did not wish to disturb him at his devotions, and as the General spoke in a low voice, he could only now and then understand a word, but not enough to connect what he said; he saw the tears flowing copiously down his cheeks! He retired quietly and unobserved.

The Quaker came agitated to his family, and as he mentioned the incident to his wife, he burst into a flood of tears. Long afterwards he related it, always with deep emotions, and drew forth tears from those who heard it—a proof positive that the incident was true, and that it had deeply affected him at the time. He added, in relating it, "If there is any one on this earth that the Lord will listen to, it is George Washington."[28]

The scene at Valley Forge not only discouraged him but moved him to prayer. The sight of his soldiers, their bare feet wrapped in rags and streaking blood in the snow drove Washington to desperation. The nearby stone church not only gave inspiration but served as a hospital for the sick. Reverend Hunter of a New Jersey brigade delivered a sermon and George and Martha Washington attended.

At one time General Washington told Brigadier General

Thomas Nelson, Jr., "That he must be worse than an infidel who lacks faith and more than wicked that has not gratitude. But it will be time enough for me to turn preacher when my present appointment ceases." When Washington resigned his commission at Annapoplis, his closing words were to commend his new country "to the protection of Almighty God." After his first inauguration in New York City he and other government officials walked to St. Paul's Church for special services, the only church in that vicinity left standing after the British set fire to lower Manhattan. In 1791 when the President visited Lancaster, Pennsylvania, he attended a Dutch Reformed Church there and told his wife that he could not understand one word of the message because it was in a foreign language. During the yellow fever epidemic in 1793 Washington set Sunday aside for church services and private letters and closed each day by reading the Bible with his family. A year later he informed his Mount Vernon manager regarding ruined crops that "I am sure the all-wise Disposer of Events knows better than we do what is best for us or what we deserve. His granddaughter, Nellie Custis, said after his death, "His life, his writings proved that he was a Christian."[29]

Washington's will began with the words: "In the name of God, Amen."[30]

Twenty-eight years ago, a book appeared which purported to answer the question of Washington's religious character or lack of it. The volume, *George Washington and Religion* by Paul F. Boller, Jr., is an interesting and informative analysis and cites a seemingly unprecedented number of quotes from Washington in regard to his pious nature and actions. The volume centers around the often-asked query, was Washington a Christian? Unfortunately when the reader is finished, he is not sure of the answer, at least not from the viewpoint of the author. One thing is clear, however: George Washington was religious, if in his own way. But that way, uniquely his own, was different enough so that comparing it with orthodoxy or the leanings of ordinary persons, does not lead to a clear conclusion nor should it be expected to. In this book, instances are given of various individuals from a small girl to a dedicated parson seeing Washington kneeling in prayer. Then others denied that Washington ever kneeled or even prayed in public. He is said to have been a deist but different from Jefferson, Franklin, and Paine in this respect. How many kinds of deists are there? (It is believed that in the preceding pages, the Callahan theory has shown that Washington was not a deist.) Indeed his frequent declarations that God works through our lives to shape our destiny, as well as Washington's fervent thanks for divine help in his military and political accomplishments, directly dispute the main tenets of deism.

Boller points out that Washington's religious views were so widely and warmly received that only two denominations in the United States, the Quakers and Episcopalians, "refrained from embroidering the record of their associations with the President." Yet according to his diary, Washington did not attend church regularly. Probably he did not always mention it or was so busy, as most national leaders, that he found it difficult to do so. The President referred in his verbal and written expressions to "Providence," "the Divine Protector," "the Almighty," "the Great Arbiter," etc. These are questioned as indications of a religious broadness so thin it meant he had little religion. But such were common eighteenth-century designations and all of them, it seems certain, lead to one God. Author William Meade is quoted as saying about Washington, "the communications of no kind, ruler, general or statesman in Christendom ever so abounded in expressions of pious dependence on God."

A close observer of Bishop William White who was a friend and frequent pastor of Washington stated that the President "manifested through life unimpeached sincerity of character and his attendance on the public services of the house of God furnish satisfactory proof of his respect for religion and his belief in Christianity."

On the eve of the departure of John Jay for England in 1794 when he was to negotiate the famous treaty, Washington wrote him to "deserve success by employing the means with which we are possessed, to the best advantage and trust the rest to the All Wise Disposer." When asked by some ministers why "the only true God and Jesus Christ" were not mentioned in the United States Constitution, Washington replied "that the path of true piety is so plain as to require but little political attention." He might have applied this to himself. If his reticence regarding his religious beliefs were not obvious to some skeptical people, perhaps he felt such should be taken for granted.

For his chef, Washington chose Samuel Fraunces of New York who presided formerly at Fraunces Tavern there (still active and home of the American Revolution Round Table). Known as "Black Sam" because of his swarthy complexion, Fraunces had long been devoted to Washington and so fitted in well. Serving under him was Hercules, a capable cook from Mount Vernon. On Tuesday afternoons, the President held a reception for men in the dining room. He stood in front of the fireplace and was described as "clad in black velvet; his hair in full dress, powdered and gathered behind in a large silk bag; yellow gloves on his hands; holding a cocked hat with a cockade in it and the edges adorned with a black feather about an inch deep. He wore knee and shoe buckles, and a long sword with a finely wrought and polished steel hilt which appeared at the left hip. The coat was worn over the sword so that the hilt and the part below the coat behind were in full view. The scabbard was of white polished leather. . . . He had the very uncommon faculty of associating a man's name and personal appearance so durably in his memory as to be able to call one by name who made a second visit." Mrs. Washington held her soirées on Friday evenings.

At meals, the President said grace before sitting down. If a clergyman was at the table, Washington asked him to ask a blessing before dinner and return thanks afterward. On Sundays, the President read a chapter aloud from the Bible after breakfast, then the whole family went to church. There seemed to be a constant stream of beggars appearing at the Presidential household, including sailors who had spent their paltry pay, distressed women, old soldiers and cripples. In the domestic records are shown such items as $50 given for a Catholic Church and $250 to Bishop William White for distribution among the poor of Philadelphia. (Such items are not noticed among the present-day deragotary descriptions of Washington's income and outgo.)

A prominent Philadelphian, Charles Biddle, described in his autobiography an incident of the President losing his temper, and justifiably: an aged mechanic recalled that he had gone to work early one morning to do a job of painting at the President's house. A worker who accompanied the painter "attempted some liberties" with the maid who let them in and she let out loud yells of protest. These brought Washington into the hall, half-dressed and half-shaved, and on hearing the girl's protests, roared, "I will have no woman insulted in my house! Whereupon he gave the offender a kick which sent him reeling down the stairs and then called on Tobias Lear to throw the man out the front door.

Those who analyze President Washington's salary and his expenses probably do not realize the cost of what he considered the proper maintenance of a respectable and dignified executive household. The family of eight with twenty servants consumed daily a large quantity of food. In addition, the weekly receptions and dinners, often with twenty or thirty guests plus holiday celebrations, "and the total expense becomes amazing." Cider had to be bought by the barrel, sugar by the barrel, molasses by the hogshead, and Madeira by the pipe. When his official appropriation did not equal his domestic expenses, Washington paid for it out of his own pocket.

> Though rated a wealthy man, his wealth was not fluid, and the receipts of his private income were often long overdue in reaching him . . . he was loath to ask Congress to increase the appropriation, consequently, he often paid out of his own pocket what were legitimate government charges . . . and toward the end of Washington's administrations, the cost of living in Philadelphia had soared.[31]

4
Yellow Fever

In the summer of 1793, what has been called one of the great tragic episodes in the history of this country occurred. It was yellow fever which broke out in Philadelphia, and its chief historian has called it "the most appalling collective disaster that had ever overtaken an American city." This fearful plague was to remain a threat for a century afterwards. For one hundred days, this dreadful disease horrified not only the citizens of Philadelphia but thousands of others who were afraid to go near the place.

More affected officially than anyone else was President George Washington and his cabinet who were forced to leave the stricken capital and endeavor to supervise the national government from outside. The fever had broken out in July and was first brought to light when on the waterfront a man developed yellow jaundice and died. The disease soon spread to other parts of the city and became a raging torrent of affliction. The situation was worsened by the fact that Philadelphia was a hot and damp low-lying coastal town with a summer climate worse than any Southern city. When the tides were in, they left decayed matter on the banks, and the swampy water was often stagnant. Dead animals were thrown into the Schuylkill River and the shallow wells were continually being polluted by garbage.[1]

President Washington was shocked and alarmed and no doubt wished that the permanent national capital which was to be occupied seven years later, were now available. As it was, the capital had to remain for the time in Philadelphia where many of the citizens were German, French, and Negroes. Personally affected besides Washington were John Adams, Thomas Jefferson, Alexander Hamilton, and Henry Knox. The plague proved to be too big a challenge for the eighteenth-century doctors although they heroically plied their primitive measures. They had no Walter Reed who later discovered that yellow fever is not contagious and is carried from one person to another by a female mosquito. Little was known about this malady but it was soon learned with dismay that the fever begins with chills and pains in the head and body. Temperature rises rapidly and bowels and kidneys are affected. Often in a few days the fever declined but soon rose again with the victim turning yellow and hemorrhaging black blood. Then came a typhoid condition, a dry tongue and rapid pulse and all too often, death. The doctors were handicapped but they did make accurate observations that helped to classify the disease for future treatment.[2]

The hero of this tragic story was not of course George Washington but Philadelphia's "most amazing citizen, Dr. Benjamin Rush." As will be seen, his mighty and persistent efforts to combat this plague have made his name a paramount one in the history of American medicine. Unorthodox, pioneering and even fanatical in his frantic fight against the yellow fever, his personal philosophy and his appealing description of the crisis were almost as distinctive as the horrible predicament itself.

The poet, Phillip Freneau was there and described the scene as follows:

> Hot, dry winds forever blowing,
> Dead men to the grave-yards going:
> Constant hearses,
> Funeral verses;
> Oh! what plagues—there is no knowing!

The first printed account of the yellow fever seen by President Washington appeared on 28 August 1793 in the *General Advertiser* in Philadelphia. This was of course not the first time that he knew of the disease but the newspaper account described how widespread and alarming it was. Dr. Rush had already identified the malady on 19 August when he and two other doctors treated the wife of a West Indies merchant and she had died the following day.

Immediate recognition of the disease was made by the College of Physicians and announced in the newspaper article; printed at the request of Mayor Matthew Clarkson, it panicked the people. The statement described the disease, its symptoms and treatment. It was believed that a ship which had recently docked from Santo Domingo containing a cargo of coffee had been damaged and rotted en route, then dumped on a local wharf where it contaminated the air of those who breathed it. Dr. Rush was at once convinced that this was the source of the yellow fever—but this was only the first of his medical mistakes. Thousands of residents quickly fled the city.[3]

Outside of Philadelphia, the weather was so hot and dry that farmers fainted in the fields. Rumors ran rife and it was reported that fever was showing up from Vermont to Virginia. Still, in Philadelphia, America's national city, and its political capital, crowds collected in the streets. People gathered in stores, churches, and clubs and on the street corners. Impressive processions were held for President Washington who became increasingly conscious of the approaching menace. Dr. William Currie said, "There was something however in the state of the atmosphere in the city or in the constitution of the inhabitants, peculiarly favorably to the operation of the contagion." On 19 August Dr. Rush emerged from his house on Walnut Street and strode toward the river. In this crisis, his last name was certainly appropriate as he dashed from one patient to another. He was gray-haired and forty-seven years of age at this time, well-dressed, erect, and slender. He could not walk too fast, however, because he had weak lungs and a chronic cough. It is a wonder that he was as spry as he was because according to the custom of that day, he bled himself occasionally.[4]

Dr. Rush had told his wife that he advised all families to move from the city, that this was the only way to escape the disease. Thomas Jefferson wrote to James Madison that "Everybody who can is flying from the city and the panic of the country people is likely to add famine to the disease." Said Oliver Wolcott, Jr. to Theodore Wedgwick, "A malignant fever is raging in this place and induces numbers to fly into the country." To his father he wrote the same day, "The apprehension of the citizens cannot be increased; business is in a great measure abandoned: the true character of man is disclosed and he shows himself a weak, desponding and selfish being."[5] As can readily been seen, the center of this momentous drama was Dr. Benjamin Rush and for him to lose a patient was a dreadful catastrophe. He also had a highly moral side which with his religion made him acutely conscious of death although he faced it often and stoically. Already he had found yellow fever patients in various stages of the disease, some without pulse, with cold clammy hands and yellow complexion. Some were feverish and bilious with bloodshot eyes, headache, and nausea. His usual initial prescription was administering calomel and bleeding. One young boy had a breaking out on his skin, his nose was bleeding and he was vomiting. A lady living nearby had the same symptoms but after treatment also died.

These cases and countless others, Dr. Rush recorded in his notebook. He still thought the cause was the rotting coffee on the wharf. Soon he pronounced the disease "the bilious remitting yellow fever." He advised his friends and other doctors to leave the city but to their credit the medical men chose to remain. Already Dr. Rush was being ridiculed but he kept on with his diagnosis and when he had time urged preparations against the disaster which would be much worse. Although this was a hideous invasion, yellow fever was not unknown in Philadelphia where it had been experienced to some extent for about every decade since the time of William Penn. But it was still hated each time and this was to be by far the worst. Before, it was of moderate dimensions but now it was soon to be a surging, bloody flood of devastation and death.

Government and private business were halted in their operation and the few which remained open did so with dread and skeleton staffs. The Supreme Court of the United States tried to meet, but in vain for lack of attendance of the judges; the Pennsylvania General Assembly adjourned after only eight days of sessions; and even the political turmoil that had descended upon the President of late dwindled to a low key under the apprehension of the "yellow menace." Indeed, the spread of fear so permeated the populace that it was in some ways worse than the disease. Although the fever itself was not contagious—as we were later to learn—fear was and it spread its dark presence throughout this eastern city leaving the imprint of its ghastly fingers upon the place that still shows the dire effects and was said to have lowered Philadelphia, which was there first, to a national position below that of New York.

A disheartening aspect of the plague was the different conceptions of its cause and nature. Some of those affected believed the disease had its origin right in their midst—and in a way they were right—because the local breeding places of mosquitoes were not surpassed anywhere in their propensity for the multiplication of the deadly little creatures. Others, as we have seen, felt that the fever arrived from abroad, brought there by ships in the harbor—and hadn't one of them in particular recently brought in a crew of filthy, infested Santo Dominicans? Although this was not true, when panic strikes there are many who will grasp at the nearest scapegoat and in this case, the new immigrants made perfect villains in the popular mind. Benjamin Rush did not improve this situation when he struck out at his medical colleagues for disputing his methods. It was difficult enough for the poor souls to try to fight the fever but to try to discern which doctor was correct made the predicament inestimably worse. The ubiquitous Fisher Ames felt that ignorance was the worst enemy of those trying to eliminate the catastrophe. In short, it was a maelstrom of looming affliction seldom seen on the earth and was compared to one of the plagues in the Bible.

Blacks were not seen to be infected for at least a month but then they began to come down with the fever. Philadelphia's Black community of over 2,400 people were mainly servants, laborers, cooks, and laundry workers. These folks found that they had no better friend than Dr. Rush, who at first had thought they were immune and that God had given them this particular protection. Unfortunately, this was not the case. Charles Willson Peale was not only a painter but he had a wonderful collection of stuffed animals and birds in his home. Just before the plague struck, he had been collecting birds for his museum. When the illness came, he shut himself up with his whole family in his house. The birds he had gathered for specimens were cooked and eaten instead; the artist then spent this time classifying his collection. As a preventive, he sprinkled vinegar over all of his family and furniture several times a day and marched through the house firing off a musket so that it would fill the rooms with smoke and hopefully ward off the disease.

Dr. Rush still tried one remedy after another. Of him, Henry Knox remarked, "The different opinions of treatment excite great inquietude—but Rush bears down all before him." As an example of his activity, Rush between the eighth and fifteenth of September saw and prescribed for over a hundred patients a day; his assistants, several more. They had to refuse many calls. The doctors gave up meat and drink and lived on broth, milk, vegetables, and water. Rush opened his Bible and read from Psalm 121, "I will lift up mine eyes to the hills from whence cometh my help." His religious affiliations however, were as varied as the remedies he used. At first, Dr. Rush was an Episcopalian, next Presbyterian, afterwards a Universalist, then returned to Presbyterianism. In his anguish and desperation, he cried out, "My only hope and refuge thou knowest, O God, is in thee." But he so persisted in bleeding his patients excessively, it is now believed that some died simply from that treatment alone. Nonetheless, people stopped Rush in the streets and told him how much they thought of him, wrote him letters of gratitude and in many ways seemed to think he was their saviour.

A Philadelphia merchant, Samuel Breck, visiting in Philadelphia at the time, observed some of the victims. He was there on the eighth of September and reported that the next day,

> Everything looked gloomy and deaths occurred that day from the fever. In the afternoon when I was returning to the country, I passed by the lodgings of the Vicomte de Noailles who had fled from the revolutionists of France. He was standing at the door and calling to me, asked what I was doing in town. 'Fly,' said he, 'as soon as you can for pestilence is all around us.' And yet it was nothing then to what it became three or four weeks later, when from the first to the twelfth of October, one thousand persons died. On the twelfth a smart frost came and checked its ravages.

Breck added that this memorable affliction was extensive and heart-rending. Its rapid march terrified physicians which caused them to use different methods of treatment. For a long time, it was noted, nothing could be done other than to furnish coffins for the dead and men to bury them. One man who tried to find lodgings had to sleep on the floor of the stable. Next morning he was found dead. Another individual visited a doctor who turned out to be a quack and instead of treating the man, he called for a coffin for him. Even so, death soon occurred and the cart for the corpse arrived at the appointed hour. Perhaps the saddest comment on the yellow fever epidemic in Philadelphia was made by Breck. Cried he, "The burning fever occasioned a paroxysm of rage which drove the patient naked from the bed to the street and in some instances to the river where he was drowned. Insanity was often the last stage of his horrors."[6]

Thousands of similar examples could be cited but a typical one is that of two French sailors who stayed in a room at a local boarding house. Also there was a Mrs. Richard Parkinson who fell ill of the fever. Then one of the sailors was stricken and although attended by a physician, died. On the next day, Mrs. Parkinson expired, followed by a couple who sickened and died within a few hours of each other. Next, the other French sailor passed away and next door two other persons likewise.

Church bells tolled constantly to announce the funerals and Dr. Rush told his wife that "the fever has assumed a most alarming appearance. It not only mocks in most instances the power of medicine but has spread through several parts of the city remote from the spot where it originated." Rush was not the only man leading the attack against the yellow fever. Mayor Matthew Clarkson was a tough and substantial businessman, rich and learned. He was formerly a New York aristocrat who had grown up in Philadelphia and was a successful insurance executive. By 1793 he had a considerable fortune but also nine children for whom to provide. He was also counselor of the American Philosophical Society, founded by Benjamin Franklin and still active today, in part giving grants to authors. Washington had known him before the Revolution when he had served as an auditor of army accounts. To him, Dr. Rush turned for help and the mayor typically responded. He warned the people that they could expect to see the epidemic to continue for some time and called on them to do their part as an essential duty.[7]

Meantime, Dr. Rush set aside eleven rooms intended to prevent the spread of the fever. Citizens were admonished to avoid infected persons, fatigue, drafts, and intemperance. When visiting the sick, vinegar or camphor should be used; every house holding sick people should be marked as such; beds should be without curtains in large airy rooms; tolling of bells should be discontinued; closed carriages should be used for burying the dead as privately as possible; streets should be kept clean; gunpowder should be burned to clear the air; and a large and airy hospital should be provided for indigent patients.[8]

Apparently not every one was ignorant of the real cause of the malady. Writing in the *American Daily Advertiser*, someone who styled himself "A.B." prophetically observed that the late rains would produce a great increase of mosquitoes. Whoever would take the trouble, the writer went on, to examine their rain-water tubs would find millions of mosquitoes swimming about in the water with great agility but not yet quite mature enough to fly off. Readers were advised to take a glass of wine and pour a teaspoon full of oil into it. The results should be the destruction of the whole brood of young mosquitoes. Some foolish measures were taken by frightened people including the recommendation of chewing garlic and tobacco; of covering oneself with vinegar; of spreading soil on the floor of a room and changing it every day. One young boy who heard that tar was a preventive fastened a tar rope around his neck one night and buttoned his collar over it. He awoke strangling and barely got it off just in time to save his life.

In a city directory compiled at that time were listed the names of some of the prominent citizens of Philadelphia. These included Samuel and James Pemberton, Benjamin Rush, Alexander Hamilton, Thomas Mifflin, Thomas Jefferson, and George Washington. Among others who could have been included were John Jay, John Adams, and Henry Knox. As well-informed as these leaders were, they were slow to react to the progress of the pestilence and for a time were undecided whether to stay or go. Nevertheless, shops were beginning to be empty of clerks, printers left town and it seemed that virtually everyone had the sickness in their families. Doctors noticed more and more people with glazed eyes, chills, nausea, and nose bleed. These symptoms were followed by cramps in the stomach, hiccoughs, stupor, purple coloring of the whole body, and then all too often, death.

Dr. Benjamin Rush in desperation turned to his Maker, "While I depend upon divine protection and feel that at present I live, move and have my being in a more special manner in God alone, I do not neglect to use every precaution that experience has discovered to prevent the infection." His prayer evidently was answered because he came through the epidemic unharmed except suffering from exhaustion and depression.

To make matters worse in late August a violent rain storm struck the city. Dust was turned to mud as more inhabitants left town. They rushed out into the country leaving their residences to the mercy of the fever and the flood.

A general exodus struck the city. Federal Government officials were no exceptions. President Washington departed for Mount Vernon on 10 September, stating that he would like to have stayed longer but that Mrs. Washington was unwilling to leave him "surrounded by the malignant fever" and that he could not think of hazarding her and the children any longer by his staying there. Jefferson fled the "nondescript disorder," as both Hamilton and wife came down with it. Washington told Hamilton that he hoped the fever would not be serious and added that the "malignancy of the disorder is so much abated that not much is to be dreaded." How little did the President know. He even invited the Secretary and Mrs. Hamilton to dinner. Only three days later, Hamilton was at the point of death.[9]

Martha Washington wrote to Mrs. Alexander Hamilton, expressing gladness that the Secretary was recovering from the fever. Said Mrs. Washington, "We are lucky to have three bottles of old wine that was carried to the East Indies, which is sent with three of another kind which is very good, and we have plenty to supply you, as often as you please to send for it." Later Martha was to write Fanny Washington that "I thank God we are all well—and not the least fear of the yellow fever while the weather is cold. Some people seem to anticipate its return in the summer—but I believe they have no cause but that of a gloomy disposition—they have suffered so much that it cannot be got over soon by those who were in the city. Almost every family has lost some of their friends, and black seems to be the general dress in the city."

That Mrs. Washington was actively aware of the loss of others is evident in a letter she wrote jointly with the President to Tobias Lear on the death of his wife. "It is the nature of humanity to mourn for the loss of our friends," they wrote, "and the more we loved, the more poignant is our grief. It is part of the precepts of religion and philosophy to consider the dispensations of Providence as wise, immutable, uncontrollable; of course it is our duty to submit with as little repining as the sensibility of our natures is capable of, to all its decrees."

As the Washingtons prepared to depart from plague-stricken Philadelphia, they invited Mr. and Mrs. Samuel Powel to accompany them. The couple declined the invitation; however, Elizabeth Powel writing to Martha on 9 August 1793, "After a long conversation with him [Mr. Powel], I collected that he saw no propriety in the citizens flying from the only spot where physicians conversant with the disorder that now prevails should be consulted; nor does he appear to be impressed with the degree of apprehension that generally pervades the minds of our friends." Seven weeks later, Samuel Powel was dead of the fever.

Now, the burden of the executive duties fell upon Secretary Henry Knox. He was instructed by Washington to send by every Monday's post information of the disease and its progress. The President also urged Knox to move the clerks and all the War Office out of the city, but evidently Knox insisted on remaining.

For several days, Knox was really Acting President. He had been asked by Washington to take charge of the government during the absence of the President, and with Hamilton ill, Jefferson gone, and Randolph also out of town, there was no one else of comparable rank to do so. Knox reported to Washington on 15 September, praising Dr. Rush for his treatment of the fever victims. All public offices, state and national, were virtually closed, except for the national war office. "All my efficient clerks have left me, from apprehension," Knox said, adding that he planned to see that no necessary duty would be neglected. "The streets are lonely to a melancholy degree," the almost-deserted Knox told Washington.

> Hundreds are dying and the merchants have fled. Ships are arriving and no consignees to be found. Notes at the banks are suffering to be paid. In fine, the stroke is as heavy as if an army of enemies had possessed the city without plundering it . . . Colonel and Mrs. Hamilton, it is said, have excessively alarmed the Morris family at Trenton, having lodged there. The people of Trenton refused to let them pass and compelled them to return again to Mr. Morris. Everybody whose head aches, like Rush . . . Mr. Meredith took, upon an alarm, 20 grains of calomel and as many of Jullop. Although it cured him of his apprehension of the yellow fever, it very nearly killed him with the gout at his stomach.

With hundreds of people dying daily and being carted through the streets to overcrowded cemeteries, Knox finally took the advice of Washington and departed from Philadelphia. He was the last of high officials to leave. He reached Elizabethtown, New Jersey, on 19 September, only to learn that quarantine had already been established in New York through which he was to pass en route home. So for four weeks, Secretary of War Knox inadvertently remained in the town whose newspaper he had founded as a propaganda sheet back in the war days. Had he not been so conspicuously large in body, Knox might have slipped across to Manhattan in spite of the quarantine guards. But in that borough, published instructions warned citizens not to take strangers into their homes. All goods that arrived there from Philadelphia were to be unpacked and aired out for forty-eight hours before being allowed to enter the city. Bedding was to be washed and smoked with the "fumes of brimstone."

During his enforced sojourn in Elizabethtown, the sturdy Knox merrily passed away the time by writing Washington and describing what was going on in the panic-stricken section. The militia were out all over New Jersey much as in the days of war. New Yorkers seemed to have gone crazy from fear of the plague, with fugitives from Philadelphia undergoing much fright because of being interned on Governors Island without having sufficient living accommodations there. A boat from New Jersey succeeded in landing some passengers in New York City, but a mob quickly gathered and drove the passengers, whom they insisted were infected, back on board, together with one of the mob, who got mixed up in the shuffle. His name was Mercier, and he insisted to mob leaders that he had not come on the boat and had not been away from the city for six years, but in their excitement and fear, they would not believe him. So Mercier had to spend the night on board the stranded vessel with people he was sure had yellow fever.

Knox also told Washington of a New York tailor who had a case of mild common fever. But hearing so much about the epidemic of yellow fever which was proving deadly, he proceeded to take such great quantities of the medicine prescribed by Benjamin Rush that he really became ill. Overanxious friends, thinking that he was going the way of most of the Philadelphia victims, ordered the man's coffin. "And to mark the monstrous absurdity which prevails," Knox added, "the people came into the sick man's room in droves to see the *curious fever*, and he has been so worried, that his life *is* in great danger." As can be imagined, Knox wanted to get through to Boston to be with his beloved wife, Lucy, and the children. He tried to get a boat to Newport, but none would take him, since that town was also full of rumors about the deadly Philadelphia fever. So it was with much impatience that Knox waited out his quarantine in New Jersey, remarking with his unfailing good humor that he was "too bulky to be *smuggled* through the country."

Back at his post in Philadelphia, Knox found that the plague was not yet over. A memorandum of his, dated 11 October 1793, states that "yesterday we were witness to what appears to me shocking. A coffin was brought to the entrance of Welch's Alley, where it stayed for some time waiting for the man to die, before he was put into the coffin. Such hurry must bury many alive; 137 were buried here in one day by a committee, besides those privately interred."[10]

By early September, Washington was becoming more and more concerned with the increasingly disastrous situation. The Philadelphia streets were deserted. Citizens scurrying along the thoroughfares made strange sights as they held their noses against the odoriferous wind. If one feared that any person he was meeting already had the disease, the pedestrian veered off in order to avoid him. Vehicles sounding down the street created fearful havoc among those in front who thought the approaching wheels might be carrying a load of corpses bound for the dumping pits.

But Washington still remained at his plantation home. As usual he had placed advertisements in the newspapers stating that anyone having accounts with his household, please settle them before he left for Mount Vernon. These advertisements disturbed some people who were concerned that their leader might be deserting them to the ravages of the epidemic. Perhaps the bravest of those remaining were the doctors. In the midst of a rainstorm they held a meeting of the College of Physicians in the building of the American Philosophical Society. This gathering was at the request of Mayor Clarkson and it was the first such meeting in which the Fellows of the organization were appealed to by the local government. These doctors were the last earthly resort and were not only medical men but also leaders of the community. Some of them had been educated in Europe and felt that they logically could disagree with Dr. Rush, himself a graduate of Princeton and the University of Edinburgh. Sixteen physicians were present at the meeting to consider what steps could be taken to combat the epidemic.

It was realized that in Philadelphia at this time there were numerous nurses and midwives, apothecaries, and even soothsayers who, though not all incompetent, could hardly be recognized as having a cure for the fever. There were even physicians from outside the country such as one from the West Indies who was more of a politician than doctor. A few French doctors were on hand but, like others from abroad, their credentials were often regarded as questionable by the Fellows of the College of Physicians. The Abolition Society, the Masonic Order, the Temperance Society, and the Society of the Cincinnati were all represented in the College as well as in the American Philosophical Society.

Dr. Rush believed that all fevers were the same and all had their basis in the air which people breathe. Dr. Currie disagreed with this theory and did not think that the air or rotting coffee could cause any kind of infection. Some thought the numerous cemeteries through the rays of the sun falling on them gave off harmful evaporations. Philadelphia was also undergoing a long drought which was blamed by some. Rush, who seemed to have no end of theories, pointed out that the trees between the city and the Schuylkill River had been cut down years before and the resulting space had increased the likelihood of fevers.

There was a book by John Moultrie, Jr., of South Carolina which he had written and published while a student at the University of Edinburgh that contended the fever was caused by too much exercise, heavy drinking, and fetid air. Another book by John Lining of Charleston contained the theory that the fever originated in the West Indies. In other words, there was much medical opinion that opposed the theories of Dr. Rush in regard to the coffee, the smells, and the filth. So it can be seen that in this meeting of the College of Physicians there was confusion. A committee was appointed to report on the best means of preventing the spread of the disease and its contagion. Naturally Rush was one of the committee and after consulting with the others, he went home through the rain and worked on the report until late at night. The report was soon adopted unanimously and sent to the mayor, the governor and lawmakers and then was published in the newspapers. Unfortunately, the report held out little solace for the public. No preventive or cure had been found and in the document the uncertainty and dread which the doctors felt was clearly shown. The main features were

Avoid infected persons.
Beware of fatigue, drafts and evening air.
Dress properly and drink sparingly.
Use vinegar or camphor on your body when visiting the sick.
If sickness is within a house, mark it on the outside accordingly. Patients should be in the largest and best ventilated rooms.
Stop tolling the bells.
Bury the dead as privately as possible.
Keep the streets clean.
Do not build fires in houses or on the streets, but burn gunpowder to clear the air.
Provide a large and airy hospital near the city to receive poor, stricken people.[11]

The report had a quick effect. Streets were cleaned, houses were scrubbed and whitewashed and gunpowder was burned. Philadelphia was an ill-smelling city. The few nervous inhabitants who walked outside left a swath of unpleasant odor from their tarred ropes, camphor bags, garlic chewing, and having been doused with vinegar. People were afraid to shake hands with each other and hesitated to wear revealing mourning bands. Sailors were so ill that ships stayed tied up to the docks, leaving no room for incoming vessels.

As work and business slowed down almost to a halt in Philadelphia, the shops and stores no longer had use for their clerks and laborers. Those who could, left the city but more of the jobless thronged the streets, became hungry, penniless, and unable even to buy medicine or pay the doctors. It was now imperative to do something about this situation. The College of Physicians had urged as its most important goal that a place be found for the deceased paupers. An organization known as the Guardians whose aim was to help with the poor came forward and took possession of the Ricketts Circus, already discussed, located at Twelfth and High Streets. Fortunately for him and his performers, they had moved on to New York before the plague struck. Now to this amphitheater came infected patients who were laid out on the floor. Some of them soon died. Nearby neighbors, learning of the presence of the sick, were horrified and fearful and threatened to burn the building.

Mayor Clarkson was aware of the situation in the circus building and of the neighbors' threat to burn it. He called the Guardians together and they resolved to do their best to find a suitable house away from the city but not too far removed, to house these indigent patients. Also needed were doctors, nurses, and supplies. Fortunately they found a place. It was on a high ground just northwest of the city and was a famous old mansion. They could not have made a better choice, for this venerable home happened to be empty. The history of the house itself was interesting. In 1723 Andrew Hamilton, an eminent attorney, had purchased from Mrs. William Penn a large estate known as Springettsbury Manor north of the city. It had an acreage as large as the city of Philadelphia itself. Hamilton had built here a magnificent resident and named it "Bush Hill." In 1735 Hamilton had successfully defended John Peter Zenger, publisher of the New York Weekly Journal against the charge of seditious libel, a landmark case which established the principle of a free political press in the colonies. Andrew Hamilton was not able to enjoy this estate very long for he died in 1741 and was buried there, having bequeathed the estate to his son James. Vice President John Adams occupied the mansion for two years. His wife Abigail admired the house greatly and thought it was a delightful residence. Bush Hill then was transferred into the hospital which the physicians had sought. From a magnificent and historic home it became "a dread charnel house of fear, dismal suffering and death."[12]

A young medical student, Charles Caldwell from North Carolina was in Philadelphia and was living with a family who fled the city. He appealed to Dr. Rush for help in finding a new place to board and was told about the hospital which had opened at Bush Hill. There, qualified students were needed to act as aides to the doctors in giving prescriptions and supervising the nurses as well as other such duties. No pay was involved but it was a good opportunity to help and study the yellow fever. Caldwell jumped at the chance and soon was busy in what he learned was a melancholy atmosphere.

Young Caldwell found that everything at the hospital was "limited, crude and insufficient, the nurses few and inexperienced, the whole establishment being, in its character as a hospital, the product of but two or three days labor by men altogether unversed in such business and was a likeness in miniature of the city at the time, a scene of deep confusion and distress, not to say of utter desolation."[13]

As has been stated, one remedy for combatting the fever which had been recommended was to destroy the plague by firing cannon and thus creating heavy smoke. Although this practice had been abandoned, one equally ludicrous was being enacted. This was the firing of small guns both indoors and out and the resulting pandemonium which enveloped the scene. Houses reverberated with the explosions of muskets. This extreme action would not have been so bad except that the bullets caused physical damage. It became so dangerous to walk in the streets that the mayor ordered the firing stopped. "Continue to commit me by your prayers to the protection of that Being who has so often manifested his goodness to our family by the preservation of my life," Rush prayed.

He evidently had a strong faith for despite his setbacks, despite his trying every remedy he could muster, the result was the same: no success. As the number of deaths increased, Dr. Rush was reminded of what Benjamin Franklin had said, that in Barbados those who came down with the fever did not begin to recover until after the doctors had run out of medicine. In his anguish and desperation, Rush continued to pray and then began examining in his library the books of famous physicians who had written about the yellow fever. But to his dismay, he found that they contradicted each other and gave him virtually no help in his predicament.

It must not be concluded, however, that Benjamin Rush was the only hero of this futile war. He was the best-known and had made a name for himself before this tragic episode. He was a signer of the Declaration of Independence, a co-founder with James Pemberton of the first anti-slavery organization in this country—and his name has been prepetuated in the Rush Medical School in Chicago. Dr. William Currie worked as hard as Dr. Rush but has not received equal credit. He composed a pamphlet, the extended title of which belied its length of thirty six pages: *A Prescription of Malignant, Infectious Fever Prevailing at Present in Philadelphia; with an Account of the Means to Prevent Infection, and the Remedies and Method of Treatment, Which Have Been Found Most Successful: By William Currie, Fellow of the College of Physicians.* This was the first publication to appear on the subject of the yellow fever in this country. In it, Dr. Currie portrays the symptoms of the fever in simple, understandable language, unlike most medical tracts. But he erred in stating that the fever was caused by bodily contact. He urged cleanliness, well-ventilated houses, proper diet, and exercise and temperance. Most of all he emphasized fresh air.

Charles Willson Peale, the painter, was exceptionally distressed by the plague as can be understood because of his artistic sensitivity. He commented that the situation could not be comprehended except by those who were present. "Fear seemed to have absorbed all the finer feelings of the heart," he said. And no wonder. The spectacle would have turned the stomach of the most hardened individual. Husbands left wives and vice versa, parents deserted their children, and human death became as familiar as that of a pet dog. Bodies were neglected in the streets. A man and his wife were found dead in bed with their small child between them still alive. Parentless children wandered along in the streets. For some reason, women are less susceptible than men. Corpses were dragged away like dead animals and then buried together in a single hole. One grimly humorous incident occurred when people came upon a drunken sailor in the street, and mistaking him for dead, called for a cart to take him to the cemetery. As he was being dragged by the heels toward a coffin, the sailor suddenly awakened and astonished his handlers by blood-curdling yells.

This terrible situation sank fully into the troubled consciousness of President Washington, and he had hesitated about leaving on his long-planned visit to Mount Vernon, as we have seen. One major concern of his was the severe illness of Alexander Hamilton who had almost died from the fever. Washington was fond of Hamilton but even more than this, it is believed, he needed the services of the Secretary of the Treasury. But now with Hamilton on the way to his recovery, the President and Mrs. Washington had finally departed for Mount Vernon. Even then he was not certain, as he wrote Henry Knox, that "the spreading of and continuance of the disorder may render it inadvisable for me to return to this city as soon I first intended. In case you should remain in the vicinity of Philadelphia, please write me a line by every Monday's post informing me precisely of the then state of matters . . . I sincerely wish and pray that you and yours may escape untouched and when we meet again, it may be under circumstances more pleasing than the present."[14]

It can easily be seen why Washington was so concerned. The newspapers were full of reports on the dreadful condition. There were calls for creditors of decedents' estates; banks asked that all notes be renewed so that their makers could leave the city. The movement of indigent patients to Bush Hill was publicized and all infected people were requested to be segregated and kept together. The illness of Alexander Hamilton had caused a controversy. Instead of using Dr. Rush, Hamilton had asked Dr. Edward Stevens of New York to treat him. Stevens and Hamilton had been friends since their boyhood in the West Indies and were at King's College together. Stevens used the West Indies treatment for yellow fever and had openly denounced the theories of Benjamin Rush. Both Secretary and Mrs. Hamilton contracted the fever but under the care of Dr. Stevens both made a quick recovery. In typical manner, Hamilton made public his reaction by writing a letter to the College of Physicians praising the method of Stevens as differing from that of Rush. This unnecessary gesture caused criticism of Hamilton from the Republicans, but praise from the Federalists who were glad he recovered. He sent a copy of his letter to Washington. As noted, others refused to leave the city, among them Charles Willson Peale who was not only a painter but had established a renowned museum. The place was so crowded it was a wonder that there was room for the large family which included four children with the appropriate first name of Raphael, Rembrandt, Titian and Rubens. Peale worked so hard taking care of his family that for two weeks did not take off his clothes. Fortunately, the Peales survived the plague.[15]

Around the middle of September, Dr. Rush was becoming exhausted. His sleep was interrupted by heavy sweating. Wearily he remarked that when it was evening he wished for the morning and when it was the morning the forthcoming labors of the day caused him to shudder as he faced them. He was so tired that often he had to lie down for awhile between visits to his patients. Then he became ill and his young assistants endeavored to take care of him. The news of his illness caused consternation.

Letters came from all parts of the city. But Benjamin Rush was too tough to die. In a few days he was up prescribing for bleeding and purging his patients. Now he was treating as many as 150 patients a day but in the evening he found time to write letters and record his observations. Not to dwell too long on this remarkable doctor, but as can be seen he was the outstanding figure of the plague although most of his methods were wrong and the real cure for yellow fever was not to become known for over a century. In 1900, Dr. Walter Reed and his associates carried out in Cuba experiments with soldiers which conclusively proved that yellow fever is caused by mosquitoes. As a result the disease has virtually been eliminated in this country and the general hospital of the army medical center in Washington, D.C. is named for Walter Reed.[16]

It is hard to imagine a catastrophe of similar proportions in the United States today, although a likely number of casualties occur each year from different causes. In that time when the nation was experiencing growing pains and consisted of only fifteen sparsely-populated states, the yellow fever was to its inhabitants a world-shaking event. In its center was Dr. Benjamin Rush, his associates and the victims; at its periphery was President George Washington, though not as physically affected but as acutely conscious and who felt the greatest responsibility for the country's welfare. The Chief Executive had been hardened by military struggles but in those there were tangible means to combat the enemy. Here he had been caught in a whirlwind of malignant activities in which the enemy was hidden behind an invisible causation. The government had been harshly interrupted and some of its highest officials threatened with death. Washington himself has been criticized for leaving the scene of the tragedy and he did so reluctantly but his long record of bravery under other circumstances belies any accusation that he was negligent or cowardly.

5

A Working Holiday

On 10 September 1793, President Washington had set out for Mount Vernon. The trip had been planned for some time but was delayed because of the yellow fever. He went for two reasons, first because it appeared necessary to leave Philadelphia during the on-going crisis and since other important government officials were absent from the city, little official business could be conducted anyway; also, he was badly needed at home to oversee the confused situation there.

No sooner had he arrived at Mount Vernon than the Chief Executive found this was to be no ordinary vacation. He hardly had time to enjoy the contrasting serenity between the stricken city and his own plantation beside the Potomac. In his Presidency in particular, the seat of government resided in its head man. Wherever he was by choice or otherwise, he bore his burden of responsibility. On this clear autumn day, Washington made his way to the site of the city which was to bear and honor his name. There he found celebration, a dazzling display of colors by members of the Masonic Lodge amid a throng of happy spectators. The cornerstone of the capitol was being laid. The ceremony seemed premature because the building was at the time only part of a foundation. This did not deter the organizers, and the colorful parade included city officials, mechanics, and members of the Masonic Lodge. The latter carried Bibles on cushions and were dressed in bright regalia set off by jewels and accompanied by bands of music. This impressive procession marched through a lane in the forest, and as yet the President could only get a glimpse of what was to be his great city. A few houses appeared along the road, these having been built before Major Pierre L. Enfant, the architect, had laid out the site.

Congress had authorized the President to erect this capitol near his Mount Vernon but they had neglected to appropriate money for the ambitious project. Local landowners had donated ground to the government in the hope that the forthcoming city would increase the value of their adjoining land. Washington and other government officials had encouraged the construction but it had been disrupted by a number of factors. L'Enfant had proved to be so temperamental and inconsistent that he had been dismissed. The landowners had fallen out with the commissioners and much interest had been lost in the entire project. The state of Pennsylvania wished to hold on to Philadelphia as the nation's capital and was offering public buildings at the expense of the state.

There had been differing plans for the design of the capitol building but Washington and Jefferson preferred one which featured a dome in the middle flanked by extending wings. Designs however did not bother the marchers as they reached a bare hilltop. There Washington was presented with an engraved silver plaque as cannon sounded, Masons officiated and a huge ox was barbecued and devoured.[1]

This was a memorable occasion for the Masonic Order and Washington, its most eminent member. Before the cornerstone was laid, the official inscription was read aloud. It said, "This southeast cornerstone of the capital of the United States of America, in the city of Washington, was laid on the eighteenth day of September, 1793 in the eighteenth year of American independence in the first year of the second term of the Presidency of George Washington whose virtues in the civil administration of this country have been as conspicuous and beneficial as his military valor and prudence have been useful in establishing our liberties."[2]

Although he received frequent correspondence from other government executives, Washington could not conduct much business at Mount Vernon because he had not brought official papers with him, not expecting to stay there very long. It seemed that everywhere he turned on his plantation, there was something wrong. Horses had been turned loose in the fields where clover was growing and had destroyed much of this valuable forage. The manager of the farm had to be replaced and the new one had not yet arrived. So Washington's relaxation was short and inadequate. How he would have liked to remain there, free from the cares of his feverish world but as in times past, this was denied him. Information came from Jefferson and Knox that Philadelphia was still not free of the yellow fever. Now back at his post in that city, Secretary of War Henry Knox had discovered this condition.[3]

With the critical contingency in mind, Washington instructed his cabinet to met him in Germantown, Pennsylvania on the first of November. He asked members of his cabinet what they thought should be done in regard to the Congress meeting if the Philadelphia epidemic continued. Since most of the actions of the national government at this time were without precedent, such decisions were not easy ones. Hamilton and Knox were of the opinion that Washington could call Congress to meet at any place in an emergency. On the other hand, Jefferson and Randolph felt that the Constitution prohibited such deviation. Washington wished to avoid any possible charge that the Executive was interfering with the prerogative of Congress. He was especially careful in this because a Southern site had been chosen as the new capital of the country and he did not wish to offend Northerners. So he decided that he would go to Germantown and the others in government could join him there, this being an apparent solution in regard to the Constitutional question.

Washington was joined at Baltimore by Thomas Jefferson who not uncommon for him in those days—was not in a good humor. En route he had been robbed of seventy dollars and was additionally upset because the yellow fever had forced him out of Philadelphia at an important time when decisions in which he was involved had to be made. He and Washington reached Germantown in a downpour of rain and there saw many disheartened refugees from Philadelphia walking the muddy streets.

As can readily be seen, the decision of Washington to meet here regardless of its Constitutionality meant that he was taking the side of Hamilton and Knox. Some historians have stressed that Knox seemed to agree with Hamilton on almost every such occasion. This was not always true but when they did agree, it was logical because both had similar beliefs, both were conservative Federalists and both were loyal to Washington (especially Knox); and in general they were really in agreement with the President. After some haggling among his staff, Washington was finally housed in a handsome mansion belonging to Colonel David Franks. In this same house nine years before, British General Sir William Howe was awakened by the news that an American army under Washington had arrived in Germantown. A fierce battle followed in which many of the American troops became lost in a fog and fired upon each other. The artillery of General Henry Knox attacked a detachment of redcoats holed up in the nearby Chew house but despite the heavy assault which used enough ammunition to dislodge a regiment, the cannon balls only bounced off the sturdy brick walls and the resulting delay contributed to the defeat of the Americans. Now the commander-in-chief was back in a contrasting, if civilian capacity, even though the nasty weather and political situation were both uncertain.

The President was of course saddened by the recent loss of a number of friends from the plague in Philadelphia, particularly by the death of Samuel Powel whose companionship and that of his wife had long been cherished by the Washingtons. There had been rumors, (like others, groundless) that Washington was romantically interested in Mrs. Powel. Such rumors, gleefully pounced upon by predatory historians and others who would like nothing better than to find flaws and tear down this great and good man, were doubtless based upon the fact that Washington enjoyed the company of most of the ladies he met, but that was all. The President was only one among many who grieved, since over 5,000 people died of the 1793 yellow fever menace.[4]

At the Germantown meeting, the question arose as to what distance from shore did American sovereignty protect its ships from raiders. It was up to the President to settle this question and thereby set another precedent. Jefferson stated that the greatest extent which had been authorized for territorial waters was the limit of sight, which was about twenty miles. The smallest distance considered was how far a cannon ball could carry, then about three miles. Washington decided on the three-mile limit.[5]

In late November, Washington was occupied with collecting and arranging materials for his annual address to Congress. There were a number of topics to be presented, Secretary Knox having presented an account of Indian and military matters on the frontiers but consideration of these could wait. The real problem was how to explain and justify the Proclamation of Neutrality. In a cabinet meeting, Jefferson and Randolph expressed opinions that the President should not declare anything further about war or peace. Hamilton as usual took the opposite side and said the Chief Executive should not hesitate to make such declarations. So now Washington was again caught in the middle; but this time he sided with Jefferson, ordering positively that all relevant papers should be laid before Congress. He told Jefferson, "I am well satisfied with the train things are in."[6]

Snow fell early that winter in Philadelphia and with its coming, the yellow fever seemed to have vanished. Though Congress now for the first time had a Republican majority, Washington's address was well received. His explanation of the policy of neutrality was simple yet convincing. He repeated his ideas as set forth in the Proclamation of Neutrality but added that it was up to the wisdom of Congress to correct or enforce this plan of procedure. The President urged Congress to consider the study of military art which he added could scarcely be attained by practicing it alone. What he had in mind was the establishment of a military academy. The first significant advocacy and materialization of this idea was that of General Henry Knox when during the Revolution at Pluckemin in New Jersey, he established what he called an "Academy" or training school in which he taught officers and men the basic principles of the use of artillery in combat. Therefore, Knox has justifiably been called "the founder of West Point" although its formal implementation did not come until early in the nineteenth century. The peace-loving Jefferson opposed the idea at this Congressional meeting but Washington strongly favored it and doubtless would have been glad to see the military school open its doors above the Hudson River at that time. The press, even the Republican publications, praised Washington's speech, describing it as one of moderation and containing no invective against the conduct of other nations. "Permit me," concluded Washington, "to bring to your remembrance the magnitude of your task. Without an unprejudiced coolness, the welfare of the government may be hazardous. Without harmony as far as consistent with freedom of sentiment, its dignity may be lost."[7]

Secretary of State Thomas Jefferson had a number of times told Washington that he wished to resign and return to Monticello. In mid-December, Jefferson recommended to Congress a general system of reciprocity with such restrictions as Britain or any other nation might lay upon American commerce. Then he delivered his last opinion as a member of the cabinet with a clear explanation and argument for the principle that "free ships make free goods."[8]

Jefferson wrote Washington reminding him that he had previously told the President that he must retire at the end of the year.

That time being now arrived, and my propensities for retirement becoming daily more and more irresistible, I now take the liberty of resigning the office into your hands. Be pleased to accept with it my sincere thanks for all the indulgences which you have been so good as to exercise toward me in the discharge of its duties. Conscious that my need of them has been great, I have still ever found them greater, without any other claim on my part than a firm pursuit of what has appeared to me to be right, and a thorough disdain of all means which were not as open and honorable as their object was pure. I carry into my retirement a lively sense of your goodness, and shall continue gratefully to remember it.

In reply, the President expressed his extreme regret at the loss of his brilliant Secretary of State. There is little doubt that a principal reason why Jefferson retired was because of the bitter opposition of Alexander Hamilton. "I will not suffer my retirement," said Jefferson, "to be clouded by the slanders of a man whose history, from the moment at which history can stoop to notice him, is a tissue of machinations against the liberty of the country which has not only received and given him bread, but heaped its honors upon his head."[9]

As a young man, Edmund Randolph's father had been a Tory before the American Revolution and had fled from Virginia with the royal governor. The son became an aide to General Washington during the war at the age of twenty-two. Later he was governor of Virginia but owned no large estate and although he practiced law, he hated the profession. Edmund Randolph was an unpopular man. Both Federalists and Republicans distrusted his unpredictability, but as Attorney General, the forty-year-old Randolph had the confidence of the President and his often-impartial views paralleled those of Washington. Jefferson did not like Randolph for other reasons mainly because of the embarrassments of the latter's private affairs which forced him to use expedients that damaged him with merchants and shopkeepers. Randolph at one time tried to borrow money from Jefferson—who was not the best money manager himself. It seems that Washington sided more with Hamilton than Jefferson although the principal biographer of Jefferson contends that "Washington sided more often with him than with Hamilton."[10]

That Jefferson was resentful at the time of his retirement, he left no doubt in his own statement in which he took a slap at Washington: "The firm tone of his mind," he wrote in regard to the President, "for which he had been remarkable, was beginning to relax; its energy was abated; a listlessness of labor, a desire for tranquility had crept on him, and a willingness to let others act or even think for him."[11]

The foregoing statement was patently more resentment than fact. Thus came to a close a year that had been as difficult a one as Washington had experienced in his two terms of office; a year of crisis, of critical conferences, of national and international strife and tension, a period that has been compared to the darkest days of the Revolution, but the great leader rose remarkably to the occasion.

Thomas Jefferson left the Washington administration in an unhappy if formal manner. In his own mind he had many reasons but it is interesting to note that his departure was less friendly than that of Alexander Hamilton although both had heretofore expressed allegiance to their chief. To Washington, the exit of Jefferson was painful but not wrenching. As has been seen, shadows had already appeared over their official relationship but it must have been a blow to the pride of the President to see his fellow Virginian passing from view across the Potomac. From the standpoint of Jefferson, he was leaving at a good time. On the part of Washington whose public standing had fallen to a new low, the loss of his valuable secretary of state was grievous. Even a strong supporter of Washington, John Marshall, later to carry out as Chief Justice many of the precedents set by Washington, commented on the unsettled situation. Much regard and respect still lingered in the minds of the President's followers but recent events, Marshall wrote, "appeared to break the last cord of that attachment which had theretofore bound some of the active leaders of the opposition to the person of the President."[12]

William Duane, a journalist who opposed Washington generally, accused the President of having a fading countenance; of being tyrannical. For his part, the President stated that he was being attacked for his opposition to every measure which tended to disturb the peace of the country. But he continued that such attacks on him would not change his conduct or have any other effect but to increase the joy of his forthcoming retirement. Said he, "Malignity may dart her shafts, but no earthly power can deprive me of the consolation of knowing that I have not in the course of my administration been guilty of a *willful* error, however numerous they may have been from other causes."[13]

It was sad, this parting of two leaders, but Washington was in a position from which he felt he could not back down. In one of his last letters to Jefferson instead of signing it "affectionately," the President had ended it with the words "with every great esteem." Probably this was caused by Washington's knowledge of Jefferson's correspondence with some who differed sharply with the President on political matters such as James Madison and James Monroe. He told Jefferson frankly that he understood that the outgoing secretary had denounced Washington although he had never suspected Jefferson of being insincere. Alluding to the differences between Jefferson and Hamilton, Washington pointed out that he had often sided with Jefferson and that he did not consider any man infallible in politics, that the President had wished to preserve the country from the horrors of war. Then the President wished Jefferson well, especially in his cherished agrarian pursuits.[14]

In modern parlance, President Washington had a bad press. This was especially true in his second administration when it would have pleased him most had the press been favorable. Yet in his generous attitude he even recommended that newspapers be free of transportation tax. Outwardly he seemed to appear comparatively indifferent to the taxing of the journals but inwardly they often aroused his ire and struck him as being unfair and unwarranted. At one time he notified the publishers that he had no time for newspapers and wished to cancel his subscriptions to the New York *Daily Advertiser*. Perhaps the most abusive anonymous letter directed against the President appeared in Thomas Greenleaf's *New York Journal* on 7 December 1793. In it was asserted that "aristocratical blood" flowed in the President's veins, that he was guilty of gambling, reveling, horse racing and horse whipping, that he was so stubborn he could not stand restraint, that he was infamously niggardly" in his personal business transactions, and was a "most hard swearer and blasphemer" despite his religious pretentions to the contrary. This was just too much for Washington's friends and a apology was demanded from Greenleaf—with which he complied.[15]

One result of the yellow fever epidemic which must have been welcome to President Washington was the demise of Philip Freneau's *National Gazette*, the newspaper that Jefferson had sponsored and which had consistently criticized Washington in the past. It was a victim of the fever—some wag characterized its final issues as "yellow journalism". Its editor, Philip Freneau, retired to his farm in New Jersey and continued to write poetry.

Who would take the place of Secretary of State Thomas Jefferson, probably the most able such man ever to hold that office?

President Washington did not take long to decide. On Christmas Eve of 1793 he invited Attorney General Edmund Randolph to succeed Jefferson. The next day during the Christmas celebration at the President's house, Randolph agreed. The new secretary was disliked by both the Federalists and Republicans but the Virginia dynasty was to go on. Washington had reason to believe that this was a good appointment. Randolph was described as being tall with fine features, dark eyes, a dignified and commanding attitude with pleasant voice and having on the whole the manner of an accomplished gentleman. For awhile he had been Washington's private attorney and never sent him a bill.[16]

In the ratification of the Constitution, Randolph had done only a fair job. At first he helped to present the Virginia Plan which became a main element of the Constitution, but then refused to sign the finished document. However, he later was convinced of its importance, changed his mind and supported the Constitution. In the first years of President Washington's terms of office, Randolph was overshadowed by the three great members of the cabinet, Hamilton, Jefferson, and Knox. When the war between England and France broke out, Washington found Randolph's opinion very useful. With his background, the attorney general could often see both sides of the question and came up with a compromise. During the yellow fever epidemic, Randolph, who still practiced law on the side, told Washington that the plague had so interrupted his business that he might have to resign because of financial need. The background of Randolph's life is important because of later crisis in the cabinet which he precipitated.

The reaction to President Washington and his administration at this time was far from being altogether unfavorable. As long as he stood fast, his most loyal supporters remained in his camp. "Tis by such a spirit, seconding the endeavors of the government," he wrote, "that we shall have the fairest prospect of preserving our peace. 'Tis by such a spirit that in any event we shall secure the internal tranquility of our country, its respectability, and shall be enabled to encounter with firmness any attempt hostile to its safety, its honor, or its welfare."[17]

An especially heartening resolution came from Caroline County, Virginia, forwarded by Edmund Pendleton. It stated: "Neither time nor dirty scribblings with which the public has been lately pestered have produced the smallest abatement in my private affection for you or my unlimited confidence in your public administration, both of which are so riveted that they are not shaken by attacks much more weighty than those trifles light as air."[18]

The journalistic abuse of George Washington in that time was similar to some expressed in the media at the present time. Two centuries have passed since Washington was in office and still the denunciation of him in some questionable quarters goes on. There have been within recent memory radio and television programs depicting George Washington in various stages of life as an awkward, bumbling figure engaged in heavy drinking, gambling, and chasing after women, these images gleaned mainly from a greedy desire to make money off of a helpless figure. In a television series the young Washington was dramatized as a soap opera type of lover too confused to know whether he should pursue married women or remain stoically with his troops. This of course was mere fancy. Certain books published in the 1980s present Washington as a low-life individual who turned in excessive expense accounts and was paid more than his services were worth. It was one thing to write and publish such pusillanimous trash but it was even worse for scholars to review these books as if they represented true history. It is fortunate that we can still view Washington's face properly high atop Mount Rushmore.

More material matters occupied the mind of Washington as the year drew to an end. There was an Indian crisis in the Northwest and as early as September, he had known that the long awaited negotiations with the Indians had broken down. American commissioners had been sent to deal with the red men but so far to no avail. The chieftans wanted the boundary of the United States to be the Ohio River. The commissioners turned their attention to British officials on the Canadian shore of Lake Erie and still were unable to make successful contact with the Indians. Washington suspected that Canadian officials were creating more difficulty than tranquility; that Great Britain wished American settlers to be restricted as far South as possible. Secretary of War Henry Knox complained that efforts for progress had been hindered by "procrastinated and fruitless but absolutely necessary negotiation."[19]

It was time for action. The one who desired it most was Major General Anthony Wayne, known as "Mad Anthony." Wayne had been a spirited officer in the Continental army and had distinguished himself in the battles of Brandywine, Germantown and Monmouth. He led a brilliant attack and captured the British garrison at Stony Point, New York, afterwards moving troops to reinforce West Point after the defection of General Benedict Arnold. Generals Harmar and St. Clair had failed to defeat the Indians, Wayne had been placed in command of American forces in the West, and Washington and Knox were confident that Wayne could do the job; still it was not quite time. In late summer the President had received a report from England that the British had issued an order-in-council by which naval commanders were authorized to seize and confiscate any cargoes of corn, flour, or meal bound for France in a neutral ship. Washington and his cabinet were astounded at such audacity.[20]

Thomas Pinckney, the American minister at London, was instructed to demand revocation of this decree which was judged to interfere with the rights of free commerce. But this was easier asked than done. Washington was afraid such depredations would increase and that American ships and men might be held indefinitely in British ports. Another worrisome possibility was that the British navy which was suffering from manpower shortages because of the war with France would step up its dreadful practice of impressing American merchant seamen. Another problem was that of thousands of Westerners who were denied use of the Mississippi River by Spain, but it was hoped that this would soon be remedied by treaty negotiations in Madrid.

There was no separate naval department of our national government until 1798, so the business of the Navy—what there was of it—was handled at first by the War Department under Secretary Knox. In the latter part of 1793, he had a bill introduced into Congress to build and equip six naval frigates for the service of the nation, especially to protect the property of the United States citizens then trading in Mediterranean ports from the damages wrought by the Barbary States pirates. Washington approved of this idea.

Knox consulted with Josiah Fox, a naval architect, and made plans for the building of the ships, he and Commodore John Barry interviewing Fox and deciding that he was capable of doing the job. Fox was subsequently employed as a clerk in the War Department specifically to do this work, and later spent many years as a naval architect in the construction of our first Navy vessels. It was not until 27 March 1794, however, that authorization was forthcoming from Congress to build the frigates. Soon afterward, Knox directed Joshua Humphreys, a well-known Philadelphia ship-builder, to prepare the plans and models for those vessels. Humphreys was appointed Naval Constructor on 28 June at a salary of two thousand dollars a year, the pay to be retroactive to 1 May because of his "incessant application to the public interest in adjusting the principles of the ship, drawing of draughts and making models."[21]

Another precedent set by Washington was that regarding the militia. During the Revolution, General Washington had often been frustrated by the lack of cooperation of the various colonies in acceding to his earnest requests for militia reinforcements. The general had no real authority to compel such action and showed remarkable patience and constraint in dealing with the situation. Many men would have given up in such dire discouragement but not Washington. One reason why he desired a strong Federal government was such a lack of unity in the loose confederation. With different attitudes and commanders, the militia was often ineffective and many of its members simply deserted.

Now that the Constitution had given the President as Commander-in-Chief authority over the militia, it still did not provide a mode of implementation. On several occasions Washington had asked Congress to provide for a uniform manner of training of the militia. He felt that by this method the loyalty of the troops would be toward the Federal government instead of the states. (The question of whether the present national guard is under the authority of its various states or the federal government is still a matter of dispute.) The President had not been very successful in such integration but he did assert the primacy of presidential claims to use the militia in national emergencies and as an instrument of national policy. He made it clear that the national interests are above any state reservations about who was in command of the militia. For example, Washington ordered militia units to join in the campaign against the Indians when General Arthur St. Clair moved against them. The President took similar action when he called out the militia from Pennsylvania, New Jersey, Maryland, and Virginia in the Whiskey Rebellion. He thought it important not only to preserve peace but also to make it a point that challenges to the national sovereignty must not go unanswered. Local grievances, he believed, should not be allowed to prevail over the common good. Still the President never waivered from his belief that in any republic, the military should always be subordinate to civilian authority.[22]

Of course George Washington was for most of his public career either engaged in a war at home or facing the consequences of conflict abroad. If he had not had extraordinary patience after the war with England, we would undoubtedly have been in another such conflict. The disasters incurred by the American armies in the West were attributed to British intrigue with the Indians. George III was pictured as unleasing bulldogs against the United States. Guns, powder and even tomahawks which the Indians used against the Americans on the frontier were believed to have been supplied by the British for the purpose of killing Americans. In addition to this, James Madison estimated that because of the Indian wars, this country was losing three and a half million dollars a year in the fur trade.[23]

In 1794, the British had 6,000 troops in North America, a thousand of whom were stationed on American soil—eleven years after the Revolution had ended. The military posts within the borders of the United States which the British had promised in the peace treaty were still in their possession and no sign was given of the redcoats moving out. With these posts the British controlled the fur trade and therefore had the loyalty of the Indians. In their eyes this made the United States appear to be a second-rate power. It was no wonder that President Washington, still trying to maintain neutrality, held the British government accountable for the frontier troubles. If not, he asked, why did England not punish its agents in the United States and Canada who stirred up the Indian wars? The American Indians who frequently warred among themselves were easily aroused anyway. They saw their tribal lands being taken over by white settlers. They often were at the mercy of lawless white bandits. One American officer said, "The people of Kentucky will carry on private expeditions against the Indians and kill them whenever they meet them, and I do not believe that there is a jury in all Kentucky which will punish a man for it." Even so President Washington said that Americans must learn to treat the Indians justly and in general he and Secretary Knox did so.[24]

Congress looked for a scapegoat in the failure of the Western military expeditions, and an investigating committee was formed, the first such to examine the situation. The committee asked Secretary of War Knox to see the papers relative to the campaigns. The request was referred to the President and he and his cabinet agreed to comply with the request "so far as the public good would permit." As a result of its investigation, the committee exonerated General St. Clair and Secretary Knox and placed the blame for the defeat upon contractors who had failed to supply the army with proper equipment. Washington was gratified but this still did not take the place of a military victory.[25]

Sentiment against Great Britain heightened. Some thought that war with another country was necessary to teach its leaders that the United States was an independent nation. Others exclaimed that they would take on "the whole mob of European kings with all their murdering legions and cut-throats." A sculptured figure of George III was removed from its base in Philadelphia in order to prevent mob violence. British officials in this country were insulted and threatened. One American cried out, "The avenging arm of America once uplifted should chastise and pursue a corrupt and base tyrant till his worthless life is terminated upon a scaffold."[26]

The bark of the Americans, however, was bigger than their bite. Although there appeared to be forthcoming an economic crisis, the Republicans particularly showed no eagerness to increase American defense. They were not afraid that Great Britain, engaged in a war with France and sapped of resources, would dare to engage in another war. Too, the United States was England's best customer—and that nation was known for its economic acumen if not greed. Weapons of trade would be enough to strangle the British bulldog, many on this side of the ocean contended. Jefferson commented that "war is not the best engine for us to resort to; nature has given us our commerce which, if properly managed, will be a better instrument in obliging the interested nations of Europe to treat us with respect."[27]

The Federalists took a different view. Led by Hamilton, they felt that the British were tough enough to stand just so much of American opposition and would eventually substitute arms for documents. The United States, after all, was still nominally an ally of France and too much active interest toward that country would convince London that we were about to take the French side, contrary to what Washington had declared regarding neutrality. War with England would mean, the Federalists reasoned, deprivation of valuable import duties and repudiation of the Hamiltonian fiscal policies. Even more reprehensible would the involvement of the United States in the tragic situation in Europe. This, it was feared, would also involve this nation in such horrors of the French Revolution which even included the guillotine. In addition, our country was occupied in fighting Indians, its militia was poorly trained and equipped with little ammunition and the seaport fortifications had fallen into disrepute. "The United States, in short, presented the spectacle of a nation armoured in righteousness and rectitude but in little else."[28] The influence of the French Revolution on America at the time has perhaps not yet been fully realized. The influence continues today. A vivid comment on the contrast was shown in a letter of Alexander Hamilton, although his viewpoint was of course extreme.

> The cause of France is compared with that of America during its late Revolution. Would to Heaven that the comparison were just! Would to Heaven we could discern, in the mirror of French affairs, the same decorum, the same gravity, the same order, the same dignity, the same solemnity, which distinguished the cause of the American Revolution! Clouds and darkness would not then rest upon the issues

as they now do. I own I do not like the comparison. When I contemplate the horrid and systematic massacres of the 2d and 3d of September; when I observe that a Marat and a Robespierre, the notorious prompters of those bloody scenes, sit triumphantly in the convention, and take a conspicuous part in its measures—that an attempt to bring the assassins to justice has been obliged to be abandoned; when I see an unfortunate prince, whose reign was a continued demonstration of the goodness and benevolence of his heart, of his attachment to the people of whom he was the monarch, who, though educated in the lap of the despotism, had given repeated proofs that he was not the enemy of liberty, brought precipitately and ignominiously to the block without any substantial proof of guilt, as yet disclosed—without even an authentic exhibition of motives, in decent regard to the opinions of mankind; when I find the doctrines of atheism openly advanced in the Convention, and heard with loud applause; when I see the sword of fanaticism extended to force a political creed upon citizens who were invited to submit to the arms of France as the harbingers of liberty; when I behold the hand of rapacity outstretched to prostrate and ravish the monuments of religious worship, erected by the citizens and their ancestors; when I perceive passion, tumult, and violence usurping those seats, where reason and cool deliberation ought to preside, I acknowledge that I am glad to believe there is no real resemblance between what was the cause of America and what is the cause of France; that the difference is no less great than that between liberty and licentiousness. I regret whatever has a tendency to confound them, and I feel anxious, as an American, that the ebullition of inconsiderate men among us may not tend to involve our reputation in the issue.[29]

Another description of that conflagration was given by Gouverneur Morris, United States Minister to France at the time. Wrote he, "In the meantime, the arms of revolutionary France were crowned with great success. Towns fall before them without a blow, and the declaration of rights produces an effect equal at least to the trumpets of Joshua. We must observe the civil, moral, religious, and political institutions," said he.

These have a steady and lasting effect, and these only . . . Since I have been in this country, I have seen the worship of many idols, and but little of the true God. I have seen many of those idols broken, and some of them beaten to dust. I have seen the late constitution, in one short year, admired as a stupendous monument of human wisdom, and ridiculed as a egregious production of folly and vice. I wish much, very much, the happiness of this inconstant people. I love them. I feel grateful for their efforts in our cause, and I consider the establishment of a good constitution here as the principal means, under Divine Providence, of extending the blessings of freedom to the many millions of my fellowmen, who groan in bondage on the continent of Europe. But I do not greatly indulge the flattering illusions of hope, because I do not yet perceive that reformation of morals, without which, liberty is but an empty sound.[30]

As noted, it had been recommended in Congress that a navy be created. Washington had employed various vessels in the Revolution but these were mainly no longer fit for duty. This was in line with Washington's statement that he was determined to preserve the peace if he could but to be prepared for war if he could not. The last of the old Continental Navy ships had been sold a decade before. Suggestions were made that instead of building one ourselves, a foreign navy be hired. It was observed that navies were foolish things and the main reason the English people were taxed so heavily. A sort of naval force had been under the jurisdiction of the Secretary of War but now it was believed a larger and more organized fleet was necessary. So Congress in February of 1794 authorized the construction of such frigates.

A bit of levity occurred when the French Revolutionist, Constantin Volney, visited the United States and made a tour of the country. In order to facilitate his reception, he asked President Washington for a letter of recommendation to the American people. Volney was known as a free thinker and the President was in a difficult spot. Wishing to avoid any controversy, Washington simply wrote on a sheet of paper, "C. Volney needs no recommendation from George Washington."

This small indication of Washington's brighter side only peeks at the inner character of the man. He has been labeled as being noble, stolid, stately, and grave but he had a lighter side when there was occasion for such—which was rare. His remarkable self-discipline has been described many times. Yet when he did lose his temper—and that was only in extremely unusual instances—it was an explosion of pent-up wrath which in one listener's words, "shook the ceiling." Washington had few close friends yet he was probably during the height of his career the most beloved President in our history, at least by the general public. True, this was a distant kind of affection mixed with awe but it was there. He was not and is not regarded as a genius but his combination of valuable characteristics were of more value to his people. He realized his limitations and often admitted them in his writings at times to an unnecessary extent. But he showed his dependence upon others by his frequent calling together of his advisors and listening to their opinions; then after deliberation, he made up his own mind. Thomas Jefferson felt that Washington's mind was slow in operation but sure in conclusion and John Adams put it more succinctly "slow but sure."

Washington's spartan life was exemplified by his daily routine. He usually rose at 5 a.m. and spent a few hours in his bedroom writing letters in his rather heavy hand in the periphrastic language of that day. When he could not finish his correspondence in the mornings, he would stay up at night, even in the arduous army days, and continue it until the late hours. If possible, he then emerged from his quarters and took a long ride with available companions. All agreed that he was a superb horseman. On his return, Washington had breakfast and then returned to his work. In the middle of the afternoon, labors ceased and a meal was served which lasted for about two hours including rest afterward. The fare varied from the simple food in the field to lavish multi-course dinners featuring meat and poultry, vegetables, pastries, and puddings. Following this repast, work was resumed until early evening when the President ate a light supper accompanied by his favorite wines, Madeira or claret. While at table, Washington usually said very little—for which he was sometimes criticized—but he preferred to listen to the chatter of his companions. There is no evidence that he indulged to excess, although he was reasonably convivial.

This can well be ascertained by the state of Washington's health which he maintained successfully throughout his sixty-seven years. Had he been a dissipated man as some of the modern accounts try to perpetrate, his health would have showed the effects long before he retired. At it was, he led a strenuous physical life as a young surveyor, farmer, and warrior and came through in excellent condition. Especially as commander of the American Revolutionary armies, he endured continuing hardships in the field and suffered great stress in camp as he worried over the bleak prospects for victory in view of lack of men, money, and cooperation of the state governments. Often he was up late at night when his subordinates had gone to bed, studying and writing in connection with his vast problems. The despair and disappointment which he endured would make a modern psychologist wonder why he did not collapse under the strain as have others of our national leaders at times. The only signs which showed the burden under which he labored was the graying of his hair and the lining of his face, both normal progressions, and the eventual need for reading glasses at the end of the Revolution. He did not become stooped or crippled, his appetite remained good and mainly natural aging shows in the portraits of him which we see now. He did have trouble with his teeth and from the time he was forty-three worse false ones.[31]

It has been stated that George Washington was fearless. If this can be true of any mortal it appears to be so in his case. He risked his life in fighting the Indians, and during the War for Independence, had several horses shot out from under him. He once rode calmly in front of enemy lines and a British sharpshooter, Major Patrick Ferguson, lined him up in his rifle sights, but Washington rode steadily on leaving the marksman so amazed that he felt the general might be divinely protected. Before his heavy duties descended upon him, Washington played cards in taverns, played wicket, and went fox hunting, but when he became a commander he forsook sports and continued to forego them after he became President. Yet he loved fun and friendly companions, men and women. Any innuendoes that he engaged in illicit sexual activities are unfounded and spurious.

It has been charged that Washington insisted on being in control of all the situations in which he was engaged. Such a psycho-historical analysis of our first President borders on a violent assumption. What great leader in all history was not in control of his achievements? If he had not been, he would not have been the leader. If there were anything extraordinary in the peerless career of Washington, it would seem that he depended too much on the opinions and participation of others. His endless staff meetings both in the army and as President bear witness to the fact and bolster the assertion that he was in control because the people *wanted* him to be in control. He was *urged* to become commander of the American Revolutionary armies and he was *unanimously* elected President after the war in the greatest demonstration of popular respect and warm admiration in American history. He wanted to retire at the end of his second term but his closest associates as well as the people fervently pressed upon him the necessity that he remain in office. He could have been king, he could have had a third term, but he magnanimously refused both.

George Washington did have a dignified manner which was by some called lofty and self-centered. It must be remembered that his were aristocratic English forebears, that it was a day of formality handed down from the monarchical motherland and that in his high position, he preferred a stately approach to life and became its symbol. Most people expect a measure of reserve in their leaders; especially in the military it has been found that a happy medium of distance between officers and enlisted men coupled with a pleasant camaraderie makes for the best discipline. and Washington was in some ways always a general. Even Gilbert Stuart trying to loosen him up, was met with a cold reminder that he need not forget who it was he was painting. True, if Washington were a candidate for public office today, he would be excoriated for unnecessary hauteur. The eighteenth century was another day. It was a time of pomp and circumstance but even so it was also the time of the Enlightenment which bestowed a brightness on the lives of people still content to hold their leaders in benign regard.

An ingrained part of Washington's life was his lasting love of the haven to which he repaired as often as his busy schedule would allow—Mount Vernon. To him, the place was like that of Antaeus, the god of mythology who returned to the earth at intervals to renew his strength. Washington related the events of a typical day there: "I begin my diurnal course with the sun; that if my hirelings are not in their places at that time, I send them messages expressive of my sorrow for their indisposition; then having put these wheels in motion, I examine the state of things further; and the more they are probed, the deeper I find the wounds which my buildings have sustained by an absence and neglect of eight years; by the time I have accomplished these matters, breakfast, a little after seven o'clock is ready. This over, I mount my horse and ride around the farms which employs me until it is time to dress for dinner. The usual time of sitting at table, a walk and tea, brings me within the dawn of candlelight; previous to which, if not prevented by company, I will retire to my writing table and acknowledge the letters I have received; but when the lights are brought, I feel tired and disinclined to engage in this work, conceiving that the next night will do as well; the next comes and with it the same causes for postponement; I have not looked into a book since I came home, nor shall I be able to do it until I have discharged my workmen; probably not before the nights grow longer when possibly I may be looking into doomsday book."[32]

Part of this daily routine was told to Washington's friend, John Marshall, who spent the might at Mount Vernon before he was to depart for Europe in the XYZ affair. So all was not pleasure on the domestic front, although the pleasing part far overshadowed the rest.

6

The Pursuit of Peace

The spring of 1794 came pleasantly to the capital but for the President there were clouds of concern. In the West, General Anthony Wayne sent word that supplies for his army were low and his enlistments were expiring; even some of the officers of his Legion were acting disloyally. He wrote to Secretary Knox, urging that something be done to relieve his alarming situation. Little progress had been made in improving the fragile relations between the United States and the French and British, particularly regarding the Western Indians. Reports also came in that soldiers were still being recruited in the South for the purpose of attacking the Spanish possessions at the mouth of the Mississippi.

Republicans in the Senate had asked the Chief Executive to send copies of his diplomatic correspondence with Gouverneur Morris, the American minister to France. The Federalists were concerned that dispatches of Morris would show him to have been in disagreement with the principles of the French Revolution. Here was another precedent which Washington had to set. Randolph was sure the papers could not be withheld from Congress but the team of Hamilton and Knox urged the President to keep them entirely confidential. As usual Washington did not adopt either extreme but of the forty dispatches, he allowed thirty-nine to go forward to Congress.[1]

Now came a pleasant parenthesis, if a brief one, in the daily grind of the President. It was on the 22 February, his sixty-second birthday, when bells rang out across the city and cannon boomed with extraordinary loudness to mark the happy occasion. In an elegant reception for him, Washington greeted with politeness the many guests, walked amiably among them and inquired about their welfare. They were served wine and cake, and for the time, this serious man could relax. Another pleasant part of the festive occasion was the arrival of Joseph Fauchet who was succeeding Edmund Genet as minister from the French Republic.

Fauchet proved to be a genial man and made a good impression in contrast to that of his temperamental predecessor, Genet. He disagreed with what Genet had done and asked that he be returned to France but as we have seen earlier, Washington was not willing to turn Genet over to the guillotine. After Fauchet had left, members of Congress dropped in and paid their respects to the President and others similarly called on him including government officials, university professors, members of the Society of the Cincinnati, clergymen, and diplomats. Prominent among the guests were Alexander Hamilton, Henry Knox, Governor Thomas Mifflin of Pennsylvania, and Governor Arthur St. Clair of the Northwest Territory.

Now that the danger of war with France had for the time subsided, the American government turned its attention to the British. The Orders in Council of June 1793 had directed naval commanders to bring neutral ships carrying provisions for France into British ports. This involved the impressment of American seamen into the British Navy. Fisher Ames, the "furious Federalist," commented, "John Bull, proud of his strength, angry, without partiality to France, ardent in his contest and straining every sinew, shows less patience and respect for us than he ought to do. The line of duty is plain—in peace, peace to the last day that it can be maintained our policy should be to dispel the danger if possible and in that same moment, to prepare a defense against it."[2]

Bills were introduced in Congress providing that the United States cease all intercourse with Britain until it had made complete recompense to American merchants and had removed every soldier from American soil. Meantime, there was a hot contest in the Senate over the Republican financial expert, Albert Gallatin (later the founder of New York University) on the grounds that he, born in Switzerland, had failed to satisfy the requirements for American citizenship. According to the principal biographer of Washington, "Gallatin was the one public man whose knowledge of fiscal affairs was thought wide enough to challenge the principles and policies of the Secretary of the Treasury." Gallatin had presented resolutions which called for a report from Hamilton on every measure and transaction of the Treasury Department since 1789. Gallatin was unseated as a result but later was to become Secretary of the Treasury under Jefferson and Madison.[3]

Secretary Henry Knox felt that the United States was on the verge of war with Great Britain, but in this regard, Washington was saddened but uncertain. He believed that instead of contemplating conflict, nations and individuals would be better off by being interested in philanthropy, industry, and encouraging manufacturing and culture rather than martial arts. He was still determined to keep this country free and do all in his power to resolve the conflict with Great Britain.

The urgency of the situation was heightened when it became necessary to send a new ambassador to England. In early March, Senator Oliver Ellsworth appeared at the home of the President with an interesting proposal. Ellsworth suggested that Alexander Hamilton would be the best man for the position. Before the Senator could finish, Washington interrupted him and said that Hamilton did not possess the confidence of the American people. However, Washington was interested in the suggestion. Soon it was learned that John Adams, Thomas Jefferson, and John Jay were being considered for the job. At this time, Senator James Monroe wrote Washington that it would be "injurious to the public interest" for himself to be considered and notified the President that he was no longer a candidate. John Jay, after weighing the matter, accepted the appointment on condition that he still remain as Chief Justice of the United States.

Washington could hardly have picked a more unpopular man than Jay. He was tall, slender, and had a long aquiline nose which extended over a pouting mouth. He had shown a middle-of-the-road attitude toward Great Britain and seemed to feel that that nation had as much right as the Americans to the peace treaties in question. As we have seen, Jay was not Washington's first choice for the position. Little could Washington know what trouble this stolid New York aristocrat would stir up in the administration. James Monroe led the opposition in the Senate and Jay was confirmed by only eighteen to eight votes. Immediately another problem was raised as to whether a Supreme Court Justice could be legally eligible for additional appointive office. Although Jay knew of this dilemma, he refused to resign. His mission to England was to solve all the political problems between that country and the United States which had arisen since the Revolutionary War. These included the giving up of the Northwestern military posts, payment of debts, the current delicate question of the British raids on American shipping, and the consequent impressment of American seamen.[4]

John Jay had only two positive stipulations: he could arrange no treaty of commerce which was adverse to American engagements with France; and he could negotiate no treaty that failed to provide for the admission of American ships to the ports of British West Indies.[5]

Another situation of importance was one closer to home. In February, Governor General Lord Dorchester of Canada had stressed to Western Indians who visited him the strong possibility that Britain and the United States would soon fight. Then the Indians and the English were to occupy much of their former territory. This was hard for Washington to believe but he had received a letter from Governor George Clinton of New York which stated that he did not doubt the authenticity of the report about Dorchester. Washington wrote Knox, who understood Indians well, asking him to keep the situation under close scrutiny and to do all in his power to make the Indian nations peaceful.[6]

Not only Thomas Jefferson had resigned but others wished to do so. Hamilton had informed Washington almost a year before that he intended to leave office. On 27 May he wrote the President again and said because the prospects of the United States remaining at peace were precarious, he could not voluntarily quit his post. He added that he could remain unless the Chief Executive had other plans. This appeared to be a quick change of mind. Washington was pleased that Hamilton would remain and told him that he was glad he would stay until "The clouds over our affairs which have come on so fast of late, shall be dispersed."[7]

Now for the foreseeable future, the President would at least have the service of two stalwarts, Alexander Hamilton and Henry Knox, although both wished to return to private life. Secretary of State Randolph showed no sign of wishing to resign. Noting a period of comparative tranquility, President Washington told his cabinet he would soon depart for a visit to Mount Vernon. Meantime, Secretary Knox held an interview with twenty Cherokee Indian chiefs who were then in the city on a mission of good will. The ceremony involved much sitting around, smoking the strong, smelly pipe of peace, passing around strong drink amid attempts at translation into English of the Indian language. As early as this period, sixty-six years before our Civil War, serious sectional differences were aroused. John Singleton Copley, the noted portrait painter, observed that in Philadelphia, talk of separation of the North and South was common, and that even civil war was mentioned. John Adams declared that "near one half of the continent is in constant opposition to the other."[8]

Senator Rufus King of New York told John Taylor of Virginia that North and South had come to a parting of the ways. The reasons given were that New England would not submit to domination of the Southern states; that the two sections never thought alike; and that a "dissolution of the Union by mutual consent" appeared to be the only way out. These diverse positions at the time grew out of the attempt to bring Great Britain into line with American policy.[9]

On 9 June 1794 Congress adjourned, much to the relief of Washington who, nevertheless, felt he might need their help. As soon as he could prepare for the trip, the President then set out for Mount Vernon. He had noted that his horses had grown fat and lacked exercise and these deficiencies were before long to be revealed. En route, the President decided to have a look at a lock which was being built on the Potomac River. As his horse entered the nearby rough ground, it "blundered and continued blundering, until by violent exertions on my part to save him and myself from falling among the rocks, I got such a wrench in my back," said Washington, that he had to dismount and when he tried to mount again, he found himself in great pain. This was said to have been his most serious injury, since it lasted several weeks, and inconvenienced him somewhat and annoyed him more. He found the accident made it difficult to get about his farms to ascertain how the crops were progressing and how his supervisors were faring in overseeing the operations. Being President and trying to live on the salary of the office, he found demanding. The Western lands which he had purchased were not bringing him a profit, in fact not even breaking even and in this respect Washington found himself "land poor."[10]

Official duties beckoned from Philadelphia. The President wrote Randolph that he planned to return to the capital as soon as he was able to ride. But when it came time to go, he found that his back still bothered him so that instead of travelling on horseback he had to use a carriage. Over the rough roads, Washington journeyed and reached the city on 7 July, after coming through a rainstorm which made his ailment worse. There, he found the Spanish problem still active, responding to comment that some Kentuckians were threatening to march against New Spain, he asked, "What if the government of Kentucky should force us either to support them in their hostilities against Spain or disavow and renounce them? War at this moment with Spain would not be war with Spain alone. The lopping off of Kentucky from the Union is dreadful to contemplate even if it should not attach itself to some other power." This statement resembles one by Abraham Lincoln some six decades later.[11]

The need to insure better relations with Spain gave Washington

concern and he turned to Thomas Jefferson who was in retirement and had done such a good job as one-time minister to
France. But before the former Secretary of State was contacted,
Washington heard from Henry Lee that Jefferson had made some
disparaging remarks about the President, hinting that the Presidential advisers were not entirely loyal to him. Washington could
hardly believe this. Replying to Lee, he said,

> There could not be the trace of doubt in his mind of predilection in
> mine towards Great Britain and her policies unless (which I do not
> believe) he had set me down as one of the most deceitful and uncan-
> did men living: because not only in private conversations between
> ourselves on the subject, but in many meetings with the confidential
> servants of the public, he has heard me often, when occasions pre-
> sented themselves, express very different sentiments with an energy
> that could not be mistaken by anyone present.[12]

When finally Jefferson received the request to serve as minister
to Spain, he replied that he was suffering from rheumatism and
besides, under no circumstances would he ever "engage in anything public." Hardly an accurate forecast in view of the fact that
within six years, he himself would be in the White House, after
participating in many political matters leading to that high office
in the intervening years. Washington then appointed Thomas
Pinckney who accepted.[13]

Furthermore, Jefferson cannot be said to have retired completely from the public scene as judged from his letter from
Monticello to his friend Tench Cox in Paris:

> Your letters give a comfortable view of French affairs and later events
> seem to confirm it. Over the foreign powers, I am convinced they will
> triumph completely, and I cannot but hope that the triumph and the
> consequent disgrace of the invading tyrants, is destined, in order of
> events, to kindle the wrath of Europe against those who have dared to
> embroil them in such wickedness and to bring at length kings, nobles
> and priests to the scaffolds which they have been so long deluging
> with human blood. I am still warm whenever I think of these scoun-
> drels, though I do it as seldom as I can, preferring infinitely to
> contemplate the tranquil growth of my lucerne and potatoes. I have
> so completely withdrawn myself from these spectacles of usurpa-
> tions and misrule, that I do not take a single newspaper nor read one
> a month; and I feel myself infinitely happier for it.[14]

If Jefferson still harbored partiality, Secretary Hamilton was
not helping matters either. Brilliant and accomplished as he was,
he did not "enjoy the confidence of the people." However, Wash-

ington felt he could not afford to lose the services of his aide, his faults notwithstanding. A fresh embarrassment occurred when a committee of the House of Representatives conducted an investigation of Hamilton's official conduct. The committee sought to have answered the question of why Hamilton reallocated money borrowed under the laws enacted in August 1790 for the purpose of payment in Europe of America's Revolutionary loans. Instead, a major part of these funds had been deposited in the Bank of the United States, which had been a favorite project of Hamilton. A related question was: had the President approved such a switch of funds? Hamilton had not written authorization so he asked Washington to give him one. This was a delicate situation and the President was unsure of what he should do. He consulted Attorney General Edmund Randolph and as a result, an equivocal certificate was issued that neither affirmed or denied Presidential sanction of the treasury transaction. This was a great disappointment for Hamilton who complained that the President had been misled. The Secretary wrote the President that "false and insidious men whom you may one day understand have found means by artful suggestions to infuse doubts and distrusts very injurious to me."[15]

The future would tell.

7
The Whiskey Rebellion

Between the American Revolution and our Civil War, the military event which challenged the constitutionality of the President's powers and received the most attention here and abroad was the Whiskey Rebellion of 1794.

It came at a most inopportune time when our relations with Great Britain and France hung precariously in the balance. President Washington was torn by the opposing views of Alexander Hamilton and Thomas Jefferson. The former in his support of a strong central government, favored not only British interests but also an effective national army. Jefferson, on the other hand, favored more independence of the individual states and shied away from anything which smacked of the current militarism of Europe. These two differing points of view were exemplified in several ways and were to lead eventually to the creation of two principal political parties in the United States. Both Washington and Hamilton had been military men while Jefferson had not. Now the President had to determine in which direction the country would head. This placed upon him an inordinately heavy burden.

The difficult situation was compounded by a proposal of Secretary of the Treasury Alexander Hamilton and enacted by Congress in 1790: it was an excise or interior tax levied for the purpose of paying state debts assumed by the national government. Madison and Jefferson had opposed this tax but in working out the compromise for the location of the new national capitol in the South, they felt it necessary to support the measure. As a result, four Pennsylvania counties west of the Alleghanies resented the tax, particularly since it hit hard their manufacture and sale of whiskey.

John Marshall, a contemporary of the Whiskey Rebellion and a conservative, believed it to be a serious threat to the United States and the most important incident of its kind up to that time under the Constitution. The origins of such an uprising go back to early

English history when the lower classes resented and feared the tax collectors—a species of disrepute in certain quarters even to this day.

As early as 1786, a state excise officer, William Graham, appeared in Washington County, Pennsylvania reputedly trying to collect taxes on distilled beverages in three southwestern counties of that state. Some of the inhabitants decided to teach Graham a lesson and one of them, disguised as the devil, encountered Graham one night and told him he was to be handed over to a satanic legion waiting outside. The tax collector was able to evade these visitors but the next day he was approached by a mob in disguise and again intimidated. They grabbed his pistols, tore up his official papers, and ordered him to stomp on them in the muddy road. They even made him resign his commission. Then they cut off half of Graham's hair, punched a hole in his hat and placed it sideways on his head. The unfortunate man was next made to march around the three counties, and forced into whiskey drinking. The crowd was never prosecuted.[1]

Hamilton had argued that if the Western people did not like his excise tax, they could stop drinking whiskey, and that Americans consumed too much spirits for their own good anyway. The College of Physicians of Philadelphia drew up a memorial supporting the Secretary of the Treasury but Congressman James Jackson, representing Western constituents, said they had a right to get drunk, "they have long been in the habit of getting drunk and that they will get drunk in defiance of a dozen colleges or all the excise taxes which Congress might be wicked enough to impose."[2]

President Washington agreed with Hamilton that a real crisis had arrived which furnished a challenge as to whether the government could maintain itself. Not only was there disaffection in Pennsylvania but also in Virginia, Maryland, Georgia, the Carolinas, and Kentucky. The Presbyterian clergy and other moderate leaders had more influence against rebellion than was expected. Also, Indians were at the rear of the insurgents, a fact that brought more fear to their hearts.[3]

One reason why excise taxes were hard to collect in this region was because the justices of the peace would not prosecute the violators for such crimes. The rural people felt that the tax was morally wrong and economically harmful to the farmers and distillers of whiskey. Anyone who was familiar with the living conditions of the region could better understand resistance to taxation. Many of the inhabitants lived in tiny hovels with floors of mud and a considerable number of lice. These western counties had a combination of such people dominated by a small number of wealthy landlords.

In the back country, the farmers of Pennsylvania who had their own stills felt that such a tax on the consumer made no sense. These consumers were often the same ones who manufactured the liquor. Money was so scarce in this part of the country that whiskey was generally used as a sort of currency. Thousands of these rural people felt removed from the eastern and more affluent part of the nation and their resentment had its origin in their European background, most of them being Scots and Irish. In the old countries, the tax collector was known for his abuses. Here the making of whiskey was their main source of livelihood. Grain grew abundantly in this fertile Pennsylvania region but it was not of much market value at its source. A wagon load of wheat or rye or even flour would bring no more that its cost if transported across the mountains. Four bushels of grain was what one horse could carry, but in the form of whiskey, twenty-four bushels could be carried in a similar single load. So these Western Pennsylvanians wanted nobody interfering with their whiskey making or its resultant business.

Washington blamed this resentful attitude on the Democratic Societies which had been formed by the influence of Edmund Genet. The President had written to Governor Henry Lee of Virginia that these societies had continued "to sew the seeds of jealousy and distrust of government among the people by destroying all confidence in the administration of it." Fisher Ames commented that these democratic clubs were "born in sin, the impure offspring of Genet. They are the few against the many; sons of darkness whose meetings were secret against those of the light. They are a false cabal attempting to rule the country and that these doctrines have been budding and blowing ever since, is not new to anyone who is acquainted with the character of their leaders and has been attentive to their maneuvers. I early gave it as my opinion to the confidential characters around me, that if these societies were not counteracted (not by prosecutions, the ready way to make them grow stronger) or did not fall into disesteem from the knowledge of their origin, and the views with which they had been instituted by their father, Genet, for purposes well known to the government, they would shake the government to its foundation."[4]

The Democratic Societies resulted from the enthusiasm for the French Revolution which had swept the United States in 1793.

Genet founded the mother society in Philadelphia resulting in forty similar ones scattered throughout the country. These societies, like the Corresponding Societies of the American Revolution, were dedicated to the extinction of aristocracy and monarchism in the United States. They campaigned in behalf of candidates, informed the American people who were their friends and enemies, lobbied Congressmen, brought out voters, and upheld the cause of France.[5]

Washington wrote to his brother-in-law, Burgess Ball, and expressed anger at the Democratic Societies: "Can anything be more absurd, more arrogant, or more pernicious to the peace of society than for self-created bodies, forming themselves into *permanent* censors and under the shade of night, in a conclave, resolving that acts of Congress, which have undergone the most deliberate and solemn discussion by the representatives of the people chosen for the express purpose and bringing with them from the different parts of the union the sense of their constituents, endeavoring as far as the nature of the thing will admit to form *that will* into laws for the government of the whole; I say, under these circumstances for a self-created, *permanent* body (for no one denies the right of the people to meet occasionally to petition for or to remonstrate against any act of the legislature, etc.) to declare that *this act* is unconstitutional and *that* act is pregnant with mischief; and that all who vote contrary to their dogmas are actuated by selfish motives or under foreign influence—nay, in plain terms are traitors to their country—is such a stretch of arrogant presumption as is not to be reconciled with laudable motives, especially when we see the same act of men endeavoring to destroy all confidence in the administration by arraigning all its acts without knowing on what ground or with what information it proceeds—and this without regard to decency or truth."[6]

By 1 August, the President was well acquainted with the disturbances in the West. Henry Knox wrote him on 4 August, (which is believed to be the first such suggestion) and recommended to Washington that troops from Virginia, Pennsylvania, Maryland and New Jersey be sent to put down the uprisings which seemed to be occurring. Knox estimated this militia strength at 12,400 and the insurgents when armed at probably 8,000. This forecast of figures proved to be remarkably close to the actual numbers later involved in the insurrection.[7]

United States marshalls had served thirty-nine writs on the

excise resisters in Pennsylvania, none of which had had any results. It was the fortieth summons when delivered that brought armed attacks. Marshalls were accompanied on this attempt by the inspector of the western survey, General John Neville, a wealthy resident. The presence of the inspector aroused great indignation among the local people. Shots were fired at the government party, a man was killed, and the fine home of General Neville was burned. Frightened and intimidated, Neville's men fled for their lives toward Philadelphia.[8]

John Neville was born into Virginia planter society in 1731, a year before the birth of George Washington. The former spent his boyhood days on his father's estate on the Occoquan River. Like Washington, he served with General Braddock in the ill-fated expedition against Fort Duquesne in the French and Indian War. For the first two years of the Revolution, Neville was commandant of Fort Pitt and then served with Washington at Trenton, Germantown, Princeton, Monmouth, and was at Valley Forge. He ultimately became a brigadier general in the Continental Army, having equipped a company of soldiers at his own expense. Following the war, Neville settled on the first large estate in the Pittsburgh region which he named "Bower Hill." The Neville mansion was an elegant clapboard structure built of materials imported from Europe, its interior papered and decorated with fine paintings in gilt frames adorning the walls. Floors were carpeted and feather beds embellished each bed. In his ornate study, Neville had a neatly mounted desk facing an eight-day clock, world maps, and a collection of swords and guns adjoining a large library. He had supported the adoption of the Constitution and became a staunch Federalist.[9]

Hugh H. Brackenridge, prominent Pittsburgh attorney, spoke to the insurgents menacing Neville and his men, urging them not to resist the government, and threatened to call out the militia. The speech calmed the insurgents for awhile but not for long. A local attorney, David Bradford, emerged as a leader of the rebels. A meeting of militia officers assembled at Braddock's field, two miles above Pittsburgh, on 1 August.

David Bradford assumed the office of major general, mounted on a superb horse with splendid trappings, arrayed in a field marshall's uniform. With plumes flowing in the air and sword drawn, he rode over the grounds, gave orders to the military and harangued the multitude. Never was mortal man more flattered than was General

David Bradford on Braddock's field. Everything depended on his will and those who despised him paid him the most servile homage in order to control and manage him.[10]

Not only did the Western Pennsylvanians in general ridicule and ignore the taxes on whiskey, but some law officers as well. Collector of Revenue John Webster in his attempts to seize illegal whiskey was assaulted and the case was brought before James Wells, a justice of the peace. Instead of penalizing the defendants, Wells told Webster that he had never known so worthless a law as the excise tax one passed by Congress and that he, the magistrate, was sorry the person who made the assault had not knocked Webster down. The defendant went free. According to one historian, Webster had made a practice of seizing liquors on the road from poor people who were carrying it to procure salt or other necessities. Sometimes, he would simply collect the tax and let the liquor pass but generally he kept both. Some he favored who drank at his tavern. It was believed that Webster did not account with the public for the proceeds. In the assault, he was forced to tear up his government papers and stomp on them. Some of the assailants were tarring and feathering him and they did set fire to his hay stacks and stables, but the more moderate ones prevailed, put out the fire and protected Webster from further attacks. Finally, he was released and allowed to return home.[11]

The residents of Pittsburgh were alarmed by a noisy march through the streets of the men who had gathered there. Anyone who owned a still and had paid the excise tax had his house destroyed. Many barns were burned and representatives of the government were tarred and feathered. Government agents were attacked and searched for any instructions regarding the insurgents. Copies of any official correspondence thus found resulted in harassment of the carriers.

President Washington studied the communications about these activities and realized that immediate and positive actions were needed. (Some modern historians of Jeffersonian leanings deny this was necessary.) Washington felt that for three years, he had tried conciliation and even considered whether the excise tax should be widened to cover more than it did. "If the laws are to be so trammelled with impunity," he said, "the minority, a small one too, would control the majority and end at one stroke Republican government."[12]

The President wrote to Governor Henry Lee of Virginia, "I consider this insurrection as the first formidable fruit of the Democratic Societies. I believe too maturely their own views may contribute to the annihilation of them."

Washington then held his first official conference concerning the crisis. Attending were the Governor of Pennsylvania, Thomas Mifflin, Chief Justice Thomas McKean, Attorney General Jared Ingersoll, and Secretary of that state, Alexander Dallas. These state officials showed reluctance to recognize the need for military action, and were inclined to minimize the seriousness of the situation. The last-minute efforts to avoid extreme measures included the appointment by Washington of Attorney James Ross, Judge Robert Yates, and Attorney General Bradford to confer with Pennsylvania representatives. Governor Mifflin and Thomas McKean asked Pennsylvanians to cooperate on the same mission. They were directed to proceed at once under instructions of the Secretary of State. Washington had already been advised that he had the authority to call out the militia under certain circumstances. The instructions provided for amnesty and full pardon for past offenses for those complying with the laws and non-intervention in the execution of them. The rebels would be told that everything had been prepared for the militia to move but that such action would not take place until the commissioners had reported their answers in the hope of preventing "the last dreadful necessity which the President so much deprecates."

As usual, Alexander Hamilton recommended extreme measures for putting down the rebellion by overwhelming force. Secretary of War Henry Knox offered two suggestions: one that Mifflin be reminded of his own responsibility and questioned about the adequacy of the Pennsylvania militia; and second that a proclamation of warning be issued before force was employed. Bradford contended that the insurrection was high treason, a capital crime and under the circumstances, force was justified in being employed. On the other hand, Secretary of State Randolph warned that it was necessary to use caution, the reason being that "if so indulged it would heap curses upon the government. The strength of the government is in the affection of the people." He also urged the postponement of military force until the commissioners had fulfilled their assignment.[13]

The important part which Randolph played in Washington's crucial decisions has not always been recognized. Randolph now laid before the President a useful summary of the origins of the rebellion and the course he thought proper to take. After all Randolph was a lawyer and viewed the matter from a legal standpoint. In his opinion, no particular law had been broken. Judging from his survey he concluded that military action was not needed immediately, that such a move might excite disorders in other discontented people because of the excise tax and also among those who were opposed to the Washington administration regardless of the issue. Randolph also felt a military expedition would prove to be a serious problem economically. The Attorney General was also doubtful about sending militia from one state to fight against citizens of another. Great Britain would benefit from what it might conceive of inconsistency toward foreign uprisings and internal disobedience. Hostile partisans of the United States would be inflamed and our government would not be considered safely established until it could prove it had sufficient military power within its own borders.[14]

Governor Thomas Mifflin also added an opposing view and wanted the matter placed in the hands of the Pennsylvania state government. He stated that it would be improper to use the military power of the state while its judiciary was competent to punish the offenders. Washington regarded this attitude as "a cool contradiction of the President's policy and the evidence." In a reply prepared by Randolph, Washington pointed out that military measures were already required and that firm, energetic conduct was necessary as a solution.

In the authorization of the use of troops, Randolph referred to the Militia Act passed by Congress in 1792 which stated,

> that whenever the laws of the United States shall be opposed, or the execution thereof obstructed, in any state, by combinations too powerful to be suppressed by the ordinary course of judicial proceedings, or by the powers vested in the marshalls by this act, the same being notified to the President of the United States, by an associate justice or the district judge, it shall be lawful for the President of the United States to call forth the militia of such state to suppress such combinations, and to cause the laws to be duly executed. And if the militia of a state, where such combinations may happen, shall or shall refuse or be insufficient to suppress the same, it shall be lawful for the President, if the legislature of the United States be not in session, to call forth and employ such numbers of the militia of any other state or states most convenient thereto, as may be necessary, and the use of the militia, so to be called forth, may be continued, if necessary, until the expiration of thirty days after the commencement of the ensuing session.[15]

At a cabinet meeting, it was decided that the President would issue a proclamation, which he did. It stated that "Combinations subversive to governing individuals and the prevalent opposition by irregular meetings, the use of fear and violence, personal and property damage, the abuse of public officials and the use of armed and disguised bandits, amounted to treason. The insurgents were ordered to disperse and all inhabitants were instructed to suppress dangerous proceedings."[16]

It was reported to Washington that although the people of consequence were in favor of obeying the laws, the common people were not. (The tax collectors demanded military protection because they were afraid of physical resistance.) Not only did folks dislike the tax on whiskey, they simply did not wish to obey any kind of government from outside. Even among Washington's troops there was a division of sentiment. The more conservative ones were eager to punish the insurgents while those of lower economic class were not so eager to come into contact with those Pennsylvanians of similar status. There was also considerable criticism of the fact that Hamilton was second in command of the army and because of his militaristic viewpoint, this expedition might result in an American standing army, something which the Republicans at this time resisted. As it was, one observer reported, "The President was happily successful in reducing the licentiousness in part of the army into subordination to the laws and in inspiring the people of the western counties with such a measure of confidence as prevented any conduct of their part that could give the army just cause of irritation."[16]

It so happened at this time that Secretary Henry Knox who had been speculating in Maine lands and was anxious to see his family in Boston, had asked to return home. Then when he learned about the Whiskey Rebellion, he reconsidered and stated to Washington, "accustomed to serving your desires, much less your orders, as paramount to every other consideration, I shall certainly defer my journey or even renounce it altogether if necessary, though permanent pecuniary ruin may result." Knox went on to explain his plan of leaving that night, 8 August, and by riding all night and arriving in New York the next morning he could catch a boat for Providence and thence to Boston. Washington listened with sympathy and was impressed by the urgency of Knox's words. Also, the President had just received information from commissioners he had sent to Pennsylvania that the disorders there were not as bad as had been feared. So the President gave Knox permission to go, and within hours he was on his way. Knox and Hamilton had agreed for the latter to take over the duties of the War Department while Knox was away. Knox was later to regret this. But he was worried, desperate and wanted to go home; and Washington knew how devoted he was to his family. On the other hand, Hamilton had always been eager to take the field as head of an army, and now this was his chance.

While Knox was away, the chief clerk of the War Department, John Staff, reported to Knox that the Pennsylvania rioters had refused to return to their homes and militia was gathering to force them to do so. Ordinarily, Knox would have rushed back at once; but this time he perhaps was beguiled by the eastern coastal breezes and the fascinating prospects of home life. He had been gone almost eight weeks when he got off a message to Washington expressing his regret that "an extraordinary course of contrary winds" had delayed him longer than he had expected. He asked to join Washington when he was at Carlisle or elsewhere to help him with the painful task ahead. Two days later, Knox wrote again to Washington saying, "I shall fly to your standard; the prosperity of the country, industry and habits of order conspicuous everywhere are the most brilliant compliments to a free government that the world has ever experienced. The consciousness that the golden age of happiness has been produced under your auspices must afford you, Sir, inexpressible sensations of the most exalted nature." This effusive missive did not, however, seem to convince Washington who replied that it might have been advantageous if Knox had been with him but it was now too late; that he would be returning to Philadelphia before Knox could arrive. Knox was sorely disappointed over his failure to get to join Washington and the troops. But his usual buoyancy returned when he was able to inform Hamilton that John Jay had settled some points of dispute between Great Britain and the United States. Of course Knox did not realize at the time the limitations of the Jay Treaty.[17]

The President found a little time to relax. He attended Christ Church in Philadelphia. The church which was built in 1774 is still standing. The President must have watched the sunlight streaming through the palladium windows with arches flanked by vertical sidelights behind the altar. The church itself had been built from the proceeds of lotteries conducted by Benjamin Franklin. The building was constructed of brick probably because of sad memories of the fire in London in 1666 which influenced the structures of future churches.

A pleasant letter came to Washington in the midst of his somber communications about the Western insurrections. The oldest granddaughter of his wife, Elizabeth Parke Custis, had just turned eighteen years of age and wrote and asked for Washington's picture. He granted her request and in doing so, indulged in some reflections on love and marriage:

> Do not, in your contemplation of the marriage state, look for perfect felicity before you consent to wed. Nor conceive from what the fine tales of the poets and lovers of old have told us, of the transports of mutual love, that heaven has taken its abode on earth. Do not deceive yourself in supposing that the only means by which these are obtained, is to drink deep of the cup and revel in an ocean of love. Love is a mighty pretty thing; but like all other delicious things, it is cloying; and when the first transports of the passion begin to subside, which it assuredly will do, and yield, oftentimes too late, to more sober reflections, it serves to evince that love is too dainty a food to live upon *alone*, and ought not to be considered further than as a necessary ingredient for that matrimonial happiness which results from a combination of causes; none of which are of greater importance than good sense, good dispositions, and the means of supporting you in the way you have been brought up . . . for be assured, and experience will convince you, that there is no truth more certain, than that all our enjoyments fall short of our expectations; and to none does it apply with more force, than to the gratification of the passions.[18]

But there was little time for such personal and diversionary correspondence. In the West, moderation did not prevail. Many of the communities continued to resist and there was considerable, resulting violence. By early September, Washington's hope for peaceful settlement of the crisis was dwindling, and regretfully he approved orders for a general rendezvous of the militia. Something over a total of 12,000 troops were being assembled in their respective states. The President, now acting as a general, started on his journey to Carlisle, Pennsylvania, where the militia of that state and New Jersey were to assemble; then to proceed to Bedford for the final gathering of the whole army. He would at that time decide whether he would advance with the troops or return to Philadelphia for the scheduled opening of Congress on 3 November. Hamilton asked to accompany the soldiers and Washington granted his request. Just as the President was preparing to leave Philadelphia, a letter was placed in his hands from Major General Daniel Morgan of the Virginia militia, stating that he was on his way with a division to join the expedition against the insurgents. From Carlisle, Washington replied to his old companion in arms,

> Although I regret the occasion which has called you into the field, I rejoice to hear you are there; and it is probable that I may meet you at Fort Cumberland, whither I shall proceed as soon as I see that the troops at this rendezvous are in condition to advance. At that place or at Bedford, my ulterior resolution must be taken either to advance with troops into the insurgent counties of this state or to return to Philadelphia for the purpose of meeting Congress the third of next month. Imperious circumstances alone can justify my absence from the seat of government while Congress is in session; but if these from the disposition of the people in the refractory counties, and the state of the information I expect to receive at the advanced posts, should appear to exist, the loss must yield to the greater duties of my office, and I shall cross the mountains with the troops; if not, I shall place the command of the combined force under the orders of Governor Lee of Virginia, and repair to the seat of government.[19]

When he was young, Daniel Morgan was a husky Virginia wagoner carrying supplies to the British over the Blue Ridge Mountains in the French and Indian War. He headed a company of volunteer riflemen who were among the first troops from Virginia to join General Washington at Cambridge, Massachusetts in 1775. Soon Morgan went to Quebec with Benedict Arnold on an ill-fated expedition to try to capture that British stronghold, was captured and later exchanged. After serving with brave distinction as a colonel in the New Jersey and New York campaigns, Daniel Morgan, having been promoted to general, led his men in a smashing and colorful defeat of the British at the Cowpens. Now he was back in the field to effectually wind up the American military move against the Whiskey Rebels.

On the first of October the President set out before breakfast and had an opportunity to view the picturesque Pennsylvania countryside. He noticed that the red earth contained bits of slate and that although the ground was rather rough it was pleasant riding along in the crisp air of autumn. He was impressed by the cultivated fields, the sturdy farm houses with adjacent red barns built in the systematic and lasting German pattern. He had time to stop briefly and observe the construction of a canal linking the Schuylkill and Susquehanna Rivers. Washington found that the work was excellent on the locks that had been completed. He admired the arched bridges on the roads which crossed the waterway. He wrote from Carlisle on 9 October to the Secretary of

State, "The insurgents are alarmed but not yet brought to their proper senses. Every means is devised by them and their friends and associates, to induce a belief that there is no necessity for troops crossing the mountains; although we have information at the same time that part of the people there are obliged to embody themselves, to repel the insults of another part."

"The Whiskey Army" was composed of prominent men, substitutes and some of the lowest classes of American society. The word "militia" came to have an unfavorable connotation, meaning to many observers, a lower class of citizens. The men were poorly clad with no service uniforms while the gentlemen dressed in flashy colors unique to each brigade. More harmful to the troops than their human opponents were the diseases which struck them such as dysentery and fever which proved often debilitating, sometimes half of a brigade being incapacitated. Enlisted men tore down fences for firewood, stole chickens and livestock for food. Officers lived better but at times were unable even to obtain a chicken to make soup for the sick. Even so, the presence of General George Washington among the troops demonstrated to the world that this young nation still had effective power.[20]

Many Easterners had left the cities believing that life would be better in the West. They had braved the dangers of the wilderness in order to acquire their own land. A considerable number of those who owned the Western lands were so distant from their tenants that grievances were hard to settle and the renters were placed at a disadvantage. Towns were small and none exceeded four hundred residents, the population of Pittsburgh, the largest of these villages, was only 376 in the 1790 census. Those without property consisted of former slaves, laborers, servants, widows and other dependent poor. They knew little of crop rotation, still used crude plows and their crops with the exception of Indian corn were those of old England: wheat, oats, barley, hemp, flax and buckwheat. One newspaper advertisement listed as acceptable for barter, "cash, flour, whiskey, beef, pork, bacon, oats, wheat, rye, corn, ashes, candlewick and tallow." Frosts and snows destroyed crops, and Indians as well as wild beasts threatened human life.[21]

Washington was quite familiar with this Western country. He had learned about its living conditions on his first Western trip in 1748. Not only did he know the land and its people, had found the Indians there but he had later made investment in Western lands. He had mapped and surveyed thousands of acres beyond the Appalachian Mountains and claimed 4,695 acres in South-western Pennsylvania alone. This section was also a buffer against England, Spain, and the Indians. In 1791 several men assaulted a tax collector in Washington County named Robert Johnson. Disguised in women's clothes, they cut off Johnson's hair, tarred and feathered him, stole his horse, and left him in the forest. Two of these "women" were recognized and a cattle drover named John Connor was hired to deliver the warrants. As a result Connor was horsewhipped, tarred and feathered, robbed, and left tied to a tree.[22]

In another instance, George Clymer, supervisor of tax collection for Pennsylvania, found to his dismay that he was hardly known in Western Pennsylvania, even though he had signed the Declaration of Independence and had travelled there. Fearing physical resistance, Clymer decided to use disguises to hide his true identity. At first he tried to pass as Secretary of War Henry Knox but failed to fool people because they knew how fat Knox was. Clymer then posed as a servant, which was also unsuccessful. He was afraid to venture out of Pittsburgh and in a few days "returned to Philadelphia with the rapidity of a post rider, accompanied by a military guard through the most peaceable part of the country."[23]

President Washington, now acting as a general and commanding more men that he had ever had at one time during the Revolution, travelled through the Pennsylvania countryside and stopped at Williamsport, Fort Cumberland, and Bedford. At this last place, with all the troops assembled, the Commander-in-Chief became convinced that his presence was no longer necessary because the rebellion had fizzled out. His expedition had accomplished its purpose, mainly that of demonstrating to the nation and to the world that this country could maintain order. So the President decided to return to Philadelphia, and by 28 October he and his aides were back in the capital preparing to face other difficulties

"The spirit which blazed out on this occasion," Washington stated, "as soon as the object was fully understood and the lenient measures of the government were made known to the people, deserve to be communicated. There are instances of general officers going at the head of a single troop and of light companies; of field-officers, when they came to the place of rendezvous, and found no command for them in that grade, turning into the ranks and proceeding as private soldiers under their own captains; and of numbers possessing the first fortunes

in the country, standing in the ranks as private men, and marching day by day, with their knapsacks and haversacks at their
backs, sleeping on straw with a single blanket in a soldier's tent,
during the frosty nights which we have had, by way of example to
others. Nay, more, many young Quakers, of the first families,
character, and property, not discouraged by the elders, have
turned into the ranks and marched with troops." Washington
added,

> Let us unite therefore in imploring the Supreme Ruler of nations to
> spread his holy protection over these United States; to turn the
> machinations of the wicked to the confirming of our Constitution; to
> enable us at all times to root out internal sedition and put invasion to
> flight; to perpetuate to our country that prosperity which his good-
> ness had already conferred, and to verify the anticipations of this
> government being a safeguard to human rights.[24]

In a letter to Governor Lee, on leaving him in command, the
general conveyed to the army, "the very high sense he entertained
of the enlightened and patriotic zeal for the Constitution and the
laws which had led them cheerfully to quit their families,
homes, and the comforts of private life, to undertake, and thus
far to perform, a long and fatiguing march, and to encounter and
endure the hardships and privations of a military life. No citizen
of the United States can ever be engaged in a service more
important to their country. It is nothing less than to consolidate
and to preserve the blessings of that Revolution which, at much
expense to blood and treasure, constituted us a free and independent nation." His parting admonition was "that every officer and
soldier will constantly bear in mind, that he comes to support
the laws, and that it would be peculiarly unbecoming in him to
be, in any way, the infractor of them; that the essential principles
of a free government confine the province of the military when
called forth on such occasions, to these two objects; first, to
combat and subdue all who may be found in arms in opposition
to the national will and authority; secondly, to aid and support
the civil magistrates in bringing offenders to justice. The dispen-
sation of this justice belongs to the civil magistrates; and let it
ever be our pride and our glory to leave the sacred deposit there
inviolate."

John C. Miller has well described the outcome stating that,

> President Washington would have been well advised to have let the
> Democratic Societies die a natural death instead of attempting to

hasten their end of singling them out for his official disapproval. By so doing, he tended to impair the real strength of his position in American politics—his Olympian aloofness from the partisan struggles that raged about him. The condemnation of the Democratic Societies planted the idea in Republicans' minds that President Washington was at heart a Federalist or—even worse—a Hamiltonian. As it transpired, there was no real necessity for the President to risk his popularity upon this issue; within a year, the Democratic Societies had ceased to exist, not so much because of Washington's censures as because of the decline and final extinction of the societies in France itself and of the increasingly critical attitude adopted by Americans toward the French Revolution.[25]

The government mountain had indeed labored and brought forth a mouse. Only twenty prisoners were brought to Philadelphia, paraded down Market Street, and kept in prison for months. Not a prominent person was among them. Only two prisoners were found guilty of high treason (levying war against the United States) but Washington pardoned both of them, one, he said, was a "simpleton" and the other insane." Jefferson said that a real insurrection never existed, while Hamilton declared that the government had gained reputation and strength by showing that it could compel obedience to the laws.[26]

The political result of the Whiskey Rebellion was mainly to strengthen the power of Hamilton and the Federalists. Some of the circumstantial evidence indicates that Hamilton encouraged the lack of understanding between the Washington administration and the Western insurgents for the purpose of promoting his own interests. The defeat of the Democrats also encouraged investors in the Western lands to accelerate their economic development.

A viewpoint opposed to that of Washington and the Federalists was expressed by writer using the name of "Franklin" in a Philadelphia newspaper:

The period is at hand when you will be called upon to exercise the right of freemen, the right to declare who shall be your lawgivers. The magnitude of this right must appear to every reflecting mind, but its importance has additional energy when the present state of our country is considered a state at which the manly and independent soul revolts, and which the friend of humanity sincerely deprecates. Scorned, injured and insulted by that nation which has no claim to humanity or civilization but what the few philosophers among them give, we have borne them with a meekness that seemed to give birth to a question of the purity of the motives which led to such submission. The common rights of nations have been denied us, and the manly and pacific means of redress within our power have been shamefully abandoned. That spirit, that elevation of soul which promoted us to resist a British tyrant's will and bore us triumphantly through one of the most glorious revolutions in the annals of mankind, seems to have slumbered in shameful apathy or to have yielded to considerations of sordid calculation. When the bold tone of freedom ought to have animated every heart to a resistance of decrees; when every man ought to have been nerved against a bloody and barbarous foe, we have slept over our wrongs and have rather kissed the rod of chastisement. Shall we then, fellow citizens, continue our confidence to men who have reduced us to such a state of degradation? Shall we continue to delegate a trust, the most important in a freeman's gift to men who are absorbed in their own calculations, and who appear to consider their country's interest as a secondary thing? Shall we foster agents at the expense of the vital principle of the body politic and neglect an exertion that shall restore our lost dignity and honor?[27]

In his speech on the delayed opening of Congress, 19 November 1794, Washington, referring to the insurrection in Western Pennsylvania, did not hesitate to denounce "certain self-created societies" as "fomenters of it." After detailing its commencement and progress, he observed,

While there is cause to lament that occurrences of this nature should have disgraced the name or interrupted the tranquility of any part of our community, or should have diverted to a new application any portion of the public resources, there are not wanting real and substantial consolations for the misfortune. It has demonstrated that our prosperity rests on solid foundations; by furnishing an additional proof that my fellow-citizens understand the true principles of government and liberty; that they feel their inseparable union; that, notwithstanding all the devices which have been used to sway them from their interest and duty, they are now as ready to maintain the authority of the laws against licentious invasions, as they were to defend their rights against usurpation. It has been a spectacle, displaying to the highest advantage the value of republican government, to behold the most and least wealthy of our citizens standing in the same ranks as private soldier; preeminently distinguished by being the army of the Constitution; undeterred by a march of three hundred miles over rugged mountains, by the approach of an inclement season, or by any other discouragement. Nor ought I to omit to acknowledge the effications and patriotic cooperation which I have experienced from the chief magistrates of the States to which my requisitions have been addressed. To every description, indeed, of citizens, let praise be given; but let them persevere in their affectionate vigilance over that precious depository of American happiness, the Constitution of the United States. Let them cherish it, too, for the sake of those who, from every clime, are daily seeking a dwelling in our land. And when, in the calm moments of reflection, they shall have retraced the origin and progress of the insurrection, let them determine whether it has not been fomented by combinations of men, who, careless of consequences, and disregarding the unerring truth, that those who arouse cannot always appease a civil convulsion, have disseminated from ignorance or perversion of facts, suspicions, jealousies, and accusations of the whole government.[28]

8

Philadelphia à la Carte

The autumn of 1794 in Philadelphia was a pleasant one especially since the yellow fever plague had virtually vanished. What a relief the government officials and others who had returned must have felt not to have to face the demonic conditions which had engulfed the city and left its permanent mark upon it. President Washington had been told by Edmund Randolph that the capital was again normal and that it was safe to return. Despite the benevolent stamp placed upon it by William Penn, his city of fraternal affection had been forced to undergo a Gethsemane that it did not deserve, and now must recover from the baneful scars.

As far as the neglected national government was concerned, however, the place was not quiet. Members of Congress were returning and Washington must busy himself in preparation for his annual message to that body. Secretary of State Randolph was supposed to have prepared a draft of the speech but the critical conditions and plague had postponed this preparation. Fortunately, the situation was eased by the delay in the gathering of the lawmakers so that the Chief Executive had more time for readying his address. Now he could review the turbulent events of the past months and deliberate on his description of them. Any negative atmosphere was lightened by reports from Hamilton that the situation in Western Pennsylvania was quieting down and that the government action there had been quite successful.

Randolph also sought to allay any fears of criticism from the press of whatever Washington might say in his address. "Let it cost what labor it may," he wrote the President, "if the measures which you will impart to Congress be properly supported against misrepresentation, you will establish perfect tranquility to the government, and your administration will be found to have passed through a trying crisis with dignity. . . . The fame of him who has so long been my patron is more dear to me than any connection with any other man."[1]

The news of General Wayne's decisive victory over the Indians would surely brighten the speech but prospects would have been better if Wayne had not also made complaints. He reported poor recruiting and urged strongly the establishment of a large permanent army. Otherwise, he told Secretary Knox, "we have fought, bled and conquered in vain." This statement touched upon a then-controversial question. From the beginning of the revolt of the American colonies, many of the people here had abhorred the presence of regular troops, exemplified by the British redcoats, not only because of their oppression but because they also represented the old European order of despotic rule by a standing army. To these settlers, anything military smacked of overbearing government by force; and after Washington's army, mostly state militia, had been disbanded after the war, attempts to restore a similar permanent organization had been opposed in legislatures and in Congress. It was not until 1802 that Congress enacted the enlistment of a Regular Army and even after that, its numbers have dwindled after each war. Washington himself did not envision a Prussian type of military forces regularly maintained but favored civilian rule and national emphasis on peace.

Washington wished that he would be able to announce improved relations between England and the United States. But the rumors from England were that John Jay was making little or no progress and this gave the Republicans ammunition for more criticism of the administration. In addition, there had been no news from James Monroe, the new ambassador to France, although it was understood that the Jacobins had fallen from power. Robespierre was executed in July. France had been unexpectedly successful in her military campaigns and the European wars were expected to continue at an accelerated rate. Randolph felt that it was important to keep France in a friendly mood so as not to jeopardize the negotiations with England.

In the Alexander Hamilton Papers at the Library of Congress is a document he had written, dated Philadelphia, 1794 in which he declares his opinion of the French Revolution. "In the early periods of the Revolution," Hamilton penned,

> a warm zeal for its success was in this country, *a sentiment truly universal*. The Love of Liberty is here the ruling passion of the *Citizens of the United States*, pervading every class, animating every bosom. As long therefore as the Revolution of France bore the marks

of being the cause of liberty, it united all hearts, concentered all opinions. But this unanimity of approbation has been for a considerable time decreasing. The excesses which has constantly multiplied, with greater and greater aggravations, have successively though slowly detached reflecting men from their partiality for an object which has appeared less and less to merit their regard. Their reluctance to abandon it has however been proportioned to the ardor and fondness with which they embraced it. They were willing to overlook many faults—to apologize for some enormities—to hope that better justifications existed—and to look forward to more calm and greater moderation, after the first shocks of the political earthquake had subsided. But instead of this, they have been witnesses to one volcano succeeding another, the last still more dreadful than the former spreading ruin and devastation far and wide—subverting the foundations of right, security and property, of order, morality and religion— sparing neither sex nor age, confounding innocence with guilt, involving the old and the young, the sage and madman, the long-tried friend of virtue and his country and the upstart pretender to purity and patriotism—the bold projector of new treasons with the obscure, indiscriminate and profuse destruction. . . . The French Revolution is a political convulsion that in a great or less degree shakes the whole civilized world, and it is of real consequence to the principles, and of course, to the happiness of a Nation to estimate it rightly.

At last the Senate convened on 18 November after waiting for a week on Aaron Burr who was probably dallying with some woman in New York. A joint committee visited the President and he announced that he would address Congress the next day at noon. Customarily, his coach was escorted by a procession of constables and he was dressed in black and wearing a dress sword, attended by the Secretary of State, the Secretary of War, and the Attorney General, Hamilton having not yet returned to Philadelphia. Washington took his place between the Vice President and the Speaker of the House. He bowed to the members of Congress who had risen from their seats, removed his eyeglasses and began to read in a clear voice from a paper he had taken from his pocket. He spent about two-thirds of the address on the causes and the suppression of the Whiskey Rebellion which he said had been cheerfully accepted by most Americans. Washington reviewed the steps taken for this purpose including the sending of commissioners but since this was not effective it was necessary to send the militia. The President stated that his "fellow citizens understand the true principles of government and liberty, that they feel their inseparable union and that they are as ready to maintain the authority of the laws against licentious

invasions as they were to defend their rights against usurpation."
He urged that all citizens "persevere in their affectionate vig-
ilance over that precious depository of American happiness, the
Constitution of the United States."[2]

George Thacher wrote his wife that "The President had delivered one of the most animating, firm and manly addresses I ever
heard from him or any other person. Though he read, he made
use of much more motion that has been usual for him on like
occasions. He felt what he said. He recounted the whole of his
conduct and motives in calling out the militia . . . I felt a strange
mixture of passions that I cannot describe. Tears started into my
eyes and it was with difficulty I could suppress an involuntary
effort to swear that I would support him." A lady in the audience,
Miss Elizabeth Smith, wrote to her brother saying Washington's
"whole appearance commanded the utmost reverence and attention. It really seemed as though we were addressed by a far
superior being than any here below."[3]

President Washington next day informed the Senate that he
planned to send Thomas Pinckney, (brother of the American
statesman, Charles Cotesworth Pinckney) then the American
minister to England, to Spain as envoy extraordinary. It was the
President's hope that such a special mission would make successful the continuing negotiation for commercial rights on the
Mississippi River. This was no compliment to Pinckney because
the position had already been offered to Patrick Henry and
Thomas Jefferson both of whom had declined. Thomas Pinckney
was educated at Oxford, had served in the Revolution, escaped
capture at Charleston and joined the Continental Army. He had
been governor of South Carolina and United States minister to
Great Britain.

Soon the Senate formally acknowledged the President's message. Vice President John Adams brought the Senators to Washington's house and read the statement which had been adopted.
The Senate approved fully the use of militia to put down the
Whiskey Rebellion and also joined with the President in condemning "the proceedings of certain self-created societies."
Washington was pleased but faced disappointment when the
House did not agree to all of his recommended measures. Congressman William Smith appealed to the House for such approval stating that its absence of such would leave the President
in a dilemma. Madison and Jefferson were pleased that the
House took this negative position and felt that the President had
made a serious political mistake in bringing up the matter at all.[4]

Edmund Randolph rushed to have published a series of articles the purpose of which was to explain why the President connected the Whiskey Rebellion to the Democratic Clubs. Dispatches from James Monroe in Paris confirmed reports of the American minister's pledge of friendship and alliance in a speech to the French National Convention. Monroe explained that such an address was necessary to win the cooperation of the French government and he was only following the spirit of his instructions. Meantime a young Englishman named William Cobbett who had come to America took up the journalistic cudgel in behalf of the Federalists. Cobbett had been a British soldier who served in Europe and became disillusioned with the anarchic conditions there. He came to Philadelphia in 1792 and for a time taught the English language to refugees from Europe. When Joseph Priestley, the renowned chemist and friend of France, fled to America in 1794 and was welcomed by Republicans in Philadelphia, young Cobbett wrote and published two pamphlets sharply criticizing Priestly and charging him with radicalism and atheism. For this, Federalists praised Cobbett and embraced him even more when he issued another pamphlet, "A Bone to Gnaw for the Democrats" that excoriated the Democratic Societies.[5]

During a lull in governmental activities, Washington found time to write letters to Mount Vernon, mostly to his manager there, William Pearce. One such missive concerned a report that a relative, Fanny Washington, had used fifty-six bottles of wine for the purpose of entertaining visitors. Washington wrote Pearce that "There are but three descriptions of people to whom I think it ought to be given: my *particular* and intimate acquaintances, the *most* respectable foreigners and persons of some distinction such as members of Congress." Although Washington welcomed orderly visitors who wished to see the buildings and gardens, he did not feel that he "should be run to any expense on account of these visits of curiosity. No gentleman who has the proper respect for his own character would use the house for the sake of conveniency." The master of Mount Vernon could be quite practical.[6]

George Washington had had comparatively little formal education but he came to realize through his experience in "the school of hard knocks" the advantages of such training. Accordingly, he told John Adams (a Harvard graduate) that he believed a national university in this country was something to be desired and wished to have a full discussion with Adams about the matter.

The President had in mind that such an institution would be built in the new Federal City and he proposed through Randolph to James Madison that information leading to such a project be made available and that Washington himself would be interested in donating his fifty shares in the Potomac Company for this purpose.

The President realized that many schools and colleges had been interrupted or closed during the American Revolution. However the war had brought a broadening of knowledge by the march of armies, and the operations of war enabled many people to make geographical discoveries around the country which would not otherwise have been made. One of the professions which had benefited from the war was that of surgery. Doctors learned from treating soldiers and sailors more in eight years that they ordinarily would have learned in several decades. For instance, Dr. Benjamin Rush discovered the method of curing lockjaw by the use of bark and wine. After American independence, journalism flourished although sometimes in awkward, prejudiced directions. Even so, men such as Benjamin Franklin, Alexander Hamilton, Thomas Jefferson and James Madison contributed learned articles through the press and pamphlets.

New England led this nation in the production of good literature and its writers contributed much to American success in the propaganda war with Britain. By the early 1770s, there were in those Northeastern colonies more than two thousand college graduates whose knowledge and abilities influenced and directed many people in the conflict with our mother country. The Revolution actually promoted literature and the speeches as well as belles letters had greatly enriched the causes of separation and the culmination of independence. Orations, letters, dissertations, and other kinds of literature inspired the younger generation to become educated. Francis Hopkinson was an able political satirist, Philip Freneau wrote poetry and edited a party newspaper, John Trumbull ridiculed British blunders and wrote a memorable poem "M'Fingal" while Joel Barlow wrote an epic poem, "Columbiad" comparing the discoveries of Columbus with the development of the new world. Noah Webster, pursuing an unbeaten track, discovered construction and beauty of the English language for his contemporaries as well as for posterity.

Against this background, President Washington wished to establish "some system of American education." He said it had always been a source of regret for him to see American students going to Europe before their minds had matured and they had "correct ideas of the blessing of the country they leave." He was afraid that our students might acquire in Europe "habits of dissipation, extravagance, and principles unfriendly to the rights of man."[7]

In an early version of his will, Washington had stated his intention that young men from all parts of the United States complete their education "in different branches of literature, arts, and sciences. They should get fixed in the principles of the Constitution, understand the laws and the true interests and policy of their country; by forming acquaintances with each other early in life, they would be cured of those local prejudices and habitual jealousies which when carried to excess, are never failing sources of disquietude."[8]

It is not certain though possible that Washington entertained in the back of his mind the thought that by locating the university in the city which might well bear his name, it could be a sort of monument to him. Here the students could watch the national government in operation and thus not only receive a general education but could become well informed in the workings of our political system. This perspicacious idea has been borne out by the visits and longer stays of American students in the city of Washington.

At this time the University of Geneva, famous for its learned faculty, was in a chaotic state because the unsettled conditions in Europe had left it financially destitute. Its professors looked longingly at the United States and wished to move their institution here. The alert John Adams favored the idea and proposed it to Washington, but the President showed little interest in bringing over foreigners who might not understand our language. For once, the European-minded Jefferson, upon learning of the possibility, agreed with Adams. But Washington was nationalist-minded, Jefferson was mainly concerned with Virginia. At the time, however, the Virginia legislature did not agree with Jefferson. In not many years he was to found the institution there which was to become one of the monuments to him.

Washington suggested to Madison that he hoped Virginia would be in favor of a national institution of higher learning; he also notified the commissioners of the District of Columbia that it was time to work for a university in their city and in this he would be glad to help. There came from Thomas Jefferson a letter suggesting that Washington give a donation to import the University of Geneva. If so, Jefferson stated such a gesture might overcome the reluctance of the Virginia legislature. He added that the university would be suitable for locating in his state. He did believe that by its being in Virginia the university would be near enough to be beneficial to both locations.

President George Washington was not a college graduate, but he knew a thing or two about domestic conditions and foreign relations. He told Jefferson that a transplanted Geneva University would exclude professors from the University of Edinburgh which had some of the most renowned faculty in the world. As to the moral atmosphere of the institution, Washington doubted that those of Geneva were any better than those elsewhere. Washington then wrote Robert Brooke of Virginia that he would like to leave all his canal shares for a national university, but if that state wished to establish its own educational institution, it was agreeable with him. The legislature then voted for its own seminary and Washington left his Potomac River shares to Liberty Hall Academy which later became Washington and Lee University, in Lexington, Virginia which, if not a national university, has a splendid reputation.[9]

Diversion played so little part in the life of President Washington especially in his last term of office, that is pleasing to note in early December he and Mrs. Washington attended a performance at the Cedar Street Theater in Philadelphia. The next week he watched from his doorway a procession of the colorful battalion of Jersey Blues militia which had returned from the Whiskey Rebellion in western Pennsylvania. A few days later, Vice President Adams for some reason brought to Washington a disreputable-looking seaman from Algiers who claimed to have letters of introduction from the Queen of Prussia and the Duke of Brunswick—which apparently turned out to be a fiasco. But the President, still being careful not to offend the current French government, refused to see the emigres, Rochefoucauld and Talleyrand who were passing through Philadelphia on a tour of the United States.

Recreational activity was soon replaced by concern on the part of the President regarding the forthcoming resignations of Secretaries Knox and Hamilton who had notified Washington that they must leave by year's end or soon afterward. Knox had given the last day of December as his time of departure. As we have seen, the letters of exchange between him and Washington were cordial and affectionate. The conscientious Knox did not leave without winding up his busy and eventful career by offering a final set of recommendations on the situation on the Western frontier. He had for years studied the red men and held a warm regard for the best of them. He even at one time stated that the best way to solve the Indian problem was intermarriage between them and white people. Knox knew the weaknesses of the Indians, but he also condemned the encroachment of the pioneers by force and fraud upon Indian lands previously guaranteed by treaty. He suggested that equal punishment be given to white and red men alike for violations.[10]

President Washington on New Year's Day 1795, signed a proclamation designating 19 February for public demonstrations of thanksgiving for the peace then enjoyed throughout the United States. He climaxed this by entertaining members of Congress at his house with wine and cake. A friend who was present observed that "The President is in fine health and seems to defy the ravages of time during life as his name certainly will after death."

The name of Timothy Pickering was sent to the Senate and confirmed as Secretary of War. He was a former adjutant general, then quartermaster general of the Continental Army. He was later postmaster general, and afterwards was to become Secretary of State. In the Jefferson administration he served in the Senate. Washington must have been disturbed by reports of John Jay's conduct in England at this time. A Southern newspaper printed an account that Jay had accomplished nothing in his seven months in England. According to the article "He kissed the Queen's hand; he dined with Pitt; he sent a spirited note to Grenville. He has already gotten as far as the status quo and there he holds fast."[11]

Washington was not omitted from abuse. Fisher Ames told Christopher Gore that a man named James Callender had proposed a toast at a public dinner in Virginia in which he said "a speedy death to General Washington." There was added unhappiness and regret at the departure of Alexander Hamilton. Washington wrote to him, "After so long an experience of your public services I am naturally led at this moment of departure from office (which it has always been my wish to prevent) to review them. In every relation that you have borne to me I have found that my confidence in your talents, exertions and integrity has been well placed. I the more freely render this testimony of my approbation because I speak from opportunities of information which cannot deceive me and which furnish satisfactory proof of your title to public regard. My most earnest wishes for your happiness will attend you in your retirement and you may assure yourself of the sincere esteem, regard and friendship of, dear sir, your affectionate friend."

Hamilton replied, "as often as I may recall the vexations I have endured, your approbation will be a great and precious consolation. It was not without a struggle that I yielded to the very urgent motives which impel me to relinquish a station in which I could hope to be in any degree instrumental in promoting the success of an administration under your direction . . . Whatever may be my destination hereafter, I entreat you to be persuaded (not the less from having been sparing in professions) that I shall never cease to render a just tribute to those eminent and excellent qualities which have been already productive of so many blessings to your country; that you will always have my fervent wishes for your public and personal felicity and that it will be my pride to cultivate a continuance of that esteem, regard and friendship of which you do me the honor to assure me. With true respect and affectionate attachment, I have the honor to be."[12]

On the same day of this letter, 2 February 1795, Oliver Wolcott, Jr. was named to replace Hamilton. Wolcott, son of a prominent Connecticut family, was already Comptroller of the Treasury, having held that post as a favorite of Hamilton since 1789. Within a short time, Hamilton was on his way with his family to their home in Albany, New York where also lived the family of Philip Schuyler wealthy father-in-law of the retired secretary. For Washington, this was the beginning of a new era; for in the last year he had lost three of his four department heads, probably the most able men a cabinet had ever had or ever has had since. Only Edmund Randolf of the original group remained.

At least the President was comforted that he still retained one fellow Virginian and confidant who had by this time become very familiar with all major phases of the workings of the government. Even now, Randolph was submitting a report for the President to present to Congress on the matter of obtaining a loan from Holland which seemed to be urgent at the time. On the last day of January, the unofficial news from England was that John Jay had concluded a treaty with Britain—but this had been done in late November. Of course this news was greeted with satisfaction by the Administration which expected that the official report would be received soon. To one less patient and inured to long delays in such trans-Atlantic transmission than Washington, this snail-like procedure would have been quite upsetting. Not so with the President who waited in silence. He consulted with the Secretary of War on some alarming information that the state of Georgia had defied the Federal Government and thrown open about fifty million acres of Indian land for purchase by speculators. This type of scurrilous practice had bothered the administration for years, but now it was being legalized by the State of Georgia, and Washington thought it might "deeply affect the peace and welfare of the United States."[13]

President Washington on 19 February 1795, went to Christ Church where Dr. William White preached a sermon on "Reciprocal Influences of Civil and Religious Duty." Whether this sermon was pointed at Washington is not known, but it well might have been. Years later Dr. White recalled that Washington was always serious and attentive in church. He could have been uncomfortable though, because it was at this time that he had to order a new set of false teeth, having lost his natural ones. He did appear in good health at age sixty-three, and on his birthday entertained visitors in his home. That evening he and Mrs. Washington were entertained at a ball sponsored by the City Dancing Assembly and directed, oddly enough, by that vitriolic critic, Benjamin Franklin Bache of the newspaper *Aurora*. Although it was raining, several hundred people were in attendance and the President seemed to enjoy the occasion. Fisher Ames commented that Bache filled his paper "with insults on the celebration and yet acted as manager but the celebration was unusually demonstrative of respect to our great chief. He rises over enemies like the sun scattering the mists."[14]

Financial problems were not confined to the government. A Charles Carter of Fredericksburg, Virginia (Washington's birthplace) had asked the President for a loan of 1,000 dollars to aid the business of his son. This amount in that day was of course considerable, so that Washington was embarrassed at the request. He answered that his friends did him a disservice when they regarded him as a moneylender. He stated that his public income was inadequate to the expense of living in the Capitol. (A common complaint today.) "To keep myself out of debt", the President continued, "I have found it expedient now and then to sell lands . . . These are facts I have no inclination to publish to the world; nor should I have disclosed them on this occasion had it not been due to friendship to give you some explanation of my inability to comply with your request." Washington did add that he would pledge $100 if nine other individuals could be found who would match that amount.[15]

To the dismay of the Chief Executive, Congress had done nothing about the Indian land problem in Georgia and this brought fears that there might be hostilities between the Creeks and white people there. In the current predicament, Washington felt it necessary to take upon himself the responsibility for some action in this direction. He wanted something done even if Congress was not in session so he directed Secretary of War Timothy Pickering to study the matter and come up with an effective program. By the end of March, Pickering had prepared definite instructions for Territorial Governor William Blount and for the Indian agent in Georgia, James Seagrove.

In the meantime, Mount Vernon beckoned and Washington was off again to visit his cherished acres. He made it a point to sound out the citizenry en route on the speculation about Jay's forthcoming treaty. There he found some favorable anticipation but kept silent concerning his own knowledge—or lack of it—of the document. At the Federal City, he encountered problems among the commissioners. One of them, Thomas Johnson, had written Washington that "The success of the city has now become important to your reputation. It is a favorite object with you and not less so with me, though the reward will be as unequal as our powers and merits. You will stand as the first figure while I shall be in the undistinguished group in the background." The dispute resulted from a claim of Johnson that he owned lots on Rock Creek which had been, other commissioners argued, acquired for speculative purposes and this should not have been allowed. Washington found the dilemma distasteful, but doubted that he could solve it. He did see Johnson and talked with other commissioners who opposed him, then continued on his way to Mount Vernon hoping that the problem would go away.

At home, Washington found peaceful quiet, but also a letter from Randolph describing a situation in which the resident Dutch minister had dismissed his consul and asked the United States to recognize this action officially. Here was another instance for which Washington had no precedent on which to rely. The matter might ordinarily seem a trivial one, but the President saw in it marked significance. At this time, the Dutch government was shaky because of the Jacobin French agitators trying to establish a "Batavian Republic" there. Washington told Randolph that the request of the Dutch minister was embarrassing and held more importance than it might seem. "To comply might have an unpleasant effect both here and elsewhere," said the President, "and not to do it would, I conceive, be a departure from the usual and established course of procedure in such cases. In a word, it seems to have placed the Executive between Scylla and Charybdis." Randolph was asked to make a cabinet study of the problem and inform him of the results when he returned to Philadelphia. Upon learning of the matter, Thomas Jefferson rejoiced and commented that the French movement would now probably extend around the world.[16]

A prospect of receiving needed personal funds arose when John Gill of nearby Georgetown came to Mount Vernon with an offer to purchase some land owned by Washington, called "Difficult Run," apparently from the irregular nature of the parcel. Washington was interested but Gill did not have the necessary cash for the purchase and apparently had no idea of improving the land if he bought it. Businessman Washington did not like Gill's attitude, but since the land was of little use and there was no other prospective buyer, a suggestion was made to Gill that he could pay part of the price down and the rest in annual payments. This idea Gill found acceptable.

Immediate chores being taken care of, the President returned to Philadelphia and was there by the first of May. Upon his arrival he became aware of strained relations between Secretary Randolph and the French minister, Fauchet. Randolph had written James Monroe that Fauchet had gotten into the habit of complaining and had written him an "indecent letter in which he collects all the charges which he thinks himself qualified to maintain against the United States . . . I am absolutely persuaded that we must lay down some new rules with respect to foreign ministers in general and prevent them from meddling as they usually do in our internal affairs." (One wonders what Randolph would have felt about the United Nations which some observers accuse of constant meddling if not trying to conduct our internal affairs.) At the same time, Hamilton wrote to Washington enclosing a letter from Gouverneur Morris warning that the new rulers in Paris intended to annul the 1778 treaties between France and the United States. Hamilton added that he hoped this report could not be true but stated that "in these wild times everything is possible."[17]

Oddly enough, Washington found time at this juncture to attend to more domestic affairs than he had while at home. He wrote several letters to his plantation manager some of which included questions about the welfare of the slaves and expressing concern regarding their living conditions. He regretted that some of the overseers treated the slaves like "brute beasts on the farm" and expressed his disapproval of such practice. Also as a personal pleasure, Washington spent some time with his old friend and associate, Henry Knox, who was preparing to leave Philadelphia for Northern Maine where he would acquire millions of acres until at one time, the former Secretary of War owned, on paper at least, a third of what is now the state of Maine. With Knox and his family went William Bingham, a prominent Philadelphia financier with whom Knox was associated in land speculation. Eventually Bingham and Knox sold over one million acres in Maine to Alexander Baring, the American agent from the great London financial house. Much of this did not turn out well for Knox however, who at one time was threatened with imprisonment for debt—as actually happened to a contemporary, William Duer, one-time assistant Secretary of the Treasury under Alexander Hamilton.

News came that Mrs. Lafayette was safe in Paris after a long imprisonment. But there was no encouraging word about her husband who was still dear to Washington's heart, and some historians have said, the nearest to a son that the President had. Warm still was the desire of Washington to help his old friend who had harbored great hopes for the future of France, but who seemed to waver between parties there until he was captured and exiled to Austria, fortunate to escape the guillotine. It was one of the President's deepest regrets that he could not bring about the release of Lafayette, but as in other decisions involving the placing of duty above personal considerations, Washington chose the former. One of the very rare times when he was reportedly in tears was when the President spoke of Lafayette and recalled the "good old days" when he and Lafayette were comrades in arms, contrasted with the latter's confinement in the prison at Olmutz.

In this spring of 1795, George Washington had little time for retrospection. Republican editors and writers had for more than a year been angry at the President for his appointment of John Jay as special envoy to Great Britain, and were highly critical of his behavior at the Court of St. James. Jay's long delay in achieving any results now caused them to turn their journalistic guns on Washington who was holding in secret the treaty which they felt that everyone should be aware of, especially those who feared to be the objects of it. The Chief Executive could not have been too surprised at the clamor of opposition because he knew when he appointed Jay, and later decided to keep quiet about what the envoy had done, that there would be a partisan outcry. The job now was to prepare for worse.

9

Jay's Treaty Mistreated

In the appointment of John Jay, the President had acted in a nationalistic spirit. It certainly was not easy for him to ignore the situation in Europe because he had ties to English ancestry and felt gratitude toward France for its invaluable help in the American Revolution. But he was head of a new nation and felt he should put its interests first regardless of any personal inclinations. In this respect, probably the most painful dilemma which he had faced was trying to choose between the positions of Hamilton and Jefferson, both of whom he respected and personally liked. In many ways he revered England and wanted nothing more than proper recognition from it. He had been sympathetic to the early reforms in France, but he did not share the views of Jefferson which he felt extended too far. The execution of its king and queen had removed any doubt of where he stood. Also he had enough of wars never to desire another. This nation did not have need for European spoils nor did it seek to destroy any other nation in order to increase our importance.

Washington wrote to Gouverneur Morris that he believed the United States should be permitted to enjoy "all the advantages that nature and its circumstances would admit including the expansion of useful arts and manufacturers so that their products might be exchanged with the nations and colonies of Europe."[1] "In every act of my administration," Washington stated to the selectmen of Boston,

> I have sought the happiness of my fellow citizens. My system for the attainment of this object has uniformly been to overlook all personal, local and partial considerations; to complete the United States as one great whole; to confide that sudden impressions, when erroneous, would yield to candid reflection; and to consult only the substantial and permanent interests of our country. Nor have I departed from this line of conduct on the occasion which has produced the resolutions. . . . Without a predilection for my own judgement, I weighed

151

with attention every argument which has at any time been brought into view. But the Constitution is the guide which I never can abandon. It has assigned the power of making treaties with the advice and consent of the Senate. It was doubtless supposed that these two branches of government would combine without passion and with the best means of information, these facts and principles upon which the success of our foreign relations will always depend; that they ought not to substitute for their own conviction the opinions of others, or to seek truth through any channel but that of a temperate and well-informed investigation. Under this persuasion, I have resolved on the manner of executing the duty before me. To the high responsibility of it, I freely submit; and you gentlemen are at liberty to make these sentiments known as the grounds of my procedure. While I feel the most lively gratitude for the many instances of approbation from my country, I can not otherwise deserve it than by obeying the dictates of my conscience. There is but one straight course, and that is to seek truth and to pursue it steadily.[2]

The mission of Gouverneur Morris was foredoomed to failure. At a time when understanding between France and the United States was indispensable, he had already aligned himself with France's enemies. Had he possessed the confidence of the government to which he was accredited, as Franklin and Jefferson had in their times, he might have tempered the misconceived policy of the Gironde. In 1793 in Paris, he was out of time and out of place. He unwittingly encouraged both France and England to continue the game of makeweight with America and he vastly increased the difficulties of establishing American neutrality. Earlier, the daughter of Vice President John Adams had reported from London that Morris "renders himself very obnoxious by an active and officious zeal in favor of the aristocracy. If Morris had not been an American, the Jacobins would have had his head on a pike long ago."[3]

When John Jay arrived in London in the spring of 1794, the British were flushed with victory over the French, and during most of the summer and autumn, Jay negotiated with Lord Grenville, the foreign secretary, against a background of British military triumph. Perhaps to his surprise, Jay found considerable cordiality within the British government. Both William Pitt and Lord Grenville were anxious to settle the dispute with the United States, and Jay was even received by King George III. The American took the occasion to praise the king's "justice and benevolence," which seemed rather odd under the circumstances. Jay attended a week-end party, frolicking with lords and ladies "and it was difficult to believe that he had once been proscribed as an enemy of Great Britain."[4]

John Jay was graduated from King's College and became a successful lawyer in New York. He married Sarah Livingston and thus was connected with another of New York's most prominent families. Though very reluctant to turn against England, he grew to be an ardent patriot and was a member of the first Continental Congress. He drafted the resolutions which authorized the New York delegation to sign the Declaration of Independence. He soon became chief justice of the state of New York and in December, 1778, was president of the Continental Congress. Jay went to Spain to seek an alliance with that country but events were so confusing he was not successful. In 1781, Jay was commissioned to act with Benjamin Franklin, John Adams, Thomas Jefferson, and Henry Laurens in negotiating the vital 1783 treaty with Great Britain. He had less confidence in France than did some others and in that treaty, Jay managed to include articles more favorable to the United States than was thought possible. On his return to America he was feted and soon became Secretary of Foreign Affairs in the Confederation Government. He brought that position, hitherto little recognized, to one of dignity and prestige. He was much in favor of arbitration in the settlement of disputes. Jay was one of the famous trio with Hamilton and Madison who wrote the *Federalist Papers* which, widely published, helped greatly to obtain ratification of the Constitution. Some important cases decided while Jay was Chief Justice, demonstrated his conservative and nationalistic views, but he was capable and had high integrity. It can easily be seen why he was chosen by President Washington to negotiate the treaty which bears his name.

Washington was uncertain as to the outlook for relations between the United States and Great Britain. He had protested that the British were stirring up the Indians, which had caused the murder of helpless woman and children along the American frontier, and felt that if such continued, there would be real trouble between the two countries. Jay's position soon became more difficult. As has been seen, James Monroe, the American minister to France, was a Republican and ardently pro-French in his sympathies. His speech to the National Assembly was looked upon with skepticism by British officials. Lord Grenville told Jay that if Monroe's attitude was the official one of his government, it would be difficult for England to regard America as truly neutral and unless the United States remained neutral, Britain was not apt to surrender the northwestern posts or to make a commercial treaty with this country.[5]

With friends like Jay in England and Monroe in France, Washington must have felt that he needed no enemies. Meanwhile France through its National Convention, resolved that it would strictly observe its 1778 treaty with America. Monroe was elated. He wanted to announce the news to the United States and proposed that Thomas Paine, who had been released from prison in October, be the courier. Monroe felt that Paine could explain the troubles France had come through, but since the latter was a member of the Convention, it might be difficult for him to receive permission. Also, Paine might be persecuted by England, if captured. But Paine, because of his position, could not accept the proposal.

When James Monroe was offered the post of minister to France, he was astonished, saying that he thought he was the last man to whom the offer would be made. The appointment was surprising, for Washington surely knew that Monroe did not favor many of the administration policies. As a youth of eighteen James Monroe was one of the first Virginians to join the Continental Army where he distinguished himself in battle and was wounded at Trenton. He was placed in charge of a regiment of men from various colonies and because of this diverse make-up, the regiment did not fit in well with the over-all military organization and Monroe's reputation was damaged. He later studied law with Thomas Jefferson who became his sponsor and friend. Monroe is sometimes portrayed as the last of the "Virginia dynasty" which started with Washington and extended through Jefferson and Madison. As a United States Senator, he turned out to be a severe critic of the Washington administration. Eventually of course he became President and made a commendable record.

In France, as American minister, Monroe was supposed to disregard his political leanings and try to do what was best for his country. But he seemed to look upon his appointment as more in the interests of France. Meantime he worked out with Jefferson a code so that he could communicate secretly with the latter.[6]

At this time relations between France and the United States were at the lowest ebb in thirty years. Relations between Secretary of State Randolph and the French Minister Fauchet were no longer cordial, the Frenchman tending increasingly to blame Randolph for the obstacles placed in the former's path. Even more serious was the shadow of the Jay mission to England, "which lay across the minds of the French minister and of American well-wishers of France like a dark cloud before a storm." Randolph had told Monroe to go to France to strengthen our friendship with that country; that France should be told of our appreciation for past services especially in view of our strained relations with England and France.[7]

With the end of the year came the long-expected departure from office of Secretary of the Treasury Alexander Hamilton. Washington notified the secretary that his resignation was reluctantly accepted. Hamilton replied with equal grace, thus exited the member of Washington's cabinet who in the long run had the most influence on the Chief Executive. Although at times they disagreed, there was mutual respect and more loyalty on the part of Washington than that of Hamilton. This was because of the noble character of George Washington and some weaknesses in that of Hamilton. Aside from any defects, he was an extraordinary human who will stand in history as a man with a great career which ended in great tragedy.[8]

On the last day of January 1795, an intriguing rumor was heard that John Jay had signed a treaty in November. Washington was filled with eagerness and anxiety over when the crucial treaty would arrive. Weeks went by and suspense deepened. Washington's patience was tried but he kept his composure and waited in silence. Washington's birthday that year was celebrated on 23 February 1795. At sixty-three, he appeared to be in fine health and good spirits and received a number of well-wishers who came to his home that morning. In the evening, he and his wife attended a dance which, as usual, he enjoyed and gave toasts to the citizens who had come to honor him.[9]

On 7 March (with a number of Congressmen on their way home), David Blaney, a Virginian entrusted by Jay, reached the office of Edmund Randolph after a hard ride from Norfolk. Blaney had been en route from England for more than three months, and the paper he delivered was not the original draft of the treaty but nevertheless, an exact copy. Here was at last "a treaty of amity, commerce and navigation" signed by John Jay and Lord Grenville on 19 November 1794. To Washington, Jay wrote, "It must speak for itself. To do more was not possible."[10]

To many the treaty brought disappointment. The best thing about it appeared in the first section which began "There shall be a firm, inviolable and universal peace and a true and sincere friendship between His Britannic Majesty and the United States of America." Washington breathed easier; for if other details were unsatisfactory, at least war was averted and he, of all people, knew what war meant. In the long and complicated document, Jay had been obliged to renounce the freedom of the seas. The principles which the United States had set forth in previous treaties with foreign powers at the recommendation of Thomas Jefferson, were free ships make free goods; neutrals are entitled to trade freely with belligerents in non-contraband goods; and the contraband list being confined to a few articles of war was surrendered by Jay as a price of Anglo-American friendship. Instead, the British concept of belligerent's rights was in the treaty. Naval stores were to be contraband; provisions could not be carried in neutral ships to enemy ports, trade with enemy colonies was prohibited; Great Britain was granted most-favored-nation treatment; and it was agreed that private debts could not be sequestered. Sales of prizes in American ports would no longer be permitted and we were not to allow our ports to be havens for ships of Britain's enemies.

John Jay had to promise that no molasses, sugar, coffee, cocoa, nor cotton would be carried in American ships to any part of the world except the United States. To Jay the inclusion of cotton in this category was especially significant because he believed that the United States ought to manufacture for itself all the cotton it grew. He did not obtain a concession which might have stipulated payment for the Negro slaves the British had carried away during our Revolution. He did not much regret this however for Jay was a strong abolitionist and doubtless was glad that the slaves had gained their freedom. Actually the British government felt that it had been generous to the United States; but the ministry had to defend itself in the House of Commons against charges of being pro-American. Here William Pitt declared that the treaty had been "dictated on both sides by a spirit of fairness and mutual accommodation."[11]

We did get something. The British government promised to surrender the northwest posts by June of 1796. The amount of compensation for spoliation, which consisted of the claims of British creditors who had been deprived of their money, was referred to arbitration. Britain agreed to pay for spoliations upon American commerce but the United States promised to pay the claims of British creditors against American citizens. Nor were there any guarantees against impressment of American sailors by the British Navy.[12]

In the twelfth article of Jay's treaty was a commercial portion in which it was stipulated that American ships were to enjoy the privilege of trading with the British West Indies which had been closed to American ships were open to vessels of seventy tons or less. "Thus while Jay succeeded in breaching mercantilistic walls which Great Britain had erected around its empire, the crack was so small, hardly more than a fishing smack could get through."[13]

President Washington was surprised and extremely disappointed in most of the treaty. Lord Grenville felt that he had gone as far as he could without losing the support of Parliament.

The treaty was to cause explosive disagreement within the United States government and among its people but not all were opposed to it by any means. Noah Webster stated

> I am of the opinion that the treaty, as modified by the Senate, makes no sacrifices that are dishonorable to us as a nation and none which are very prejudicial to the United States . . . I believe in the present state of America, it would be good policy to carry it into effect as a temporary agreement. The Northern states will, if left to themselves, acquiesce in the ratification of the treaty, if that should be or is the determination of the President. The Democratic clubs are not yet strong enough to even threaten any general disorder. At the same time, the societies are secretly extending their force, and in my apprehension some decisive legislative remedy must be speedily applied to extirpate the evil or we must ultimately be governed by irregular town meetings. In this thing much, however, depends on the war in Europe. But in the Southern states the danger appears to be more real. The circumstances which led and still lead the people of those states to a close connection with French politics, you very well know. The opposition to our government then is general; and to me it bodes an ultimate separation between us and them. The peace of our country stands almost commited in either event. A rejection of the treaty leaves all the causes of hostility unadjusted with the addition of a double exasperation of temper. A ratification threatens evil commotions, at least in the Southern states. A rejection sacrifices Mr. Jay and perhaps many of his friends, and ratification threatens the popularity of the President, whose personal influence is now more essential than ever to our Union.[14]

The principal reason why John Jay was not able to obtain from Great Britain the desired concessions was one of which at the time Washington had no knowledge. Alexander Hamilton's actions were the reason. In July of 1794, Hamilton assured British Minister George Hammond that the United States would never enter an alliance or an armed-neutrality agreement with European nations to the disadvantage of England. This gave Lord Grenville the very information and weapon that he desired. Said he, "With great seriousness and with every demonstration of sincerity, Hamilton had told him that it was the settled policy of this government in every contingency, even in that of an open contest with Great Britain, to avoid entangling itself with European connections." So Grenville had no reason to make undue concessions, and Jay's mission was thereby sabotaged.[15]

The United States Constitution requires the advice and consent of the Senate for the ratification of a treaty before it finally reaches the Presidential desk. The Senate by this time had adjourned and was not to convene again until the special sessions planned for 8 June. So the treaty would have to remain for three months in the custody of the President. He and his Secretary of State agreed that the text of the treaty should be kept in strict confidence until delivered to the Senate for its verdict. Also, by that time, Jay would be home from England and be able to answer any attacks on his treaty.

The treaty itself contained technical parts which Washington did not clearly understand, particularly the commercial provisions. Doubtless, it would have been useful for him to have consulted an expert on such. But Alexander Hamilton had retired from the government and the President did not feel it appropriate to consult him at this time nor did Washington talk to any other members of his cabinet about the matter except the Attorney General and the Secretary of State. These officials were ordered by the President to conceal the text from everyone until the treaty should be delivered to the Senate.

Like Henry Knox who always longed to go home, Washington felt the same way about Mount Vernon. At this time despite his worries, he spent a week there but had to return because of the pressure of official business. Meantime, editors of opposing newspapers who had been angered over Jay's appointment as a special envoy to London, now aimed their printed attacks at Washington himself because he had seen fit to keep the treaty secret. Especially violent were the assaults in Benjamin Bache's *Aurora*, Philip Freneau's *Jersey Journal*, and Thomas Adams's *Independent Chronicle* of Boston. However, Federalist newspapers came to the defense of the President including John Fenno's *Gazette of the United States*, Benjamin Russell's *Columbian Centinel* of Boston, and the *United States Chronicle* of Providence, Rhode Island.

Diverting somewhat from this criticism was the arrival in Philadelphia of a new envoy from France. This was Pierre Adet who replaced the representative Jacobin, Joseph Fauchet. Washington met Adet who like Fauchet had to speak through an interpreter but the new envoy seemed friendly, quiet and intelligent. For this, the President was grateful because not only had Edmund Genet been a tremendous problem but also his successor.

Vice President John Adams brought the Senate to order Wednesday, 24 June. A new Senator, Jacob Reed of South Carolina, a Federalist, made the surprising motion that England should be required to make compensation for the Negroes its military forces carried away during the Revolution. Nowhere did the treaty deal with this old grievance. This idea had the support of every Southern Senator except James Gunn of Georgia. The Southerners then asked for an immediate roll call on the original motion to consent to all the treaty except Article 12. This carried but lacked the two-thirds vote which the Senate required.[16]

President Washington had his differences with Alexander Hamilton but when it came to important matters, especially economic ones, the opinions of the former Secretary of the Treasury were still highly respected and now much desired. So, on 3 July, almost four months after Jay's treaty had arrived, Washington wrote to Hamilton in his own hand. "My desire," he stated, "is to learn from dispassionate men who have knowledge of the subject and the ability to judge of it, the genuine opinion they entertain of each article of the instrument and the result of this in the aggregate." He apologized to Hamilton for interrupting him in his busy practice of law but indicated that his advice was greatly needed. "It is much more than ever an incumbent duty on me," the President continued, "to do what propriety and the true interests of this country shall appear to require. My wishes are to have the favorable and unfavorable sides of each article of the treaty stated and compared together that I may see the bearing and tendency of them and ultimately on which side the balance is to be found."[17]

While Washington awaited a reply, the Fourth of July was celebrated in Philadelphia. Not a happy part of the occasion were the words of the newspaper, *Independent Gazette,* stating that "Mrs. Liberty was dead from a dose of subtle poison administered by the British king. She is to be publicly interred this day. . . . Our sun with awful splendor has sunk in pristine darkness. Farewell thou radiant goddess who once inspired our souls. May we weep on thy tomb until our abject forms are changed to marble."[18]

Nevertheless, the people of Philadelphia in their best clothes enjoyed the good weather. Bells rang and President Washington received the felicitations of all types of citizens. However, late in the evening a noisy crowd of shipwrights and mechanics paraded in the streets and overhead could be seen an illuminated life-sized effigy of John Jay, in one of whose hands were scales and in the other a bag of gold. He was represented as saying to the Senators, "Come up to my price and I will sell you my country." The demonstrators marched to the suburbs of the city and there burned the effigy amid loud shouts until they were dispersed.

Washington compared the harsh criticism of the treaty to the barking of a mad dog. Jay stated that he could have found his way across the country by the light of his burning effigies which showed him selling his country for British money. In New York City, Alexander Hamilton was pelted with stones when he tried to speak in favor of the treaty. In the meantime, Jay had been elected governor of New York and conveniently resigned as Chief Justice of the United States. "In whatever line you may walk," Washington wrote Jay, "my best wishes will always accompany you. They will particularly do so on the theater you are about to enter."[19]

The President thanked Hamilton for his extensive comment on the treaty and controversy surrounding it and indicated that he was concerned himself over what British ships might do to American seaports. Washington showed Hamilton's letter to Randolph who replied with his own reasons why he believed that Washington should approve the treaty: that peace would be obtained; that there was not much chance that any negotiations could produce a more favorable treaty; that as time went on, Britain might be even more demanding. Randolph moreover suggested that he call on the British minister to ascertain what could be done by that personal method. He would convey the sentiments of the President in desiring harmony with England and specially see what was the reaction to Article Twelve of the treaty. Washington agreed with Randolph and accordingly the Secretary of State visited the British minister Hammond. He soon returned and told Washington that the minister gave him no satisfactory answer.

James Madison was the leading authority on the Constitution in the House of Representatives. In fact he has come to be known as "the Father of the Constitution." Therefore he felt that his interpretation of that document was better than that of Washington. Madison's views were contained in a resolution in 1796 and introduced by Senator William Blount to the effect that although the House of Representatives did not claim an integral part in the making of treaties, that even when one was ratified by the Senate it was the Constitutional right of the House to deliberate on the expediency or independency of carrying out the treaty. It was not necessary, the Madison-Blount resolutions stated, for the House to give a purpose for which information was wanted; it was only sufficient for the House to express such a desire. Based on this theory, Madison contended that the House had a right to withhold the necessary appropriation and thereby nullify the treaty.

William Blount, a North Carolinian and political leader, served in the Revolution and was a member of Congress in the 1780's. He was governor of the Northwest Territories and elected United States Senator from Tennessee in 1796. He was more interested in land speculation that he was in government, although he was loyal to his regional interests. Blount had become obsessed with the idea that Spain was in general an enemy of the new United States. He also was fearful of Indian raids since some in the southeast had murdered white settlers including women and children. Many times, Blount had urged the Washington administration to send regular troops to put down the Southern Indian uprisings but those troops were busy on the Western frontier with Indian troubles of their own. With Wayne's victory, these concerns were lessened but Blount still insisted the Americans must kill the red men or the Indians would kill the whites. Secretary of War Pickering soon came to dislike Blount, accusing him of using his office for private gain through illegal contracts. Eventually Blount came to distrust the national government and began to turn toward the Democrats in his attitude. He secretly devised a plan for American attacks on Spanish possessions near New Orleans and Pensacola. A British fleet would assist in these illegal operations. This plot came to the attention of the Secretary of War and others in Philadelphia through a letter Blount had written to an associate who, while drinking too much, revealed its contents. Blount was called before the Senate and accused of abuses of public trust and high misdemeanors. After much evasion and denial, by him, William Blount was convicted and expelled from the Senate, the first American to attain this dubious distinction.

Soon after Blount was expelled from the United States Senate, he returned to Tennessee where, oddly from today's viewpoint, he was acclaimed as a hero and greeted by Governor John Sevier. In 1798, Blount was elected Speaker of the Tennessee House of Representatives. His impeachment trial had been postponed because of his absence, and his counsel argued that the Senate did not have jurisdiction over Blount because he was no longer a member of the Senate and had committed no crime. As it was, the case never came before the House, and in January 1799, the Senate dismissed the impeachment for want of jurisdiction since its members were now considered not impeachable as civil officers. This, however, proved to be a hollow victory because the next year William Blount died.[20]

After he had refused to send the Jay's Treaty document to the House, President Washington went further in his claims by asking the Senate's approval for the appointment of commissioners to carry out the provisions of the treaty. While the House still resisted him, Washington insisted that the issue was "agitating the public mind in a higher degree than it had been at any period during the Revolution." But he wisely during the controversy kept quiet and wrote down no opinions which would be argued about later. In the House after several speeches, the Republican leader of the opposition, Albert Gallatin, made an eloquent and persuasive speech. He argued that the government was in no danger of collapse and doubted that England would go to war with this country. Federalist listeners made fun of the Swiss immigrant Gallatin because he spoke with a heavy French accent. He was answered by Fisher Ames, the principal Federalist orator who was ill in Massachusetts but regardless hurried to the House to speak. He proclaimed emotionally that the treaty had already been ratified.

The Republicans argued that Britain was not in a position to quarrel with the United States. The anti-French coalition had fallen apart; Holland had broken away from Britain and joined her enemy; Spain and Russia had withdrawn from the struggle; Austria had problems of her own; and young Napoleon Bonaparte would soon impose upon her a victorious peace. In England sentiment for peace was strong, the country suffered from bad harvests, and the leadership was desperate for means to continue the war. John Quincy Adams wrote from Holland to his father that despite "deeprooted malignity towards us which governs the British cabinet, they have however so much at present upon their hands that they will not quarrel with us." Also, the United States was indispensable to England because the two countries were each other's best customers and the trade between them resulted in a favorable trade balance for England which was America's largest creditor. The Federalists made Jay's Treaty the keystone of American foreign policy. But Republicanism was gaining rapidly in America so that the struggle over the treaty contributed enormously to the rise of a Republican majority in this country. The accompanying dissension had echoes abroad. About it Winston Churchill wrote, "The atmosphere was charged afresh with distrust, and the seeds were sown for another war between Britain and the United States."[21]

Still undecided about signing Jay's Treaty, President Washington in mid-July set out for Mount Vernon. As his carriage went along, he asked people he met what they thought of the treaty. He found many who did not favor it. Furthermore, he was not allowed to enjoy his visit at home for long. He received a message from Randolph that the governmental crisis was the greatest which had yet occurred. The secretary wanted to come to Mount Vernon to consult Washington about it but the latter replied that it would be better if he himself returned to Philadelphia. The President was concerned that the mass meetings of protest in America would induce the French government to believe that the treaty was in favor of Great Britain at their expense. "I have never seen," he said, "since I have been in the administration of the government such a crisis which in my judgement has been so pregnant of interesting events; nor one from which more is to be apprehended."[22]

What worried Washington most at this time was a report from Hamilton and Jay that British cruisers were seizing as contraband, cargoes of American grain ships bound for France. This so angered the President that he considered not signing the treaty at all. However, he calmed down enough to agree that he would consider such signing if the British government removed or revised Article Twelve of the treaty. On the whole, Washington felt that the treaty was in the true interest of the United States and should be accepted.

Washington's stay at Mount Vernon was all too typical of those short cherished visits afforded him in this chaotic era. While he wanted to keep his mind on the supervision of his farms, being with his family and overseeing his slaves, this was impossible because, as has been pointed out, wherever he was, there was the government. He had lost three key members of his cabinet and now had to rely mainly on the opinion of Randolph, although as we have seen he did get important help from Hamilton.

Alexander Hamilton was at this time really not out of government although he had no official capacity except as an advisor.

He took the liberty of writing to Jay in England, pushing the Federalist policies to which Jay responded confidentially not letting Secretary Randolph know of their communication. Hamilton's excuse was that Randolph was not keeping Jay informed. Hamilton seemed to assume that Washington would approve of his informal actions and as a rule the President did. But not always. In one instance on learning that Hamilton had indicated that the President approved of his extracurricular activities, Washington reminded Hamilton that whatever was communicated or done should be agreeable to the laws.

John Jay was known as a hard-headed New Yorker who because of family background was coldly proud and deeply religious. He was said to be the best trained diplomat in America. Through all the criticism of his treaty, Jay remained calm and declined to apologize for its contents and effects. In keeping the treaty secret from the public and from any of his cabinet except Randolph, the President must have suspected that had any others known about it, it would have leaked out prematurely. While this gave time for Washington and Randolph to analyze carefully, it also prolonged the uncertainty about it in their minds. Even while the treaty was under Senate consideration, Washington did not consult verbally with other cabinet members except Randolph. He did ask the opinions of Pickering, Wolcott and Bradford in writing. All three recommended Washington's acceptance of the treaty.

Washington told Hamilton, "The string which is most played on, because it strikes with the most force the popular ear is the violation, as they term it, of our engagements with France; or in other words the predilection shown by the Jay Treaty to Great Britain at the expense of the French nation."[23]

Heavy rains added to Washington's depression. These not only damaged his crops but washed the topsoil from the ground into the Potomac River. It was even difficult for his servants to travel back and forth to Alexandria for the mail. At any rate, Washington decided that "In the face of violent expressions, mass meetings and all manner of protests against the treaty in particular and the government in general, peace is the issue and duty demands ratification."[24]

As the year 1795 was ending, President Washington had cause for considerable satisfaction. He said this in his address to Congress and called attention to the situation in Europe where wars had devastated the economy to the extent of widespread starvation and the destruction of arts and culture. In contrast, the

United States for the time was enjoying general tranquility and although trade had been disturbed, the benefits derived from the neutral position of the nation regarding foreign affairs more than offset this annoyance. Washington believed that his country was in the best position it had ever been and his desire to preserve the achievements was "the favorite wish of my heart."

The President declared, "Born sir, in a land of liberty; having early learned its value; having engaged in a perilous conflict to defend it; having in a word, devoted the best years of my life to secure its permanent establishment in my own country; my anxious recollections, my sympathetic feelings and my best wishes are irresistibly excited whensoever, in any country, I see an oppressed nation unfurl the banners of freedom. But above all, the events of the French Revolution have produced the deepest solicitude as well as the highest admiration. To call your nation brave were to pronounce but common praise."

On the President's sixty-fourth birthday, the House of Representatives denied by a vote of fifty to thirty-eight a motion to adjourn for half an hour so that the members could call on the President. Even so the President was given something that very day which pleased him immensely, and that was the Treaty of San Lorenzo negotiated by Thomas Pinckney with Spain. This good news was extremely welcome in view of the unfortunate conditions existing within the nation. The situation then was somewhat like that of the recent Reagan and Bush administrations. Yet it is easy to understand that Washington was justified in opposing any power of the House to have a general veto over ratification of treaties. The House at that time had many varied types of members, some conservative and experienced but many otherwise. It was Washington's belief that it was only "after time has been given for cool and deliberate reflection that the real voice of the people can be heard."

Washington received a letter from Secretary of War Timothy Pickering which stated, "For a *special reason* which can be communicated to you only in person, I entreat therefore that you will return . . . this letter is for your own eyes alone." Washington thereupon hurriedly returned to Philadelphia and on 11 August at dinner, he received Pickering and Secretary of State Randolph. Washington asked Pickering to come into another room and there inquired why he had written him such a secret type of letter. Pickering replied that Edmund Randolph was a traitor.[25]

Of all the disturbing and melancholy moments in the career of

George Washington, through the tempest of the Revolution and his period as President, never had he felt himself in such a painful and difficult situation. As hard as he had tried to bring peace here and abroad, there seemed to be no peace. No man of his time and in his place could have faced this dark horizon with such faith, courage, and resolution.

10

An Old Friend Departs

Although the historian who attempts to delve into the mind of his subject runs a precarious risk, the shock which Washington felt at the news of Edmund Randolph's alleged treachery must have been tremendous. This extraordinary Chief Executive who had led his new country to victory in war now was faced with a problem within his own peacetime staff which was in its ways more acute than that of the battlefield. Though Washington was phenomenally strong, this internal calamity was an awful challenge which not only imperiled this government and his cabinet but was a dire personal disappointment. His rugged heart though accustomed to strain must have suffered greatly at this tragic revelation—if it were true. The tree is not strong that has not withstood the storm, but this mighty oak of humanity was shaken to its roots.

The Randolph affair was the most shocking such occurrence since the time that Washington had faced the perfidiousness of General Benedict Arnold, who had been known as one of Washington's best generals, but gone over to the British and betrayed his country. Even that dilemma was more susceptible of solution than the current one because it could have been solved simply by a court-martial. Now it appeared to the distraught Washington that he was judge and jury and must decide the fate of his erstwhile trusted subordinate. He had known Edmund Randolph since he was a boy, a fellow Virginian of aristocratic lineage and presumably devoted to the same Southern ideals as his chief. Of all of Washington's colleagues, with the exception of the loyal Henry Knox, Randolph had been the most affectionate and expressive of warm friendship. Yet Randolph had not been proven guilty of wrong and Washington determined that he himself would remain silent until he could come to a just conclusion.

Washington had written to Randolph a friendly letter from Mount Vernon as recently as 29 July 1795, a private one saying,

I am excited to this resolution by the violent and extraordinary proceedings which have been and are about taking place in the Northern parts of the Union: and may be expected in the Southern: because I think that the memorial, the ratification, and the instructions which are framing are of such vast magnitude as not only to require great individual consideration but a solemn conjunct revision. The latter could not happen if you were to come to this place; nor would there be that source of information to be had, as is to be found and continually flowing to the seat of government; and besides, in the course of deliberating on these great matters; the examination of official papers may more than probaby be found essential, and these could be resorted to nowhere else. I view the opposition which the treaty is receiving from the meetings in different parts of the Union in a very serious light. Not because there is more weight in any of these objections which are made to it than was foreseen at first; for there are *none* in *some* of them; and gross misrepresentations in others; nor as it respects myself personally for this shall have no influence on my conduct and I am accordingly preparing in mind for the obloquy which disappointment and malice are collecting to heap upon my character. . . . To sum the whole up in a few words, I have never since I have been in the administration of the government seen such a crisis which in my judgment has been so pregnant of interesting events; or one from which more is to be apprehended whether view on one side or the other. (He was referring to Jay's Treaty).[1]

In one of Fauchet's intercepted dispatches which related to the Whiskey Rebellion and Washington's proclamation regarding it was the following statement of the French minister about Randolph,

Two or three days before the proclamation was published, and of course before the cabinet had resolved on its measures the Secretary of State came to my house. All his countenance was grief. He requested of me a private conversation. 'It was all over,' he said to me; 'a civil war is about to ravage our unhappy country. Four men, by their talents, their influence, and their energy, may save it. But, debtors of English merchants, they will be deprived of their liberty if they take the smallest step. Could you lend them instantaneously funds to shelter them from English prosecution? This inquiry astonished me much. It was impossible for me to make a satisfactory answer. 'You know my want of power and deficiency in pecuniary means.' . . . Thus, with some thousands of dollars, the Republic could have decided on civil war or peace. Thus *the consciences of the pretended patriots of America have already their price.* What will be the old age of this government, if it is thus already decrepit?[2]

Fauchet had left Philadelphia on 26 June for Newport, Rhode Island, where he was to board the French frigate *Medusa* for the voyage home. Contrary winds forced his packet-boat into Stonington, Connecticut and while being delayed there he learned from a French vice-counsul that the British warship *Africa* was off Newport waiting to intercept him. Therefore, Fauchet continued his journey by land and when he arrived in Newport learned that the United States vessel *Peggy* had been stopped by the British and a search made for Fauchet and his papers. This was a violation of the United States sovereignty in America territorial waters and was protested to the American and British governments. Notwithstanding, the *Africa* remained in the vicinity of Newport until six weeks later when, under a dense fog, the *Medusa* slipped out to sea with Fauchet aboard.[3]

As one authority has ponted out, Randolph's dereliction might have gone undetected had it not been for British disregard of the three-mile limit established by the United States for ships offshore. The captain of the British ship hailed and searched it in the hope of capturing Fauchet. On the ship they found Fauchet's papers but not him. The British intentionally retained these papers until July 1795 when Jay's treaty was hanging in the balance. Then, the British minister presented these documents to the United States government. Rather extensive, the papers suggested that Edmund Randolph who had opposed using force in the Whiskey Rebellion had given state secrets to Fauchet and then appealed to him to try to bribe several prominent American officials. "Officials of America have already their scale of prices," Fauchet reported to his government, "Alexander Hamilton has made of the whole nation a stock-jobbing, speculating selfish people."[4]

It was a sad evening of 11 August when President Washington, alone in his study, began to read the Fauchet papers. In them was mentioned "Precious Confessions of Mr. Randolph." This alone alarmed the reader. He apparently did not notice closely the reference in the paper to Randolph's influence on him. As he read on, Washington became more and more convinced that as much as he would like to avoid the conclusion, that Randolph had been deceitful, venal, and possibly, what Pickering had called him, a traitor. In the case of Benedict Arnold, that individual was addicted to living beyond his income; and similarly, Edmund Randolph was constantly in impecunious circumstances and trying to borrow money. Was there a parallel here?

The next morning, Washington called a meeting of his cabinet. His colleagues greeted Randolph civilly but with unusual coolness. The President's demeanor did not change. Of course he had not yet told Randolph what was in store. The latter was asked to read Fauchet's dispatch and as he did, the President, Secretaries Pickering and Wolcott watched him intently. Randolph was surprised, but seemed more disturbed at the manner in which the meeting was conducted than his own possible involvement. When asked to explain his conduct, he gave rather evasive and vague replies as if he were trying to gain time for his answers. It has been observed that the meeting which Washington set up resembled a court-martial. If the format were this the outcome might have been different. It can also be pointed out, that a court-martial is only a trial—not a foregone conviction as the popular conception often indicates—and experience has shown that many military trials can reach fair conclusions more expeditiously than do civilian courts.[5]

In the manner of a court-martial, Washington did ask Randolph to retire to the next room while he conferred with Wolcott and Pickering. This of course upset Randolph. At the end of the conference, he angrily announced that he could not remain in office after the treatment he had just received. His letter of resignation as Secretary of State was on the President's desk the next day where it was received with sadness.

If Randolph had quietly let the matter lie, the consequences might have been different. Washington could have remained silent on the matter and Randolph could have gone home peacefully to Virginia. Instead he chose to challenge the President, a formidable opponent indeed. He wrote Washington complaining that the Chief Executive had consulted others before letting him know and questioned the idea of sending him into another room while the President conversed with them. Randolph stated that he did not mean to relinquish the inquiry; that he would pursue it until he found out the truth and let Washington know. In the meantime, he hoped that the President would keep the matter secret. To this, Washington agreed.[6]

Meanwhile Washington nourished the hope that Randolph could vindicate himself and so told him. But rumors to Randolph's discredit, probably spread by Pickering or Wolcott, were soon going the rounds. In response to these, Randolph lashed out at Washington, writing Madison that "I feel happy at my emancipation from attachment to a man who has practiced on me the profound hypocrisy of a Tiberius and the injustice of an assassin."[7]

Edmund Randolph complained that Pickering was prejudiced against him before the President had knowledge of Fauchet's intercepted dispatch. "I hold Pickering's letter," Randolph wrote to Washington, "to be important to one of the views which the question will bear and therefore request the consideration of it. . . . You must be sensible, Sir, that I am inevitably driven into the discussion of many confidential and delicate points. I could with safety immediately appeal to the people of the United States, who can be of no party. But I shall wait for your answer and rely that you will consent to the whole of this affair, howsoever confidential and delicate, being exhibited to the whole world."

Disturbed, Washington summoned Secretary Pickering to his office and they composed an answer to Randolph which the President signed and mailed on 21 October 1795. "It is not difficult from the tenor of your letter," the answer stated,

to perceive what your objects are. But that you may have no cause to complain of the withholding of any paper . . . I have directed that you should have the inspection of my letter of the twenty-second of July, agreeably to your request; and that you are at full liberty to publish, without reserve, *any* and *every* private and confidential letter I ever wrote to you—nay more, every word I have ever uttered, to or in your presence, from whence you can derive any advantage of your vindication. I grant this permission inasmuch as the situation manifestly tends to impress on the public mind that something has passed between us which you should disclose with reluctance from motives of delicacy which respect me. . . . As you are no longer an officer of the Government and propose to submit your vindication to the public, it is not my desire nor is it my intention to receive it otherwise than through the medium of the press. . . . I request that this letter may be inserted in the compliation you are now making, as well to show my disposition to furnish you with every means I possess toward your vindication.

I have no wish to conceal any part of my conduct from the public. That public will judge, when it comes to see your vindication, how far and proper it has been for you to publish private and confidential communications which oftentimes have been written in a hurry, and sometimes without even copies being taken. And it will, I hope, appreciate my motives, even if it should condemn my prudence in allowing you the unlimited license herein contained.[8]

Apparently this letter so provoked Randolph that he penned a quick response.

Whatsoever my objects may be supposed to be, I have but one, which is to defend myself. Your unlimited publication is therefore, as you must be persuaded, given without hazard. For you never could believe that I intended to exhibit to public *all* and *everything* which was known to me. I have indeed the sensibility of an injured one; but I shall disclose even what I am compelled to disclose, under the necessity which you yourselves have created. I have been the meditated victim of party spirit. . . . To the people I always meant to appeal. The people will see that I have not imitated some others in treasuring up your letters or observations, from any expectation of producing them at a future day; that I have never betrayed your confidence; and that even where your 'prudence' may be condemned, your 'unlimited license' is no more than a qualified effort to do justice. It would have been less equivocal if it had not been accompanied with a kind of threat. And the candor which your letters seems to wear would have been more seasonable had it commenced with this injurious business.[9]

In similar argumentative manner, the President replied,

Your letter of the twenty-fourth of October is full of innuendoes. To whom or for what purpose you mean to apply the following words—I have been the meditated victim of party spirit—will be found, I presume, in your defense without which I shall never understand them. I cannot conceive they are aimed at me, because a hundred times you have heard me lament them from the bottom of my soul that differences of opinion should have occasioned those which are disquieting the country. . . . I am free to declare that I cannot at this moment see what relation there is between the treaty with Great Britain and the details and suggestions which are contained in the intercepted letter of Mr. Fauchet. And I am still more at a loss to understand the meaning of these other words in your letter—But I shall disclose even what I am compelled to disclose under the operation of the necessity which you yourself have created. Can these expressions allude to my having put Mr. Fauchet's letter into your hands in the presence of the heads of departments? Or to the acceptance of your resignation, voluntarily and unexpectedly offered? Or to the assurance given and most religiously observed on my part, not to mention anything of the matter until you had had an opportunity of clearing it up, while you on the other hand were making free communications thereof in all quarters and intimating to your friends that your vindication would bring things to view which would affect me more than any which had yet appeared? . . . But I do not write from a desire to obtain explanations nor shall I proceed any further in discussions of this sort unless necessity should call for a simple and candid statement of the business to be laid before the public.

This "letter" would have been even more interesting—but Washignton hesitated, thought more calmly and then decided not to send it.[10]

On 18 December, Randolph published a pamphlet entitled "Vindication" of 103 pages much of which was in the form of a letter to the President. In the pamphlet was included all of Fauchet's incriminating dispatches and material gained from French sources. Herein was stated that Fauchet had given Randolph an affidavit saying that he never made indiscreet disclosure or asked for or received French money. As far as the phrase "Precious Confessions" in the papers which had aroused Washington's suspicion, Randolph said that these did not go beyond general statements on politics. Randolph also charged that the President was now incompetent and had allowed himself to be deceived by persons who wished to sacrifice Randolph and the French to the British. He even lectured Washington on his judgement, he accused the President of being hypocritical and not a sincere friend.[11]

President Washington controlled his temper. He could not afford to dignify such invective by indulging in it himself. He doubtless felt that Edmund Randolph was at least guilty of venality, perhaps of treason.[12]

Washington was not the only one who implicated Randolph and offered to prove it. Some modern historians have disagreed. John A. Carroll and Mary W. Ashworth, successors to Douglas Freeman in his definitive biography of Washington, pronounced Randolph innocent. Irving Brant, biographer of James Madison has agreed, placing the blame on "Two of the most malevolent men who ever decorated the Presidential cabinet, Timothy Pickering and Oliver Wolcott."[13]

"From an early period of my life," Randolph had written,

I was taught to esteem you. As I advanced in years, I was habituated to revere you. You strengthened my prepossessions by marks of attention and, if by some others you have been insidiously pampered with more lavish assurances of an affectionate attachment, from me you have experienced a sincere anxiety to continue your reputation upon its ancient basis, the hearts of the people. But the season is come, Sir, when, if my obligations to you have not been balanced by laborious and confidential services, the whole account is settled without ingratitude on my part. . . . Before you saw Mr. Fauchet's letter, the British partisans had been industrious in disseminating the most poisonous falsehoods. And while I was absent at Rhode Island, they seized the advantage of utter uncontradicted slanders, boasting and insisting that in the controversy between us, I must be sacrificed. I hesitate not to pronounce that you prejudged the question, that you ought to have withstood the impulse which hurried you into a prejudication, and that he who feels a due adhorrence of party ma-

neuvers will form a conclusion favorable to myself. That you prejudged my case is proclaimed by your actions. The system of
concealment, which has been practiced under the united auspices of
the British Minister and the American Secretary of the Treasury, was
not thought unworthy of your adoption. Why was all this strategy
observed towards him of whose fidelity you had never entertained a
doubt? From a temper which, under the exterior of cool and slow
deliberation, rapidly catches a prejudice and with difficulty aban-
dons it, you determined that your impressions could not be effaced.
The immediate ratification of the treaty with Great Britain can be
traced to no other source than a surrender of yourself to the first
impression from the letter, which instantaneously governed you with
respect to that instrument and myself. The facts speak too strongly to
be resisted and I must repeat them here. When was the letter delivered to Mr. Wolcott? On the twenty-eighth of July. When was the letter
communicated to you? On the eleventh of August. When did Mr.
Hammond leave Philadelphia for New York? On the fifteenth of
August. When did he actually sail from thence? On the seventeenth
in the morning. When was the letter exhibited to me? On the nineteenth at noon. . . . You invited me in a strain of the warmest friendship to the office of Attorney General. Unsolicited you offered me the
Department of State. My conduct towards you, your knowledge of
me, was a guarantee that a corrupt collusion with a foreign minister
was impossible. . . . Disdaining to consult your prejudice, I have yet
cherished your character. I forebore to remove the suspicions which
were uttered at my having relinquished Republican ground when I
became Secretary of State. I forebore this too under circumstances not
a little trying, for I soon perceived that your popularity had been the
fund upon the credit of which all your acts, when unpalatable in
themselves, had been made current, and that this fund was not
eternal. . . . Had Mr. Fauchet's letter been shown to me in private, I
should have thanked you and gone immediately in quest of the proofs
which I now possess. I never attempted to depreciate in your esteem
any of my colleagues in office nor ever to magnify or blazon any merit
of my own. The species of influence to which I directed my labors
was not that of raising myself on their ruins. I came from Virginia as
Attorney General irresistibly impelled by the friendship of your
invitation. I was ushered by you into the most confidential business,
and I believe without the privity of heads of departments. The germs
of confidence unequivocally disclosed by you I indeed cherish, by
telling the truth without hesitation, without a momentary acquiescence in the prejudices of any man, by defending your character with
zeal and by advising measures which should spread over the President of the United States glowing colors in which General Washington had been painted to mankind. The destruction of me was a
little something, the groundwork for a more important assault on
others. In me you saw a man of no party. But having been driven by

self-defense to speak freely, I stand upon the truth of what I have spoken.[14]

Thus went the wrathful and even piteous response of Edmund Randolph—a retort to an employer who had discharged him. Washington felt he must resolve the problem; Randolph chose, instead of letting the matter lie, to attack a colossus.

Perhaps the most convincing argument in favor of Randolph's innocence has been presented by Irving Brant, a newspaperman who applied investigative reporting to the question. He pointed out that "the Randolph case is the first example under the Constitution of a high government official accused of treasonable relations with a foreign power." It was shown that Randolph's personal economic needs were so severe that while in the cabinet he asked Madison to obtain a house for him at not over $14 a month. The basic charge, it was observed, was that Randolph sought French money to promote a civil war on the very day that he gave Washington the most powerful argument for its suppression—that this was a British maneuver to detach and annex the West.

Brant held that the statement by Fauchet, in the form of an attested certificate, was a complete exoneration; that the French minister said he never had the most distant suspicion that Randolph was seeking money for himself. This author believed that Randolph's reputation was ruined by a combination of injustices and accidents: Washington's integrity being imposed upon by the malevolence of Secretaries Pickering and Wolcott; the need of Fauchet to fortify his position in France after the execution of Robespierre; and among other things, total failure in the cabinet and the country because of domestic partisanship and passions aroused by the French Revolution, to apply common sense to the charges. As Madison said "Randolph's greatest enemies will not easily persuade themselves that he was under a corrupt influence of France, and his best friend can't save him from the self-condemnation of his political career, as explained by himself."[15]

Edmund Randolph was not to see the last of his troubles. After he was forced from office and retired to his Virginia farm, he was charged with having a deficit of over $50,000 in his former department and since he was held accountable for such shortages, he and his family had to make good the entire amount.

Up to this time, the President had tried to achieve unanimity and unity by giving representation in the cabinet to persons of different political viewpoints. But after the Randolph affair,

Washington declared that he would not appoint to any office of consequence a man "whose political tenets are adverse to the measures which the general government are pursuing; for this, in my opinion, would be a sort of political suicide.[16]

It had become necessary to replace some of the cabinet members who had left for one reason or another so Washington was faced with a problem. Personally, he longed for companions like the good ones of old but this was not to be. He offered the position of Secretary of State to William Paterson of New Jersey but was turned down. Then he offered the position to Thomas Johnson of Maryland, with the same result. Thereupon Washington urged Charles Coteworth Pinckney to accept the position, telling him that the country was in a violent state of affairs; but Pinckney also declined the offer. Henry Lee advised the President to ask Patrick Henry, which seemed an odd suggestion, because Henry had opposed the adoption of the Constitution of the United States and had opposed Washington in other matters. (In later years, President Harry Truman refused to attend a commemoration ceremony for Patrick Henry because he had refused to support the Constitution.) Washington wrote Henry a letter in which he expressed an ardent desire "to comply strictly with all our engagements, foreign and domestic but to keep the United States free from political connections with *every country*. To see that they may be independent of all and under the influence of none." The letter was forwarded by Edward Carrington, an important Virginia Federalist, but Henry declined the offer.

The attacks on Washington continued unabated. With the publishing of Randolph's "Vindication" and its widespread distribution, it seemed that newspapers everywhere condemned or praised it, mostly the latter.

The *Independent Chronicle* of Boston asserted that it was absurd to think that Washington's mind was superior to that of Jefferson and Madison. A writer in the *Aurora* described the President as "Saint Washington," a man with the "seclusion of a monk and the supercilious distance of a tyrant; "that he had "dark schemes of ambition and political degeneracy," a "frail, mortal person whose passions and weaknesses are like those of other men." There was added the ominous allegation that Washington took part in the American Revolution only for personal glory; that he was a bad general and was lucky to have won the war; that he won the Presidency with an "insipid uniformity of a mind which had been happy in proportion to the contracted sphere of its operations; and that "nature had not been lavish in her favors when she gave him birth" and that he had little education.[17]

The diatribes reached such a state of abuse, contempt, and even personal insults that perhaps no man except Washington would have tolerated it. After he had studied carefully the Randolph pamphlet which of course extremely disturbed and worried him, he asked the advice of others; and eventually, the one whom he considered the best authority, Alexander Hamilton, advised him that the wisest thing Washington could do was to ignore the pamphlet, stating that "it contains its own antidote."[18]

For some time, Thomas Pinckney had wished to be relieved from his post as American minister in London. But the difficulties arising from the Jay Treaty and of finding a substitute for him had caused a delay. Hamilton observed that the importance of our security and commerce, of a good understanding with Great Britain, rendered it very important that an able man agreeable to that government should be there. Now such a man seemed to be Rufus King of New York. He had defended the treaty with his pen and by his eloquent speeches in the Senate. Hamilton knew him well and wrote to President Washington, "Mr. King, is a remarkably well-informed man, a very judicious one, a man of address, a man of fortune and economy, whose situation affords just ground of confidence; a man of unimpeachable probity who is known, a firm friend of the government, a supporter of the measures of the President; a man who cannot but feel that he has strong pretensions to confidence and trust."

Washington must have been pleased by the comment of a New Hampshire Federalist, William Plumer who said, "I do not believe President Washington was ever influenced by any other motive than love of country and of fame. An exalted character, acquired not by adulation but by the practice of the noblest virtues and blessed by a strong, discriminating mind and possessed of an easy fortune—what could induce him to deviate from his duty? He daily rises in my esteem."[19]

Encouraging also was the outcome of the long-simmering dispute regarding Spain, particularly in its relation to the Anglo-American relations. Spain, anxious to negotiate a settlement of its own differences with the United States, signed a treaty engineered by Ambassador Charles Cotesworth Pinckney, in which Spain granted to the United States rights to navigation on the Mississippi River and the right of deposit at New Orleans free of duty for ocean-going American goods; it recognized the 31st parallel as the northern boundary of Florida, agreed to restrain

Indians from border raids. President Washington had reason for satisfaction with this settlement. This favorable turn of affairs was good not only for his embattled administration and his part in it, which had reached a new low, and the only way it could go was upward.[20]

As if the President had nothing else to be concerned about, a writer in the newspaper *Aurora* charged him with overdrawing his salary appropriation of $25,000 per year. Secretary of the Treasury Oliver Wolcott immediately wrote Benjamin Bache, editor of the newspaper, explaining that the Treasury Department customarily advanced money to the President's secretary for household expenses and admitted that at times the disbursements might have exceeded the official amount allowed. But if this procedure was to be criticized it was not the fault of the President but of the Treasury Department and Congress. Typically, Bache did not accept the explanation but in his newspaper called it "a complete acknowledgment of guilt" and added that if Washington had received more than his appropriation he should be impeached. It was true that Washington had overdrawn his allotment to the extent of a few thousand dollars.[21]

Secretary Wolcott wrote to Hamilton that the President had never received any money which Congress had not appropriated and at no time had he drawn in advance as much as a quarter's allotment. Even so, this embarrassed President Washington and the Federalists, and delighted their opposition who through newspapers castigated the Chief Executive as being a "miser for every penny before it came due." But Washington had an able defender in Alexander Hamilton who published in the *New York Daily Advertiser*, of 11 November a logical argument in favor of the disbursement policy of the Treasury and offered proof that Washington had not requested the advances. Republican newspapers did not accept this defense and even revived some old British forgeries criticizing Washington as a betrayer of his own troops. In response, the Bridgeport, Connecticut *American Telegraph* stated that Bache and his henchmen had made the charges "prompted more by ill nature than by any love for the good of the people. A similar comment from the Cerberus of Democracy, Bache, barks more furiously than ever and snaps so much that its fangs will lose their power of wounding unless it makes a speedy exit by madness."

This unfortunate situation of Washington's finances while doing little damage to his reputation then and now, still has resulted in giving birth to a spate of articles and books excoriating Washington in the present day. Authors posing as historian-authorities and apparently bent on cashing in on the peerless character of our first and greatest president have lamentably made a public splash in the minds of some all-too-credulous readers. As one genuine authority has said, perhaps the worst aspect of these bubbles of misinformation has been their recogntion and review by credible individuals. Fortunately, it follows inevitably that such insidious and unjustified frothiness will inexorably be wafted away like the clouds which sometimes gather around the pinnacle of the Washington monument.

George Washington's head may have been bloodied but it was unbowed. He had undergone the slings and arrows of outrageous fortune but this was no ordinary man. Always to some extent a military leader, he had not been called "the old fox" by Lord Cornwallis at the battle of Princeton for nothing. Now he would counterattack but would overwhelm his opponents with kindness rather than force. His opportunity came with the meeting of the fourth Congress in Philadelphia in the first week of December 1795. When he entered the chamber of the house he was greeted cordially.

His seventh annual address was shorter than the previous ones and to the surprise of his listeners, instead of indulging in a long harangue in answer to the abuse to which he had been subjected, he began on a note of high optimism. Said he, "I indulge the persuasion that I have never met you at any period, when more than at present, the situation of our public affairs has afforded just cause for mutual congratulations." He mentioned the favorable condition of the Indian relations to the West, he was pleased with the negotiations with Spain, and said that after full and mature deliberation, "Our agriculture, commerce and manufactures prosper beyond former examples. Our poplation advances with a celerity which, exceeding the most sanguine calculations, proportionately augments our strength and resources and guarantees our future security. . . . Our country exhibits a spectacle of national happiness never surpassed if ever before excelled." His surprised audience heard a tastefully-worded address, moderate in everything except his keen exuberance. This simply was salesmanship well contrived, confidently appealing for national unity in an hour of growing political disparities.[22]

In both internal and external affairs, Washington found cause for satisfaction. He pointed out that Europe was involved in destructive wars and its art was being destroyed, their people starved. By this he of course referred to the French Revolution which was raging in bloody turmoil. On 12 December, Vice President John Adams and members of the Senate presented their formal reply to the President's message. The reaction was generally favorable and Washington was warmly gratified. "I have little doubt," he told John Jay, "of a perfect amelioration of sentiment after the present fermentation has evaporated a little bit more." To Gouverneur Morris he wrote, "I am sure that if this country is preserved in tranquility twenty years longer, it may bid defiance to any power whatever, such in that time will be its population, wealth and resources."[23]

The unexpected conciliatory address by President Washington caught the Republicans off guard. Had he launched a tirade of counter-criticism as they had expected, they would have been prepared to oppose it with typical forcefulness. But now they were weakened and even Jefferson admitted that the Federalists had outsmarted his faction. It was now more and more realized that the popularity of George Washington was something that the vicious assaults on him could not greatly diminish. Doubtless the skilled defense which Hamilton had presented in behalf of Jay's Treaty had aided immediately in bringing about the calming of the storm. Businessmen were reluctant to rock the boat of government too vigorously or it might sink along with its support of their interests.[24]

The year 1796 had hardly begun when the President was confronted with a challenging problem of diplomatic etiquette that further tested his judgement and political acumen. James Monroe had crossed on the ship *Cincinnatus* happy in his anticipation as envoy to Paris. He was overly optimistic because French suspicion of the United States was greatly heightened by the Jay-Granville negotiations. Monroe however was not discouraged for apparently he thought that he could smooth ruffled feelings by showing admiration for France. He even embraced the president of the National Convention, and helped to free Thomas Paine who had backed the wrong revolutionary government. By throwing his household doors open to some revolutionaries, Monroe showed bad judgement. Then he had climaxed his activities by openly opposing the mission of John Jay. It seemed also that Monroe had made a gift of the American flag to the National Convention in France. This act was unofficial but was so welcome by that body that it received tremendous applause. These radical lawmakers then gave the flag a place of honor in their meeting hall. The American Congress was also in session and there was a Republican majority in the House. French Minister

Pierre Adet seized the occasion to return the favor. On New Year's Day, he delivered to Washington a colorful silk flag sent by his government. It was a tricolor of three vertical stripes of blue, white and red set off by fringed edges and bright tassels of gold. An accompanying message stated "The connections which nature, reciprocal events and a happy concurrence of circumstances have formed between two free nations, cannot be indissoluble." It declared that Franco-American relations were forever cemented by common political principles, those of commerce and industry and the sacrifices which both nations had made for liberty and equality.[25]

Washington was not caught off guard. His answer was enthusiastic and complimentary to France. Said he, "my best wishes are irresistibly excited whensoever in any country, I see an oppressed nation unfurl the banners of freedom . . . to call your nation brave, were to pronounce but common praise. Wonderful people! Ages to come will read with astonishment the history of our brilliant exploits. My fellow citizens will cordially join me in purest wishes to the Supreme Being that the citizens of our sister republic, our magnanimous allies, may soon enjoy that liberty which they have purchased at so great a price." There was probably sarcasm in this reply but so well concealed, so well expressed, that now it seems excusable. However, the President said that the French tricolor which he had received would be deposited in the archives.

This last decision did not please Minister Adet who had felt that the flag would be displayed conspicuously in Congress, but now for it to be hidden away was disgraceful. He complained to Secretary Pickering. The President was flexible enough to allow the flag to be exhibited temporarily. That was the end of it. The Republicans were delighted that the President would make such an effusive statement about France so they made good use of this speech of conciliation. Meantime, Dr. James McHenry, a former Revolutionary aide of Washington, accepted the post of Secretary of War. Senator Oliver Ellsworth of Connecticut became Chief Justice. Washington was relieved at the completion of his cabinet but Vice President Adams expressed his regret that his cabinet did not compare well with the first one.[26]

Soon would arrive the President's sixty-fourth birthday for which he was greeted by Bache's newspaper *Aurora* with an insulting statement comparing him with all the "insolence of an emperor of Rome." But this was a voice crying in the wilderness. On 22 February 1796, Philadelphia was filled with joy and festivity. Bells rang out, cannon were fired, and the President greeted a large crowd of well-wishers at his house. In the afternoon, members of Congress called and paid their respects, as chimes resounded throughout the day. A gala was held that evening in a local hotel and a ball at a theater with candelabra and other colorful decorations adorning the large room which held more than a hundred dancing couples. The President and Mrs. Washington led the gay activities. Even the Republican, James Madison, commented on the "unexampled splendor" of the occasion. Some events of late had mottled the administration with doubts and apprehension but on this occasion and most to come, the Father of his Country still held his multitude of ardent followers warmly in his hand. More veneration was to follow.

11
Political Parties Appear

The military experience of President Washington proved invaluable in his civilian administrations. As Commander-in-Chief of the then-limited armed forces of the United States, he had learned some valuable lessons and had benefited from the experience. In the army, General Washington had an obedient staff as well as the other officers who virtually followed his orders but they also advised him. Of course they realized that such counsel would be followed only if he decided it was best. As President, he followed this practice in seeking advice from his cabinet members.

Washington found that it was not only necessary to give proper directions but to consider more the reaction and attitude of those to whom they were given. His tasks were now to endeavor to please the public and he had to take into account the beliefs and personalities of his aides. These civilians, unlike the military, if they became unhappy or proved to be unfitted, could resign. As time went on, the President grew to realize that the political sphere was one that often required painful adjustment. He had said more than once that he detested factions but regardless of his position, such did arrive despite his strenuous efforts, mainly in the form of political parties.[1]

One element of the origin of our political parties has been traced to a committee appointed in 1790 by the Virginia legislature to protest the funding-assumption acts of Alexander Hamilton. He himself had admitted that his differences with Madison about discrimination between the original holders and purchasers of government securities had "laid the foundation of the great schism which has since prevailed." Madison had agreed, and charged that Hamilton had created enemies of the Federal government and forced them to choose "between the loss of the union and the loss of what the union was meant to secure." These differences, according to John C. Miller, led to the creation of the two political parties representing the two dominant economic groups in the country: the planting-slave-holding-farmer interest and the mercantile-shipping-financial interest. The differences between the Republicans and Federalists were greater than those between the two major American political parties today.[2]

Interestingly enough the two political parties first appeared in Congress and then entered the electorate. The alert Hamilton saw that opposition to his policies was growing in Congress so he immediately dubbed his opponents "Antifederalists", a characterization which was resented by the more moderate of the Republican members. Especially antagonistic to Hamilton was Jefferson who adroitly operated behind the scenes as an unannounced leader of the Republican party. At first he worked through James Madison but although Jefferson expressed disgust with political parties, almost every letter of his on public affairs ended with suggestions on how to carry on the political campaigns.

One reason the Southerners distrusted a strong federal government was a fear that such a government would try to abolish slavery. Early in Washington's administration, a memorial from the Pennsylvania Society for Promoting the Abolition of Slavery alarmed Southern members of Congress.

They were reminded that Congress had already enacted laws preventing it from interfering with the freeing of slaves and also anything respecting their welfare, education, and religion. By 1793, Congress by a large majority passed a Fugitive Slave Law permitting owners to seize a runaway slave and return him to servitude by presenting an affidavit of ownership. The Southern agricultural viewpoint was vividly expressed by John Taylor of Caroline, a Virginia planter and politician who served in the United States Senate from 1791 to 1793. He believed that the "moneyed aristocracy was strongly oppressing the American farmer; that stocks and bonds had triumphed over wheat and tobacco." Taylor felt that an agricultural state "prescribed the agricultural virtues as the means for the admission of their posterity into Heaven." He was convinced that the less government the better.[3]

One of the most trenchant factors in the development of Southern agriculture and its resultant attitude was the invention of the cotton gin by Eli Whitney in 1793. It made possible the tremendous growth of cotton cultivation and its concomitant black slavery. This portentous development was probably the most significant economic one during the Federalist period, especially since most American cotton was exported to England, a significant interdependent factor. Their party leaders consistently criticized the doctrine of states' rights. The Federalists believed that a central government should resist the passions of the people. One related statement was: "Reason will not answer—reason will not protect your houses, ships and stables from thieves. You must have for protection the controlling fear of God and fear of Government."[4]

In observing this period of political incubation, Chancellor James Kent of New York commented regarding the divisions of the then-existing society: "There is a constant tendency in the poor to covet and to share the plunder of the rich; in the debtor to relax or avoid the obligations of interest; in the indolent and profligate to cast the whole burden of society upon the industrious and virtuous; and there is a tendency in ambitious and wicked men to inflame those combustible materials."

The Federalists had drawn upon the experience of the Articles of Confederation at which time some states had passed laws that invalidated the rights of creditors, limited freedom of speech and of religious minorities. Now the Federalists had the opportunity of upholding minority rights in general but instead the party upheld only the right of property. Noah Webster put it this way, "A Republican government can be rendered durable in no other way than by excluding from elections men who have so little property, education or principles that they are liable to yield their own opinions to the guidance of unprincipled leaders."[5]

The greatest advantage the Federalists had was in their leader, President George Washington. Under his shelter, Alexander Hamilton was to realize his plans for changing the American economy on to a lasting plateau, the main structure of which lives today. Had it not been for Washington our economic precedents would have been quite different. Washington differed with Hamilton in believing not only in solid and superior leadership of the country but in its people as well. The Federalists regarded the President as their "rock of salvation." The President was depended upon for the execution of laws, leadership in both foreign and domestic affairs and "the cement of our Union, the representative of the whole people."[6]

The first party caucus held in Congress was in connection with Jay's Treaty. The purpose was to commit the Republican Party to a course of action opposing the treaty. The meeting did not produce agreement but it was a step toward the creation of an organized party responsible to its leaders. The divergent ideals and economic interests of the American people propelled them into two groups of opposite views. Washington inevitably became involved and regrettably found himself in the middle. Although he detested being put in such a position, he eventually was forced to choose sides. Before he became deeply involved, something occurred which showed that the power of the Chief Executive was still paramount and that Washington could set another precedent. In March of 1795 the House of Representatives had called upon him to submit to its examination all the papers relating to Jay's Treaty excepting "such papers as any existing negotiations may render improper to be disclosed." In taking this action, the House attempted to test the theory that it must concur in giving validity to treaties by virtue of its control of appropriations. Such a request had not arisen before, at least not in this form and Washington turned to his cabinet for advice. He also consulted with Hamilton. As a result, the President decided to deny the request. In a message to Congress, he declared that treaties duly ratified by the Senate and signed by the President became the law of the land. He reminded the lawmakers that in the Constitutional Convention, a proposal to give the House a voice in treaty-making had been rejected.[7]

James Madison took issue with this decision. He was regarded as the leading authority on the Constitution. His views were contained in a resolution introduced by Senator William Blount (later expelled from the Senate). As has been noted, he stated that when a treaty must depend for its execution on laws passed by Congress, the House had the Constitutional right to deliberate on the expediency or inexpediency of carrying such treaty into effect.

Hamilton came to the rescue. He mobilized businessmen behind the President, public meetings were called to condemn the action of the House, and a flood of petitions poured in upon the Representatives. The Senate threatened to postpone the ratification of some other treaties desired by the House if it did not acquiesce on the Jay Treaty. Then Fisher Ames of Massachusetts arose and delivered one of the most eloquent speeches yet heard in the House. At first he pretended to be ill and emphasized his bad physical condition, playing freely upon the sympathy of the members who as they listened expected him to collapse. Ames declared that the Congress embarked upon great risk by such delay. At risk were national honor, division at home, reopening of the dispute with Great Britain, sacrifice of neutrality, and the resumption of Indian wars. He warned the House that by rejection "we light the savage fires, we bind the victims. The darkness of midnight will glitter with the blaze of your dwellings. You are a father—the blood of your sons shall fatten your cornfields: you are a mother—the war whoop shall wake the sleep of the cradle." Moved by such oratory, members of the House shed tears, except as John Adams said, "Some of the jackasses who had occasioned the necessity of the oratory. These attempted to laugh but their visages grinned horrible, ghastly smiles."[8]

Though differing with the President in their political positions, there were still prominent Virginians who defended Washington. Congressman Robert Rutherford from that state arose to say that

> "To tell the people that a *Washington* presides, and therefore all must be right, is feeble language. Though we all concur respecting that honest man, we know at the same time that he must ere long yield to an immutable clause in the universal law. And have this people any security for the upright actings and doings of his successor, perhaps a mere Negro, though he has been an Octavius, an Alfred? We are not contending about the virtues of the President or of the Senate. All regard the President as a common parent and reverence the Senate for all their virtues. . . . I call to my Eastern Federalist patriots, colaborers and conjure them not to be duped by an opinion that malignity and party spirit actuate Republican members to bitterness against the President and the Senate for sinister designs."[9]

Tackling Great Britain, Uriah Tracy of Connecticut cried that the empire

> possesses the posts, the confidence of the Indians, the many millions of dollars despoiled from our commerce, the benefits of our trade, and proceeds to make more invasions on our property and our rights! And yet the gentleman Gallatin says we will not go to war! Would Americans tamely see their government strut, attempt to look big, call hard names—and the moment they were faced, like an overgrown, lubberly boy shrink into a corner? Is this the American character? . . . The citizens of New England are not of the stamp to cry 'hosannah' today and 'crucify' tomorrow; they would not dance around a whiskey pole today and upon hearing of a military force, sneak into a swamp. I for one cannot feel thankful to Gallatin for coming all the way from Geneva to give Americans a character of pusillanimity.

This outburst drew hot protests from Republican members but calls for order were not sustained by the presiding officer, Frederick Muhlenberg.[10]

The great debate was highlighted by Fisher Ames from Massachusetts who melodramatically but effectively again protested his poor state of health as a risk factor before most of his speeches. Nevertheless he orated for an hour an a half on this occasion, speaking without notes and projecting the tenets of the Federalist party in applying them to the Constitution and the role of the House of Representatives in regard to treaties. He ridiculed the idea that he and his colleagues could consider any great issue without heated consideration. "The hazard of great interests cannot fail to agitate strong passions," he exclaimed. "We are not disinterested; it is impossible we should be dispassionate. The only constant agents in political affairs are the passions of man. . . . Shall we say that man ought to have been made otherwise? It is already right because He, from whom we derive our nature, ordained it so and thus acting, the cause of truth and the public good is the more surely promoted." Ames denied that

the President and the Senate are agents and instruments of a scheme of coercion and terror to force the treaty down our throats. Such misconceptions are unfair in their very texture and fabric and pernicious in all their influences because they block the path to inquiry. They will not yield to argument for as they were not reasoned up, they cannot be reasoned down. They are higher than a Chinese wall in truth's way and built of materials that are indestructible. . . . It is vain to say to this mountain, be thou cast into the sea. I repeat it, we must conquer this persuasion that this body has an interest in one side of the question more than the other. That word, that empty work, coercion, has given scope to an eloquence that could not be tired and did not choose to be quited. . . . If a treaty left King George his island, it would not answer even if he stipulated to pay rent for it. It might be well if Britain were sunk in the sea but Americans need never fear the return of English influence to their councils. France has had too much influence on our policies. Any foreign influence is too much and ought to be destroyed. I detest the man and disdain the spirit that can bend to a mean subserviency the views of any nation. It is enough to be Americans. That character comprehends our duties and ought to engross our attachments. . . . What is patriotism? Is it a narrow affection for the spot where a man was born? No Sir. It is an extended self-love, mingling with all the enjoyments of life and twisting itself with the minutest filaments of the heart. It is thus we obey the laws of society because they are the laws of virtue. In their authority we see the venerable image of our country's honor. Every good citizen makes that honor his own. What would his enjoyments be in a country odious to the eyes of strangers and dishonored on his own? Could he look with affection and veneration to such a country as his parent? I see no exception to the respect that is paid among nations to the Law of Good Faith. . . . No let me not even imagine that a Republican government, a government whose origin is right and whose daily discipline is duty, can upon solemn debate, make its option to be faithless, dare act to what despots dare not avow![11]

This ringing peroration left members of the House with tears in their eyes and favor in their votes. It was like that of Daniel Webster some five decades years later in the Senate. The vote was barely enough to pass and enable the Federalists to win and the Jay's Treaty to be ratified and secured. It was perhaps the most extreme act dividing the two political parties and quickening the growth of the rival systems, which has prevailed to this day. Washington was exuberant. He wrote John Jay:

> I am sure that the mass of citizens of the United States *mean well* and I firmly believe they will always *act well* whenever they can obtain a right understanding of matters. But in some parts of the Union where the sentiments of their delegates are adverse to the government and great pains are taken to inculcate a belief that their rights are assailed and their liberties are endangered, it is not easy to accomplish this— especially as is the case invariably when the inventors and abettors of pernicious measures use infinitely more industry in disseminating the poison than the well-disposed part of the community to furnish the antidote. To this source all our discontents may be traced and from it our embarrassments proceed. Hence serious misfortunes, originating in misrepresentations, frequently flow and spread before they can be dissipated by truth.[12]

Hamilton in his first years in office left a lasting imprint on American history. He was self-assured, charming, witty and very persuasive. He did not fear aristocracy and thought the Constitution was endangered only by the weakness of government. Hamilton favored an imperial presidency and a strong centralized army which he would have been perfectly willing to command. Not only did he believe in big business but in a private capacity he tried to establish a great manufacturing center at Paterson, New Jersey. Ironically this enterprise turned out to be a total failure. The Bank of the United States which he persuaded Congress to charter, partly under public control and partly a private corporation, became a useful financial instrument for the Treasury Department and a source of financial stability and attraction for investors. But Hamilton's policies divided Washington's administration, Congress and the country. By the time Hamilton retired in 1795, to repair his private fortunes, a political cleavage, extending beyond little knots of Federalists and Republicans in Congress, had begun to divide the nation, and embroil its people in a new wave of party warfare. This division was made more dramatic and intense by the furious hatreds and attachments that arose from the most world-shaking event of the era—the French Revolution.[13]

The life of Alexander Hamilton represents the ultimate American tragedy. A brilliant young genius, he heralded in early life his distinguished career by excellent writings and forceful presentations. Well educated, handsome and early noticed by General Washington, he marked his military career in a superior manner. Even more outstanding as Secretary of State and founder of the Federalist Party, he rose to meteoric heights, only to fall in a disgraceful duel and end a mostly splendid life.

For his part in the debates, Hamilton was praised. The *Independent Chronicle* even declared Hamilton "the virtual President of the United States" but continued to attack Washington and his stand on the treaty. John Jay reported general approval of the document in New York and Christopher Gore wrote from Boston that "the President's answer has been universally pleasing here. Some have become so enamoured with the thing that they have had it printed in white satin and are having it framed and glazed." From New Hampshire came a comment from William Plumer that the enthusiasm in that state was overwhelming. Said he, "The incomparable answer of our great Chieftain is very popular with the sovereign people. More than nineteen-twentieths approve it. With all the better sects it has increased his fame. His name is pronounced with rapture. What Ramsey said of Lord Dorchester may with greater propriety be applied to Washington— 'His presence alone is a host.' " Even some Republicans had admitted that the treaty would be approved. William Giles of Virginia said, "The weight of the President, twenty Senators, funded gentry, British gentry, land gentry, aristocratic gentry, military gentry and a gregarious tribe of sycophants and rummad speculators will be found to be as much as the shoulders of the House will be able to bear."[14]

James Madison was forced to admit that the New England states had risen in mass against the House of Representatives, influenced by aristocracy, Anglicism and mercantilism. "Shall we," declared Federalist Harrison Gray Otis, denouncing Albert Gallatin, "join a vagrant foreigner in opposition to a Washington, a foreigner who ten years ago came to this country without a second shirt on his back, a man who in comparison to Washington is like a Satyre to a Hyperian?" Otis may have been intemperate but so were the Republican newspapers. In Virginia, the loyal John Marshall reported that sentiment for the treaty was just about equal to the noisy objections to it.

The effects of partisanship showed in Washington's sensitive nature. Writing to a friend, Colonel David Humphreys, Washington said,

> The gazettes will give you a pretty good idea of the state of politics and parties in this country, and will show you, at the same time, if Bache's *Aurora* is among them, in what manner I am attacked for perserving steadily in measures which, to me, appear necessary to preserve us, during the conflicts of belligerent powers, in a state of tranquillity. But these attacks, unjust and unpleasant as they are, will occasion no change in my conduct, nor will they produce any other effect in my mind than to increase the solicitude which long since has taken fast hold of my heart, to enjoy, in the shades of retirement, the consolation of believing that I have rendered to my country every service to which my abilities were competent—not from pecuniary or ambitious motives, nor from a desire to provide for any men, further than their intrinsic merit entitled them, and surely not with a view to bringing my own relations into office. Malignity, therefore, may dart its shafts, but no earthly power can deprive me of the satisfaction of knowing that I have not, in the whole course of my administration, committed an intentional error.[15]

Washington himself had received a letter from Gouverneur Morris stating that a new and special representative would be sent by France to the United States who would protest and then sever relations with this country. As we have seen, he was to be accompanied by a fleet. The President felt this to be a false rumor but stated that so many strange things were happening that he would not be surprised at anything. But if the report were true, Washington added that his answer would be "short and decisive to this effect. We are an independent nation and act for ourselves. Having fulfilled and being willing to fulfill (as far as we are able) our engagements with other nations, and having decided on and strictly observed a neutral conduct toward belligerent powers, from an unwillingness to involve ourselves in war, we will not be dictated to by the politics of any nation under heaven, farther than treaties require of us."[16]

A letter to Gouverneur Morris from Paris appeared in a New York newspaper regarding the relations between France and the United States. It stated,

Could you imagine, my Dear Sir, that any American citizen could be so abandoned as to invite France to attempt, by coercion, to prevent the free exercise of the judgement of our country concerning its own interests, and to awe it into a surrender of its opinion to the mandate of a foreign country? Yet, so the fact undoubtedly is. Influential men on your side of the water have invited the French government to speak to ours a decided language against the execution of the treaty with Great Britain and even to go so far as to claim our guarantee of the French West Indies; placing before us the alternative of war with France or Great Britain. The idea has been listened to by the government, and it has been in contemplation to send a new minister with a fleet to carry the plan into effect; tho I am inclined to hope that it has recently been set aside. The extreme embarrassments of the affairs of their country, especially with regard to its finances, and more serious reflections on the hazard of driving us into an election to take side with Great Britain, as well as from the exposed state of our commerce as from the resentment which a dictatorial nation would naturally inspire, have at least produced a halt, and I trust the hestitation which has begun will end in a resolution not to risk so unjust and so mad a proceeding. Would to heaven that this was was at an end! For we shall not be safe from the machinations of this wicked portion of the globe until that event takes place—justice and morality have fled from Europe—but alas! are they flying from America also?[17]

So it was that political parties already existed. A great debate in Congress had been mainly along partisan or party lines. In The House, virtually every Congressman spoke for or against the treaty. Outstanding among the Republicans was Albert Gallatin who made a powerful argument which challenged Jay's Treaty and felt that it should have the ultimate sanction of the House. Robert Rutherford of Virginia attempted to refute Gallantin's speech and said he had "had the honor of the President's acquaintance well nigh on to 44 years and though senior in point of years, yet I uniformly look to him as a parent, my lead and my guide." In the Senate, it was remarked that this was a contest between the Executive and the House of Representatives of a more serious nature than had ever taken place in the political affairs of the Union. "Party spirit never ran so high before," said Senator John Brown of Kentucky."[18]

Despite Washington's declaration that no assent of the House was required by the Constitution to validate, a treaty, a powerful tool was still in the hands of the Representatives. The House could demolish the treaty by refusing to appropriate money for its implementation. This they did not hesitate to attempt. After a frenzied debate and strong points raised on both sides, the contest virtually ended with the fiery speech of "Furious Federalist" Fisher Ames, and as a result, the Federalists squeezed by with a margin of one vote for approval of Jay's Treaty. Chairman Frederick Muhlenberg had broken the tie, forty-nine to forty-nine casting his vote for the treaty and thereby committed political suicide because, due principally to this vote, he was never re-elected.[19]

President Washington had won—but at what effort! His official position was not to be the same again. As John C. Miller has observed, "It brought the President into the center of the maelstrom of American politics. True, he had much encouragement even with the strong opposition. John Jay had written to him 'Attachment to you as to our country, urges me to hope and pray that you will not leave the work unfinished. Remain with us at least while the storm lasts and until you can retire like the sun in a calm, unclouded evening.' " That evening was to come before long and it could not come too soon for George Washington.

That the President was acutely conscious of the rise of factional parties, he had expressed very clearly. "Party disputes are now carried to such lengths and truth is so enveloped in myths and false representation that it is extremely difficult to know what channel to seek," he commented. "This difficulty to one who is of no party and whose sole wish is to pursue with undeviating steps the path which would lead this country to respectability, wealth and happiness is exceedingly to be lamented."

For the most part during the debates, Washington had remained silent but after they were over, he felt he could justifiably express his own opinion and he stated that the real question was not whether the Jay Treaty "was a good one or bad one but whether there should be *a treaty at all* without the concurrence of the House. It was conceived that no occasion more suitable might ever occur to establish the principle and enlarge the power. On that precedent now to be set will depend the future construction of our Constitution."[20]

The final approval of the treaty and its implementation brought rejoicing among the Federalists. Reports from New York were that the news made everybody happy, although these were exaggerated. In Philadelphia, Robert Morris said there was a holiday throughout the city and from New Hampshire came the report that it was the best news they had had in years. Although Washington was pleased with the outcome, he was saddened by the scars left from the conflict. Some of his old friends he would never see again and others he would not be associated with. It is interesting to note that he had either fallen out or lost friendly connections with a number of his fellow Virginians. These included Patrick Henry, Thomas Jefferson, James Madison, James Monroe, and Edmund Randolph. To the northward, although Alexander Hamilton was a friend, there were times when he was not loyal to Washington. Farther north, Henry Knox, was a close friend of Washington until almost the end of the latter's life when war with France was threatened and Washington was called on to again command the armed forces, he had selected Hamilton, a former lieutenant colonel, ahead of Knox who had been a major general—both in the Revolutionary army.

There was no more staunch Federalist in high office than Henry Knox. Almost a half century ago, the late Douglas Freeman remarked that in his twenty-five years of research and writing on George Washington, the biggest informational gap he had found was an adequate life of Henry Knox. No one had completely explored the voluminous Knox Papers in the Massachusetts Historical Society. Three persons had attempted this formidable task but reportedly died before finishing. It was high time that this was remedied.

Henry Knox was born in Boston in 1750 and died in 1806. In his fifty-six years he lived a storied life, having dropped out of school to help support his parents. As a young man he operated a bookstore in Boston where he met the daughter of a Tory official and married her. The couple were to lead a happy life and had twelve children, nine of whom died in childhood. Knox early became interested in military affairs and made a study of artillery. (Fort Knox is named after him.) In the beginning of the Revolution, the portly Knox caught the eye of General Washington and was soon placed in charge of the American army artillery. He took part in all the battles in which Washington engaged and was given credit for the *coup de grace* in the defeat of the British at Yorktown. Rising rapidly in the ranks, Henry Knox became the youngest American major general in the Continental Army, becoming known as "Washington's favorite general."

After the war, Knox founded the Society of the Cincinnati and served as secretary with Washington as President. During the war, Knox had suggested the idea of a military academy and has justly been called the founder of West Point. He served as Secretary at War in the Confederation government and was the only such official to be carried over into the new national government as Secretary of War. In 1786 when Shays' Rebellion broke out in

Massachusetts, Secretary Knox threw national support to the Massachusets militia and thus aided in suppressing the rebellion and boosting Federal authority within the states.

Henry Knox served with distinction as Secretary of War and for all too long was virtually ignored by historians. He was devoted to President Washington and for that reason alone was inclined to agree with him on most important issues. True, he nearly always sided with Alexander Hamilton and was, if possible, an even more consistent Federalist. The fact that he was in step with Hamilton so often does not mean that was simply an echo of the Secretary of the Treasury. For Knox was himself conservative and actively interested in things financial. At times he was almost too much so, speculating on the side in Maine land to the extent of millions of acres. The Secretary of War was especially adept at dealing with the Indians. He seemed to understand them better than most white men and helped immensely in keeping peace with the Southern Indians. When those in the West continued to be hostile in spite of repeated efforts, Knox planned, behind the scenes, the three military campaigns which eventually ended in Wayne's victory at Fallen Timbers.

Federalist from the first, Henry Knox was a stalwart partisan when Washington needed him and fared well in his high administrative capacity until almost the end of his cabinet service. The skillful, manipulative Alexander Hamilton managed to inject himself into the Whiskey Rebellion campaign while Knox was away at his home on leave in Massachusetts and this was not lost on Washington who regretted that his Secretary of War was not present.

This did not elevate Knox in his estimation. The sentiment expressed, however, when Knox resigned was indicative of the esteem in which he was held. Said the *Gazette of the United States,* "there is none which we have greater cause to lament than the resignation of the Secretary of War. (A biography of Henry Knox has been published and reprinted, which it is believed fills Dr. Freeman's gap.)[21]

The Federalists styled themselves "Friends of the Constitution," and in the first Congress had a large majority in both houses. They believed that those who owned the country should run it, and of course they were referring to themselves. The Federalists were not confined to particular sections of the country because both Northerners and Southerners were members of their party. With power based upon a coalition of Northern businessmen and Southern planters, this party was not something to last. In his administrations, Washington was told that many who had been ardent supporters of his government were changing because they felt that their interests were not similar to those of Virginia.

Alexander Hamilton can be called the father of American political parties because although he favored national power, his positive stand led to opposition and the creation of two political parties. Hamilton believed in government by "the wise, the rich and the well-born," this seeming ironical in view of his own illegitimate birth. To him, democracy meant mob rule. He remarked at one time that "The people is a beast." Federalists were suspicious of allowing state governments to interfere in contractual obligations which usually favored debtors against creditors. With all his immense power and prestige, George Washington could not prevent the rise of two political parties, as much as he would liked to have done so. Washington eventually embraced conservative views of Alexander Hamilton, as the second term became a Federalist one. After the departure of Edmund Randolph, Washington's cabinet was composed entirely of Federalists. Clinton Rossiter has said that if Hamilton was a conservative in practical politics and his concern with property, he "was reactionary in his devotion to monarchy and heredity aristocracy, visionary in his schemes for industrial America and his eagerness to reduce the states to an inferior position." The poet, Thomas Green Fessenden of Boston voiced the Federalist view when he wrote

> Next, every man throughout the nation
> Must be contented with his station,
> Nor think to cut a figure greater
> Than was designed for him by Nature.

The personification of the Federalist Party was Alexander Hamilton himself. He was one of the most fascinating characters in American history and his story has been told many times. Hamilton may have been a great man but he was not a great character, for he had his Achilles heel and it was shown in his affair with a woman during his tenure as Secretary of the Treasury. In this situation, he was accused of using government funds in his relationship with her but made a frank and public confession about the affair and insisted that any money spent came out of his own pocket. He was determined to have his way. In so doing, he encountered the bitter opposition of Thomas Jefferson and others including John Adams and Aaron Burr, who ended Hamilton's life with a pistol in New Jersey in an unnecessary duel and a great loss to the nation.

Hamilton has been said to have fully appreciated that America then was an agricultural nation and that his financial measures could do little more than give impetus to the possibilities of industrial development. He admired England, the importance of the Bank of England in the development of the British economy, and his impressive figures helped cause Congress to charter the first Bank of the United States. In a series of state papers, Hamilton argued the importance of promoting commerce and manufactures. One of his most important achievements was persuading the government, first to assume the debts of the old Continental Congress and second, those of the individual states. Probably no man was more admired and hated in his day than Alexander Hamilton.[22]

Opposition to Hamilton began among the Southern planters. James Madison had turned against Hamilton in 1790 during the debate on the public credit proposals. Madison was somewhat more balanced in his views but he felt that Hamilton favored the domination of the moneyed interests. In the controversies about the national bank, Madison was joined by Jefferson and the two men began to find allies in the South with a number of influential men who had reasons for disliking Hamilton. In the North, George Clinton governor of New York and Aaron Burr (who was involved with a Democratic political club know as "The Tammany Society") formed an alliance with the Southern leaders. This odd combination became the nucleus of the new Republican Party, now supported by Samuel Adams of Massachusetts and Albert Gallatin of Pennsylvania. Aaron Burr had distinguished ancestors including clergymen and college presidents but was an unscrupulous adventurer with no morals. Jefferson, who was generally inclined to be suspicious, thought that Hamilton was secretly trying to destroy the republican government of the United States and set up a European-style monarchy; and that his doctrine of "implied powers" would increase Federal authority. The Republicans advocated "strict construction" of the Constitution and declared that Federal power must be limited in accordance with this theory, while states' rights should be strongly defended. Hamilton thought Jefferson was a "contemptible hypocrite" and that his impracaticality would lead to anarchy and perhaps dictatorship by a demogogue or military leader as such as actually happened in France.

The two-party organizations materialized in 1791. Members of Congress and state legislators joined one party or the other. Each party had its own newspaper, the editor of the Republican paper, *National Gazette*, being Philip Freneau who, as we have seen, had already strongly attacked the Washington administration. On the other hand, the Federalists had John Fenno and his newspaper, *Gazette of the United States*. As a consequence, Americans divided, the wealthy of New York, Philadelphia, etc. wanted nothing to do with the so-called "Democrats," considering them to be radicals plotting to subvert law and order and bring about anarchy. The Republican craftsman and farmers felt that American liberties were being endangered by a monarchist group. These "Anti-Federalists" said their principal purpose was to preserve the Constitution from "the profane hands of Federalists who wished to pervert it into a consolidation of a Union and the Republic one and indivisible."[23]

Professor Richard Hofstadter observed that the, "Federalists feared above all power lodged in the majority. Jefferson feared power lodged anywhere else." In his more moderate, later days, Thomas Jefferson wrote, "If we can hit upon the line of conduct which may conciliate the honest part of those who were called Federalists, I shall hope to obliterate or rather to unite the names of Federalists and Republicans."[24]

The Chief Executive was thus caught in the middle although he generally sympathized with the Federalists. He believed that the government should be controlled by neither party and therefore kept both Hamilton and Jefferson in the cabinet. Although these two could not get along, at the end of Washington's first term, both requested that he remain because they felt that the government could not maintain itself without him.

There appeared in the newspaper *Aurora* an anonymous article that seemed to disclose confidential questions asked by Washington to members of his cabinet regarding references to England and France. Feeling that Washington might think that he was the author, Jefferson wrote to the President denying any knowledge of it. Washington replied,

If I had entertained any suspicions before that the queries, which have been published in Bache's paper, proceeded from you, the assurances you have given me of the contrary, would have removed them; but the truth is I harbored none. . . . As you have mentioned the subject yourself, it would not be frank, candid, or friendly to conceal, that your conduct has been represented as derogating from the opinion I had conceived you entertained of me; that to your particular friends and connections you have described, they have denounced me as a person under a dangerous influence, and that, if I would listen more to some other opinions, all would be well. My answer invariably has been, that if I had never discovered anything in the conduct of Mr. Jefferson to raise suspicions in my mind of his insincerity; that, if he would retrace my public conduct while he was in the administration, abundant proofs would occur to him, that truth and right decisions were the sole object of my pursuit; that there were as many instances within his own knowledge of my having decided against as in favor of the opinions of the person evidently alluded to; and, moreover, that I was no believer in the infallibility of the politics or measures of any man living. In short, that I was no party man myself, and the first wish of my heart was, if parties did exist, to reconcile them. In this I may add, and very truly, that, until within the last year or two, I had no conception that parties would or even could, go the length I have been witness to; nor did I believe until lately, that it was withn the bounds of probability, hardly within those of possibility, that, while I was using my utmost exertions to establish a national character of our own, independent, as far as our obligations and justice would permit, of every nation of the earth, and wished, by steering a steady course, to preserve this country from the horrors of a desolating war. I should be accused of being the enemy of one nation, and subject to the influence of another; and to prove it, that every act of my administration would be tortured, the grossest and most insidious misrepresentations of them be made, by giving one side only of a subject, and that, too, in such exaggerated and indecent terms as could scarcely be applied to a Nero, a notorious defaulter, or even to a common pickpocket. But enough of this; I have already gone further in the expression of my feelings than I intended.[25]

An interesting glance during this period at the personal side of Washington was given by Mrs. Robert Liston, wife of the British minister. Chatting with her, a genial lady, he said that in his youth he became a surveyor because of his need to make a living and that later he had studied the military profession as one which he expected to follow. Mrs. Liston was impressed by Washington's manners and knowledge of etiquette. "His education," she wrote in a memoir,

had been confined; he knew no language but his own, and he expressed himself in that, rather forcibly than elegantly. Letter writing seemed to him a peculiar talent. His style was plain, correct, and nervous. Ill-natured people said that Washington did not write his own public letters, answers to addresses, etc. This is not true. I have known him to write in his usual impressive manner when no person was near to aid him; and what may seem conclusive, he has always written better than the gentlemen to whom the merits of his letters were ascribed. His first and last pleasure appeared to be farming; and on that theme he always talked freely, being on other topics extremely cautious not to commit himself; and never spoke on any subject of which he was not master.[26]

The Jeffersonian farmers and small businessmen were opposed to the Federalists because farmers wanted easy loans and inflationary economic policies. This group disliked the wealth and aristocratic airs of their employers. They believed that the less government the better. Jefferson, from his experience in France believed that the purest form of democracy lay in the agrarian life, that farming was the only good way of living. What he could not foresee was the industrial nation which was to follow. Jefferson's principal contribution to the Republicans was behind the scenes. Although he was a shrewd leader, as Secretary of State he preferred to work through others rather than let his own hand appear. He would rather write a letter than speak and seemed to be every man's friend, a position he favored to engaging in quarrels. His constant correspondence organized a militant opposition to Hamilton. Jefferson felt that universal suffrage should wait upon universal education. The Federalists opposed this because they thought that government should be run by special kind of people. Gouverneur Morris predicted that if suffrage were expanded that people would sell their votes to the highest bidder—in which he was unfortunately somewhat prophetic.[27]

While Jefferson was the principal leader of the opposing party, it was evident in the foregoing letter, which was somewhat more formal than the usual ones between the two men, that it indicated a cooling of relations between them. Thomas Jefferson, a remarkable man and a fellow Virginian, at an early age was graduated from William and Mary College and studied law under George Wythe. Active in local politics, he did not enter the military ranks in the Revolution but instead became governor of Virginia and did not distinguish himself when Colonel Banastre Tarleton, the dreaded British raider, swept down upon Richmond and wrecked the state capital. Governor Jefferson mounted his horse and hurriedly left the scene, leaving behind some important official papers for the British to peruse. But after the war, Jefferson's influence rose. He engineered the Bill of Rights, was ambassador to France, and as we have seen, later the first

Secretary of State in Washington cabinet. The antithesis of Alexander Hamilton, Jefferson could not be expected to work in harmony with him. President Washington did a masterful job of conciliation between the two extremists; but no one could have brought them together.

So the American party system as it exists today holds elements fathered by both Hamilton and Jefferson; and their differences are often as manifestly explosive in print and otherwise as they were in the beginning. However, attempts to change the two-party system have always failed and bid fair to do so in the future.

12

Farewell to the Arena

As early as 1792 President George Washington had decided that he would not run for office again. With the aid of James Madison, Washington had even prepared a farewell address. Because of the turbulent foreign relations and demanding domestic affairs the nation's leaders begged him to stay to handle the precarious situation. The government was still in the experimental stage and the different sections of the country were still separated by diverse social and commercial differences. It was clear that Washington's matchless leadership was still needed. Even the opposing Republicans urged him to remain. Jefferson commented that "the confidence of the whole nation is settled in you. North and South will hang together if they have you to hang on." (An apparent premonition of our Civil War.)

Now in the last year of his second administration, Washington was worn out by the arduous demands of an office that he had never sought; so this time he insisted on retiring at the end of this term which would be in early 1797.

Even so he found time to work on personal matters. On 1 February 1796, he had written an advertisement offering for sale his western lands located in what is now known as the Middle West. He also announced that he would rent out his four Mount Vernon farms and a mill, the advertisement specifying the characteristics of each farm including their black laborers and their children but no mention of the slaves. Although Washington owned slaves, he believed they should be freed eventually. These advertisements were placed in newspapers on the frontier and nailed to the doors of taverns. The Mount Vernon real estate, he advertised in England, Scotland and Ireland, explaining that he wished to get from Europe farmers "who knew how to keep land in an improved state rather than use the slovenly individuals in this country who thought nothing of working a field until it no longer will grow anything."[1]

As has been mentioned, Washington was unhappy with his

false teeth. In those days dentistry was in such a primitive stage that his teeth had to be made of wood or ivory. His front teeth projected too far which caused both lips to bulge out as if they were swelled. This was evident in the painting of Washington by Gilbert Stuart. Regarding Washington who was found to be an uneasy patron, Stuart said

> There were features in his face totally different from what I had observed in any other human being. The sockets of the eyes for instance, were larger than what I had ever met with before and the upper part of the nose broader. All his features were indicative of the strongest passions; yet like Socrates, his judgement and self-command made him appear a man of different cast in the eyes of the world. Had he been born in the forest, he would have been the fiercest man among the savage tribes. His shoulders were high and narrow and his hands and feet remarkably large.[2]

Stuart, wishing to make a portrait that would be pleasantly attractive—or enticing for sales—wanted Washington to relax, a difficult job indeed. Said Stuart, "Now Sir you must make me forget that you are General George Washington." The President looked at him coldly and then replied, "Mr. Stuart, you need never forget that I am George Washington." It is said that the reason Gilbert Stuart did not complete the famous Athenaeum portrait of the President which hangs in our schools today and shows only his face above the neckline, was because the painter wished to continue making copies and did not want to give the original to Mrs. Washington and thereby lose control of the portrait—and its sales.

Another story is told that in talking one day to Henry Lee, Stuart remarked that Washington had a terrible temper but held it under wonderful control. A few days later, Lee at breakfast reported to the Washingtons this remark. Mrs. Washington responded, "Upon my word, Mr. Stuart takes a great deal upon himself to make such a remark." "But dear Lady," Lee added, "he said that the President had it under control." With a hint of a smile, Mr. Washington cut in, "He is right."[3]

Some idea of the home life of the Washingtons in Philadelphia was given by a visitor to Mount Vernon, an Englishman named Thomas Twining. He recalled that

> At 1 o'clock today I called on General Washington with the picture and letter I had for him (from Tobias Lear, former private secretary to Washington). He lived in a small red brick house on the left side of

High Street. . . . There was nothing in the exterior of the house that
denoted the rank of its possessor. Next door was a hair dresser . . . I
was shown into a middling-sized, well-furnished drawing room.
Mrs. Washington first greeted me . . . she was a middle-sized lady,
rather stout. The door opened and she said 'the President' and introduced me to him. Never did I feel more interest than at this moment,
when I saw the tall upright venerable figure of this great man advanc-
ing towards me to take me by the hand. There was a seriousness in
his manner which seemed to contribute to the impressive dignity of
his person, without diminishing the confidence and ease which the
benevolence of his countenance and the kindness of his address
inspired . . . so completely did he look the great and good man he
really was that I felt rather respect than awe in his presence. . . .
Although his deportment was that of a general, the expression of his
features had rather the calm dignity of a legislator than the severity of
a soldier.[4]

In contrast to some other matters, Washington was pleased as
we have seen, with the outcome of the settlement with Spain.
That country had determined to pull out of the European war by
making a separate peace with France at the risk of offending
Great Britain. Spain had been an ally of Britain in the French
Revolution and apparently was anxious to bring about good
terms with the United States in order to shore up its military
position.[5]

It was becoming obvious that anyone as sensitive as Washington could not continue long in a post which was so vulnerable
to partisan attack. In regard to France which was still undergoing
its bloody Revolution, James Monroe had promised the French
government to show them the Jay Treaty in time for their opinion
on whether the United States should revise it. Monroe had no
copy and French authorities felt that he was being purposely kept
in ignorance of the treaty, something which they did not like.
Monroe unwisely sent these complaints to the Republicans in
the United States. Relations with France had reached a low
point. Washington assured the French that the United States was
an independent nation, having fulfilled its engagements to others
and was strictly observing a neutral conduct.[6]

Washington blamed James Monroe for this situation and although he was not entirely responsible, Monroe had been of little
help in keeping friendly relations between the two countries,
especially in sending his friends in the United States copies of
confidential communications he was receiving from his government.

Word came to Washington that an American ship, *Mount Vernon* which had been named after his estate, had been seized by a French privateer off the Delaware coast. Aside from any personal feeling, the President was apprehensive that this event signalled a new policy of resentment by France against American commerce. He commented, "It is the buzz of the Democrats," and believed that the newspapers "are evidently preparing the public mind for the event as a natural consequence of the British treaty."[7]

A meeting of the cabinet was called for opinions on the subject. Washington also asked Hamilton and Jay for their views, "For," he explained, "having no other wish than to promote the true and permanent interests of this country, I am anxious always to compare the opinions of those in whom I confide, with one another; those again (without being bound by them) with my own, that I may extract all the good I can."[8]

In this statement, the President set forth specifically his custom of calling in his advisers on virtually every important matter, asking their opinions, usually in writing, and then making up his own mind based upon the consensus, but not always in agreement. The Presidential cabinet is not specifically designated as such in the Constitution and this was another precedent set by Washington and which has been followed ever since.

The Chief Executive also wanted to know whether he had the power during the recess of the Senate to send a special envoy to Paris for the purpose of requesting and obtaining information regarding the strained relations between two countries. He also wondered what should be done about James Monroe. His advisers agreed that Washington should not appoint a special representative to France during the Senate recess but they felt that he could replace the regular minister with another one. Any substitute for Monroe would seem to be desirable. The cabinet criticized the failure of Monroe to present his own government's views faithfully. Whether his dereliction was because he liked France so much or used mistaken judgement, the results were the same and something should be done. In addition, Monroe had sent a private letter to Dr. George Logan of Philadelphia in which was the statement that "this is written in order to keep you apprised of the course of events, whereby the community at large may be more correctly informed of the progress of the revolution than are heretofore or can be from the English press."[9]

Thomas Paine had come to America from England in 1774 and

his eloquent pen had supported the colonial cause in an admirable, trenchant fashion. During that time, Paine had developed a favorable opinion of General Washington. Now in contrast, his hatred of the President grew from his belief that Washington had mistreated him. Paine had returned to France in 1787 to support the French Revolution in his typical, radical style. He became a French citizen, a Girondist and was elected to the National Convention, but after Robespierre came to power, Paine was imprisoned and denied his French citizenship. He asked Washington and Gouverneur Morris to obtain his release, but it was not granted for the reason that Washington did not wish to interfere in the affairs of France, as he had so clearly set forth previously. After Robespierre fell and James Monroe became the new American minister, the latter favored Thomas Paine and recognized him as an American citizen. In a letter to Washington, Paine stated that "Almost the whole of your administration was deceitful if not perfidious . . . in time, the eyes of America will be opened upon you. As to you Sir, treacherous and private friendship (for so you have been to me and that in the day of danger) and a hypocrite in public life, the world will be puzzled to decide whether you are an impostate or an imposter; whether you have abandoned good principles if you ever had any." Washington's answer was to ignore this personal attack.[10]

Instead, the President issued an official communication on French affairs. This communique stated in part, "Conscious of its fair dealings toward all the belligerent powers, and wrapped up in its own integrity, this government has little expected the upbraidings it has met with. Not with standing, it now, as it always has been, the earnest wish of the government to be on the best and most friendly footing with the Republic of France." From Thomaston, Maine, Henry Knox wrote that he had recently launched a vessel for the West Indies but had been unable to procure a proper cargo for it. "French have gone mad with relation to us," said Knox, "our Jacobins have influenced them regarding the treaty with England."[11]

There has been too much debate by historians over the authorship of Washington's farewell address. After all, he and each succeeding President have had secretaries and speech writers who fashion the basic framework for the ultimate delivery. As long as the address itself represents the purposes and conclusions of the Chief Executive, it makes little difference who supplies the appropriate words for his expression.

It was Washington's studied purpose that his farewell address
be his most important and significant legacy to posterity. And so
it has become, having been along with the Declaration of Independence and Lincoln's Second inagural address as one of the
three most important American historical documents. And in
keeping with his custom of seeking the advice of others, Washington turned to the man whom he considered to have been his
most valuable counselor and amanuensis, Alexander Hamilton.
Ever since the days of the Revolution when Hamilton was Washington's aide, he best expressed in a convoluted style similar to
Washington's, the ideas and sentiments of his chief. Now the
President turned to Hamilton for the last time in this respect.
Before sending him the draft, Washington went over it again
himself and made changes and additions including his hope that
party disputes would subside and alliances with foreign powers
be avoided. Hamilton replied that he would be happy to help
revise the address. By the middle of June, he had gone over the
draft, and wrote Washington that he was preparing a new version.
When this was received by the President, he was amazed at the
length of it. He told Hamilton he would give the new draft "the
most attentive consideration."[12]

Although Washington made some revisions, on the whole he
liked the speech now written by Hamilton. But there was one
important omission; that was a request for a national university,
so Washington included a paragraph on the subject which
proved to be one of the most perspicacious parts of his address.
In condensed form below are its principal tenets, some in his
own words:

"While choice and prudence invite me to quit the political scene,
patriotism does not forbid it."

He looked forward to the joys of private life, also backward at the
honors bestowed on him by the people.

"My wish is that your union and brotherly affection may be perpetual
and that the free Constitution which is the work of your hands may
be sacredly maintained."

May there be no major differences in religion, habits and regional
economic interests. Only the surest standard of experience should
inspire changes, and the government must be strong enough to with-

stand the enterprises of faction and protect the rights of persons and property.

"The unity of government is the main pillar of your independence, the support of tranquility at home and peace abroad. Whatever the peculiar interests of the North, South, East and West, each must first be American."

The power to make and the power to alter the Constitution presupposes the duty of every individual to obey the established government.

"The spirit of party should be discouraged and restrained lest alternate domination of one faction over another lead to despotism. Religion and morality are the two great pillars of human happiness, indispensable to private and public felicity. The union of arts and minds transcends state, party and sectional considerations, and American character wholly free of foreign attachments."

To promote as an object of primary importance institutions for the general knowledge.

Cherish public credit. One method of preserving it is to use it as sparingly as possible.

Observe good faith and justice toward all nations. Cultivate peace and harmony with all.

The United States has a set of primary interests in which Europe does not share, and Europe in turn has interests peculiarly its own. He warned against long-term alliances with other countries but circumstances might make short-term alliances essential to the security of the Republic.

"Though in reviewing the incidents of my administration I am unconscious of intentional error . . . it is probable that I may have committed many errors. Whatever they may be, I fervently beseech the Almighty to avert or mitigate the evils to which they may tend."

"I anticipate with pleasing expectations that retreat in which I promise myself to realize without alloy the sweet enjoyment of partaking in the midst of my fellow-citizens the benign influence of good laws under government—the ever-favorite object of my heart—and the happy reward, as I trust, of our mutual cares, labors and dangers."

(How tempting it is to compare this momentous message with our world today).

Now that the farewell address was written, the question was, how to convey it to the public? Washington certainly wished to avoid having it emasculated by a hostile press. Unlike today, he did not have public relations people to contact the media in as favorable way as possible. He had no regular channel for transmitting his address to the citizenry, so he anticipated some cautious, modern practices by summoning to his office, one David Claypoole, owner of the *American Daily Advertiser.* Needless to say, Claypoole was delighted to have one of the biggest newspaper scoops in history and he immediately had the address set in type, carrying proofs to the President at least three times.

The address appeared in this newspaper on 19 September 1796. It was not featured but was on Page 2 and filled all of that page and half of the next. At the end of the address, in type somewhat larger, were the words, "G. WASHINGTON, United States, Sept. 7, 1796."

Other newspapers soon reprinted the address and this brought forth a milder reaction than usual from the hostile ones. The splendid document was just too much for the opposing editors such as Benjamin Bache. Even they were perceptive enough to realize that this was something beyond their level of appreciation. In time, the address found its way into most of the newspapers of the country and several European journals. The *London Times* stated that "General Washington's address is the most complete comment upon English clubs and clubbists, upon factions and parties and factious partisans. The authority of this Revolutionist may be set up against the wild and wicked revolutionists of Europe, if not as altar against altar at least as altar against sacrilege."[13]

President Washington had written to Hamilton on 1 September stating that there was a subject in his draft of the Farewell Address which was not sufficiently touched upon. "I mean education," wrote Washington,

> generally as one of the surest means of enlightenment and giving just ways of thinking to our citizens, particularly the establishment of a university; where the youth from all parts of the United States might receive the polish of erudition in the arts, sciences and belles letters; and where those who were disposed to run a political course might not only be instructed in the theory and principles, and with this seminary being at the seat of the General Government where the legislature would be in session half the year, and the interests and politics of the nation of course would be discussed, they would lay the surest foundation for the principal part also. But that which

would render it of the highest important, in my opinion, is that the juvenile period of life when friendships are formed and habits established that will stick by one; the young men [he omitted women] from different parts of the United States would be assembled together and would by degrees discover that there was not that cause for those jealousies and prejudices which one part of the union had imbibed against another part; of course, sentiments of more liberality in the general policy of the country would result from it. What about the mixing of people from different parts of the United States, who during the war, rubbed off these impressions? A century in the ordinary intercourse would not have accomplished what the seven years association in arms did; but that ceasing, prejudices are beginning to revive again and never will be eradicated so effectually by other means as the intimate intercourse of characters in early life, who, in all probability, will be at the head of the councils of this country in a more advanced stage of it.

Washington continued,

Can it be doubted that the General Government would with peculiar propriety occupy itself in affording nutriment to those higher branches of science which though not in the reach of general acquisition are in their consequences and relation, productive of general advantage? Or can it be doubted that this great object would be materially advanced by a University erected on that broad basis to which the national resources are most adequate and so liberally endowed as to command the ablest professors in the several branches of liberal knowledge? It is true and to the honor of our country that it offers many colleges and academies highly respectable and useful— but the funds upon which they are established are too narrow to permit any of them to be an adequate substitute for such an institution as is contemplated and to which they would be excellent auxiliaries. Amongst the motives to such an institution the assimilation of the principles, opinions, manners and habits of our countrymen by drawing from all quarters our youth to participate in a common education well deserves the attention of Government. To render the people of this country as homogeneous as possible must lend as much as any other circumstance to the permanency of the Union and prosperity.

The President then turned his attention to a related subject. "The eligibleness of a Military Academy depends on that evident maxim of policy which requires every nation to be prepared for war while cultivating peace and warns it against suffering the military spirit and knowledge wholly to decay. . . . A Military Academy instituted on proper principles would serve to secure to our country a solid fund of military information which would always be ready for nationl emergencies." Washington also urged a strong navy for our protection and advocated adequate financial rewards for those in public service. He added that "it is essential to the prosperous course of every government that it be able to command the services of its most able and virtuous citizens by increasing the compensation which the government allows." How remindful is this recommendation of the current situation regarding especially the pay of members of Congress and similar public officials.[14]

Although the reception of the Farewell Address was generally favorable, it was not long before Bache succumbed to temptation to take a parting shot at Washington. The grandson of Benjamin Franklin, Bache was nicknamed "Lightning Rod, Jr.," because he could administer such "electric shocks" to Federalists in his newspaper, The *Philadelphia Aurora*. He pronounced Washington to be ". . . the source of all the misfortunes of our country. If ever there was a period for rejoicing, this is the moment. Every heart in unison with the freedom and happiness of the people ought to beat with exultation that the name of Washington from this day ceases to give currency to political iniquity and to legalized corruption." On Washington's exit from office, Bache commented, "Lord now lettest thy servant depart in peace for mine eyes have seen thy salvation." (He was quoting the Biblical Simeon who had just seen Jesus.)

The great majority of Americans disagreed. Federalist rowdies wrecked the office of Bache's newspaper and manhandled him.[15]

"The passing of the years," said one English historian, "has made Washington's farewell address almost as important a bequest of the first President as the drafting of the Constitution itself. It is read in both the Senate and House of Representatives at noon on each 22 February as a tribute and a reminder." During the Washington administrations, five new states were added to the eleven that had accepted the Constitution. They were: North Carolina (1789), Rhode Island (1790), Vermont (1791), Kentucky (1792), and Tennessee (1796).

"No man," said John Adams, "has influence with the President. He seeks information from all quarters and judges more independently than any man I ever knew. His standards for appointments were higher than for those in European countries and he selected men who "would give dignity and luster to our national character. Rarely has an office, that was to grow into the most important elective office in the world, been so clearly given the stamp of one man's character."[16]

On a Sunday in mid-December, President and Mrs. Washington attended the Presbyterian church on Market Street in Philadelphia to join the American Philosophical Society in paying homage to the late David Rittenhouse, noted astronomer and first director of the United States Mint. The eulogy was delivered by Dr. Benjamin Rush "with all the ability of an orator and all the feelings of a friend." Washington probably remembered that Rittenhouse had ground the lenses for his first spectacles in 1783. He had worn these publicly for a few minutes in the presence of his Revolutionary officers at Newburgh, when they had met to question the uncertain situation in the Continental Army, triggered by the lack of pay. The officers gathered to consider a revolution that the army take a stand against the civil government in order to remedy this situation. At a very dramatic juncture in the ominous proceedings which threatened a mutiny, Washington took out his new glasses and put them on for the first time. He then announced that he had not only grown gray in their service but was also growing blind. This touching gesture had its effect, and thus was averted military rebellion.

As the calendar indicated, 22 February was to be Washington's last birthday while in office and this was a special occasion indeed. In contrast to the sadness among those who realized the significance of this date was the celebration in the capital, ushered in by the ringing of bells and the firing of cannon. Children were released from school and the uniforms of the militia marching along the streets were highly colorful and strikingly elaborate. People were evident in their best clothes, and gay festoons fluttered from ships in the harbor while flags rippled in the breeze atop the main buildings. The weather was clear and pleasant and the swarming crowds saw the President and his wife attend the theater. This was followed by festive dancing, and supper was served to more than a thousand persons. The tall figure of the President was conspicuous among the celebrants and he stayed and took part until after midnight. Said Judge James Iredel, "I never saw the President look better or in finer spirits but his emotions were too powerful to be concealed. Sometimes he could scarcely speak."[17]

Washington did not wish to interfere in the choice of his successor but naturally he could not help but have an interest in the continuation of the government which he had done the most to establish. In contrast to the Presidential campaign of 1792 when there was only one candidate, the one of 1796 had several. John Adams and Thomas Jefferson stood out as the foremost contenders. In the *Gazette of the United States,* a writer observed that Jefferson was too democratic, but also charged Adams with being too monarchical and chose Thomas Pinckney as a happy medium. This view was supported by the younger Wolcott who wrote his father that "Mr. Pinckney is an honest man and cannot be made the tool or dupe of faction. Mr. Adams has the superior claims of age, station and firmness and understanding and it will hurt our public character and betray levity and ingratitude if he is not elected." At the time, each Presidential elector was to cast two ballots of equal status so that the candidate with the plurality of votes would be President and the one with the second highest would be Vice President, regardless of their similarity or disparity of beliefs. Hamilton had decided to back Pinckney and became apprehensive that Jefferson would win the top job. But when Pickney's chances lessened, Hamilton opposed Adams. Even the reprobate Aaron Burr was in the running.

Pennsylvania had an early election, it being on 4 November 1796. The contest there presented to British Minister Robert Liston a sad spectacle. In view of the insults and brow beatings in Philadelphia, he pronounced the American governments "on the road towards corruption." Sailors there walked the streets threatening people with clubs. Dishonest votes were cast and accepted while some valid ones were thrown out. Some individuals were prevented from voting at all. For President Washington, the political altercations seemed a sorry mess. Soon he stated,

> It has been my constant, sincere and earnest wish, in conformity with that of our nation, to maintain cordial harmony. . . . This wish remains unabated; and I shall perceive in the endeavor to fulfill it, to the utmost extent of what shall be consistent with a just and indispensable regard to the rights and honor of our country; nor will I easily cease to cherish the expectation that a spirit of justice, candor and friendship on the part of the republic, will eventually insure success. In pursuing this course, however, I cannot forget what is due to the character of our government and nation; nor to a full and entire confidence in the good sense, patriotism, self-respect and fortitude of my countrymen.

Looking backward, Washington continued, "The situation in which I now stand for the last time . . . naturally recalls the period when the Administration of the present form of government commenced; and I cannot omit the occasion to congratulate my country on the success of the experiment; nor to repeat my fervent supplications to the Supreme Ruler of the Universe and

Sovereign Arbiter of Nations, that his Providential care may be extended to the United States; that the virtue and happiness of the people may be preserved and that the government which they have instituted for the protection of their liberties may be perpetual.[18]

It was quite natural that the President should favor his own Vice President John Adams; for in him, Washington felt, the ideas which had been presented and executed in the two terms of office would continue active. Nor was it difficult for the outgoing President to predict that for Adams as well as had been for himself, hard roads would lie ahead. Critics would howl and harass any forceful government but though "we may be a little wrong now and then, we shall return to the right path with more activity."

Despite any concerns for the future, social festivities grew to an almost frenzied commotion during the last weeks of the term. Dinners, balls, and guest lists increased and Washington believed, as always, that these functions were important and should be attended to even in the midst of official duties. It was fortunate that both the President and his wife were in good health. At three separate dinners in February, the members of the House of Representatives, one-third at a time, sat at the Washington's dinner table. Also during that month, all the army and navy officers in the city dined with their Commander-in-Chief. He expected his guests to be on time—as he was—and was said to wait only five minutes on any late-comers. Washington explained, "I have a cook who never asks whether the company has come but whether the hour has come."

One of the President's last official acts was to take formal notice of the forged letters that were circulated in 1777 in a malicious effort to defame him during the Revolution. For twenty years, Washington had never even admitted that the spurious letters existed, that they were meant to "wound his character and deceive the people." Now he felt it his duty to himself, his "country and to truth, to detail the circumstances and to add my solemn declaration that the letters herein described are a base forgery and that I never saw or heard of them until they appeared in print."[19]

"The President declining to be again elected," wrote Thomas Wolcott Sr.,

> constitutes a most important epoch in our national affairs. The country meets the event with reluctance, but they do not feel that they can make any claim for the further services of a man who has conducted

their armies through a successful war; has so largely contributed to establish a national government; has so long presided over our councils and directed the public administration, and in the most advantageous manner settled all national differences, and who can leave the administration where nothing but our folly and internal discord can render the country otherwise than happy.[20]

The House of Representatives stated in a resolution to George Washington

May you long enjoy that liberty which is so dear to you, and to which your name will ever be so dear. May your own virtue and a nation's prayers obtain the happiest sunshine for the decline of your days, and the choicest of future blessings. For our country's sake, and for the sake of republican liberty, it is our earnest wish that your example may be the guide of your successors; and thus, after being the ornament and safeguard of the present age, become the patrimony of our descendants.[21]

The votes from the election were counted in February and John Adams received the highest number and was declared President-elect. Thomas Jefferson, obtaining the next highest number of votes, under the existing system, became the new Vice President. Washington had received a letter from Henry Knox bidding him an affectionate departure from office and wishing him in his retirement "a glorious setting of the sun." In his last personal letter as President, Washington responded to Henry Knox with equally affectionate regards. Wrote he,

To the weary traveller who sees a resting place ahead and is bending his body to lean thereon, I now compare myself; but to be suffered to do this in peace is too much to be endured by some . . . the consolation, however, which results from conscious rectitude and the approving voice of my country, unequivocally expressed by its representatives, deprives the sting of its poison. The prospect of retirement is most grateful to my soul, and I have not a wish to mix again in the great world or to partake in its politics, yet I am not without my regrets at parting with (perhaps nevermore to meet) the few intimates whom I love, and among these be assured, you are one.[22]

4 March 1797 was on Saturday and at noon, Washington walked alone to Congress Hall in Philadelphia. Now instead of being the Commander-in-Chief and President, he was entering upon the resumption of life as a private citizen. He was dressed

in a handsome but modest black suit and wore a hat of military appearance with a black cockade, his hair fully powdered. It was a solemn day and everyone knew it.

George Washington took his place in the lower chamber of the House of Representatives. Soon Thomas Jefferson entered in a long blue frock coat. President-elect John Adams arrived in a new carriage, wearing a broad-cloth suit, a sword, and a cockade, although why this non-military man would wear a weapon is hard to understand. He took the oath of office which was administered by Chief Justice Oliver Ellsworth. The new President later described the scene as one "affecting me by the presence of the general whose countenance was as unclouded as the day. He seemed to enjoy a triumph over me. Me thought I heard him say "I am fairly out and you are fairly in! See which of us will be happiest."[23]

The scene was so touching that tears were in the eyes of almost everyone except Washington who kept his outward composure. But after the new President Adams had departed, Washington motioned for Vice President Jefferson to follow him and then made his own way to the door. Immediately, the crowd rushed after him and huddled so closely it was hard for him to make his way out. In the street, Washington, now a civilian, waved his hat in answer to the cheers of the resounding multitude. Commented one of them, "His countenance assumed a grave and almost melancholy expression. His eyes were bathed in tears and his emotions were too great for utterance and only by gestures could he indicate his thanks and convey his farewell blessing."[24]

At last, Washington could realize his long-cherished expectations, to restore his equanimity, oversee his crops and dwell "under his vine and fig tree" as he had said before. He could be with his friends in welcome retirement and personal life. "It was no easy task," Clinton Rossiter has observed, "to be the first occupant of a mistrusted office under a dubious Constitution. It is unmistakably true that Washington made the government of America work as only he, at his point in time, could. He built the peace on which it was based."[25]

In his conclusive estimate of Washington's character, Douglas Freeman wrote, "In Washington this nation and the western hemisphere have a man, greater than the world knew, living and dying; a man dedicated and responsible, an example for long centuries of what character and diligence can do. Other historians have stated, "Washington's precedents are almost as binding as those of the Constitution."[26]

Even for a historian who has spent many years in studying the life of George Washington, it is difficult to assess his place in history. How a landed Virginia aristocrat could leave his cherished home, take arms against his mother country at the risk of his life, and choose instead of a rich and peaceful pursuit, to lead his countrymen in a war against an overwhelmingly powerful British Army in which the odds were greatly to his disadvantage, is extremely hard to fathom. Then to be willing to lead and nurture his new nation through all its early struggles, rise above the awesome opposition, and finally to emerge as a matchless figure in our history, taxes an inquiring mind.[27]

One thing, however, is certain. President George Washington clearly demonstrated that in his trail-blazing second term of office in which he set so many precedents that are followed even today, he stands out as an incomparable figure, and without doubt in this mind, the greatest of all Presidents.

After the Washingtons had reached Mount Vernon, Martha wrote to her friend, Mrs. Henry Knox, expressing the delight she and her husband felt at being home. Said she,

> I cannot tell you, my dear friend, how much I enjoy *home* after having been deprived of one so long; for our dwelling in New York and Philadelphia was not *home*, only a sojourning. The General and I [she called him General after he left office] feel like children just released from a taskmaster, and we believe that nothing can tempt us to leave the sacred roof-tree again, except on private business or pleasure. We are so penurious with our enjoyment that we are loath to share it with anyone but dear friends, yet almost every day some stranger claims a portion of it, and we cannot refuse.

In what she termed the time in which "the twilight is gathering around our lives," Martha wrote Elizabeth Powel that the General joked about how long he would live. Referring to the end of his life, she said that "he is glad to hear *beforehand* what will be said of him on that occasion, conceiving that nothing extra will happen between *this* and *then* to make a change in his character for better or for worse; and besides, he has entered into an engagement with Mr. Morris and several other gentlemen, not to quit the theater of this world before the year 1800."[28]

He almost made it. George Washington died on December 14, 1799.

Appendix
Washington's Farewell Address

United States, September 17, 1796. Friends and Fellow-Citizens: The period for a new election of a citizen to administer the Executive Government of the United States being not far distant, and the time actually arrived when your thoughts must be employed in designating the person who is to be clothed with that important trust, it appears to me proper, especially as it may conduce to a more distinct expression of the public voice, that I should now apprise you of the resolution I have formed to decline being considered among the number of those out of whom a choice is to be made. . . .

The impressions with which I first undertook the arduous trust were explained on the proper occasion. In the discharge of this trust, I will only say that I have, with good intention, contributed toward the organization and administration of the Government the best exertions of which a very fallible judgment was capable. Not unconscious in the outset of the inferiority of my qualification, experience in my own eyes, perhaps still more in the eyes of others, has strengthened the motives to diffidence of myself; and every day the increasing weight of years admonishes me more and more that the shade of retirement is as necessary to me as it will be welcome. Satisfied that if any circumstances have given peculiar value to my services they were temporary, I have consolation to believe that, while choice and prudence invite me to quit the political scene, patriotism does not forbid it. . . .

Here, perhaps I ought to stop. But a solicitude for your welfare which can not end with my life, and the apprehension of danger natural to that solicitude, urge me on an occasion like the present to offer to your solemn contemplation and to recommend to your frequent review some sentiments which are the result of much reflection, of no inconsiderable observation, and which appear to me all important to the permanency of your felicity as a people.

Interwoven as is the love of liberty with every ligament of your hearts, no recommendation of mine is necessary to fortify or confirm the attachment.

The unity of government which constitutes you one people is also now dear to you. It is justly so, for it is a main pillar in the edifice of your real independence, the support of your tranquillity at home, your peace abroad, of your safety, of your prosperity, of that very liberty which you so highly prize. But as it is easy to foresee that from different causes and from different quarters much pains will be taken, many artifices employed, to weaken in your minds the conviction of this truth, as this is the point in your political fortress against which the batteries of internal and external enemies will be most constantly and actively (though often covertly and insidiously) directed, it is of infinite moment that you should properly estimate the immense value of your national union to your collective and individual happiness; that you should cherish a cordial, habitual, and immovable attachment to it; accustoming yourselves to think and speak of it as of the palladium of your political safety and prosperity; watching for its preservation with jealous anxiety; discountenancing whatever may suggest even a suspicion that it can in any event be abandoned, and indignantly frowning upon the first dawning of every attempt to alienate any portion of our country from the rest or to enfeeble the sacred ties which now link together the various parts.

For this you have every inducement of sympathy and interest. Citizens by birth or choice of a common country, that country has a right to concentrate your affections. The name of American, which belongs to you in your national capacity, must always exalt the just pride of patriotism more than any appellation derived from local discriminations. With slight shades of difference, you have the same religion, manners, habits, and political principles. You have in a common cause fought and triumphed together. The independence and liberty you possess are the work of joint councils and joint efforts, of common dangers, sufferings, and successes.

But these considerations, however powerfully they address themselves to your sensibility, are greatly outweighed by those which apply more immediately to your interest. Here every portion of our country finds the most commanding motives for carefully guarding and preserving the union of the whole.

The North, in an unrestrained intercourse with the South, protected by the equal laws of a common government, finds in the productions of the latter great additional resources of maritime and commercial enterprise and precious materials of manufacturing industry. The South, in the same intercourse, benefiting by the same agency of the North, sees its agriculture grow and its commerce expand. Turning partly into its own channels the seamen of the North, it finds its particular navigation invigorated; and while it contributes in different ways to nourish and increase the general mass of the national navigation, it looks forward to the protection of a maritime strength to which itself is unequally adapted. The East, in a like intercourse with the West, already finds, and in the progressive improvement of interior communications by land and water will more and more find, a valuable vent for the commodities which it brings from abroad or manufactures at home. The West derives from the East supplies requisite to its growth and comfort, and what is perhaps of still greater consequence, it must of necessity owe the secure enjoyment of indispensable outlets for its own production to the weight, influence, and the future maritime strength of the Atlantic side of the union, directed by an indissoluble community of interest as one nation. Any other tenure by which the West can hold this essential advantage, whether derived from its own separate strength or from an apostate and unnatural connection with any foreign power, must be intrinsically precarious.

While, then, every part of our country thus feels an immediate and particular interest in union, all the parts combined can not fail to find in the united mass of means and efforts greater strength, greater resource, proportionately greater security from external danger, a less frequent interruption of their peace by foreign nations, and what is of inestimable value, they must derive from union an exemption from those broils and wars between themselves which so frequently afflict neighboring countries not tied together by the same governments, which their own rivalships alone would be sufficient to produce, but which opposite foreign alliances, attachments, and intrigues would stimulate and imbitter. Hence, likewise, they will avoid the necessity of those overgrown military establishments which, under any form of government, are inauspicious to liberty, and which are to be regarded as particularly hostile to republican liberty. In this sense it is that your union ought to be considered as a main prop of your liberty, and that the love of the one ought to endear to you the preservation of the other.

Is there a doubt whether a common government can embrace so large a sphere? Let experience solve it. To listen to mere speculation in such a case were criminal. It is well worth a fair and full experiment. With such powerful and obvious motives to union affecting all parts of our country, while experience shall not have demonstrated its impracticability, there will always be reason to distrust the patriotism of those who in any quarter may endeavor to weaken its bands.

In contemplating the causes which may disturb our union it occurs as matter of serious concern that any ground should have been furnished for characterizing parties by geographical discriminations—Northern and Southern, Atlantic and Western—whence designing men may endeavor to excite a belief that there is a real difference of local interests and views. One of the expedients of party to acquire influence within particular districts is to misrepresent the opinions and aims of other districts. You can not shield youngsters too much against the jealousies and heartburnings which spring from these misrepresentations; they tend to render alien to each other those who ought to be bound together by fraternal affection.

To the efficacy and permanency of your union a government for the whole is indispensable. No alliance, however strict, between the parts can be an adequate substitute. They must inevitably experience the infractions and interruption which all alliances in all times have experienced. Sensible of this momentous truth, you have improved upon your first essay by the adoption of a Constitution of Government better calculated than your former for an intimate union and for the efficacious management of your common concerns. This Government, the offspring of our own choice, uninfluenced and unawed, adopted upon full investigation and mature deliberation, completely free in its principles, in the distribution of its powers, uniting security with energy, and containing within itself a provision for its own amendment, has a just claim to your confidence and your support. Respect for its authority, compliance with its laws, acquiescence in its measures, are duties enjoined by the fundamental maxims of true liberty. The basis of our political systems is the right of the people to make and to alter their constitutions of government. But the constitution which at any time exists till changed by an explicit and authentic act of the whole people is sacredly obligatory upon all. The very idea of the power and the right of the people to establish government presupposes the duty of every individual to obey the established government.

Toward the preservation of your Government and the permanency of your present happy state, it is requisite not only that you steadily discountenance irregular oppositions to its acknowledged authority, but also that you resist with care the spirit of innovation upon its principles, however specious the pretexts. One method of assault may be to effect in the forms of the Constitution alterations which will impair the energy of the system, and thus to undermine what can not be directly overthrown. In all the changes to which you may be invited remember that time and habit are at least as necessary to fix the true character of governments as of other human institutions; that experience is the surest standard by which to test the real tendency of the existing constitution of a country; that facility in changes upon the credit of mere hypothesis and opinion exposes to perpetual change, from the endless variety of hypothesis and opinion; and remember especially that for the efficient management of your common interests in a country so extensive as ours, a government of as much vigor as is consistent with the perfect security of liberty is indispensable. Liberty itself will find in such a government, with powers properly distributed and adjusted, its surest guardian. It is, indeed, little else than a name where the government is too feeble to withstand the enterprises of faction, to confine each member of the society within the limits prescribed by the laws, and to maintain all in the secure and tranquil enjoyment of the rights of person and property.

I have already intimated to you the danger of parties in the State, with particular reference to the founding of them on geographical discrimination. Let me now take a more comprehensive view, and warn you in the most solemn manner against the baneful effects of the spirit of party generally.

This spirit, unfortunately, is inseparable from our nature, having its root in the strongest passions of the human mind. It exists under different shapes in all governments, more or less stifled, controlled, or repressed; but in those of the popular form it is seen in its greatest rankness and is truly their worst enemy.

It serves always to distract the public councils and enfeeble the public administration. It agitates the community with ill-founded jealousies and false alarms; kindles the animosity of one part against another; foments occasionally riot and insurrection. It opens the door to foreign influence and corruption, which find a facilitated access to the government itself through the channels of party passion. Thus the policy and the will of one country are subjected to the policy and will of another.

There is an opinion that parties in free countries are useful checks upon the administration of the government, and serve to keep alive the spirit of liberty. This within central limits is probably true; and in governments of a monarchical cast patriotism may look with indulgence, if not with favor, upon the spirit of party. But in those of the popular character, in governments purely elective, it is a spirit not to be encouraged. From their natural tendency it is certain there will always be enough of that spirit for every salutary purpose; and there being constant danger of excess, the effort ought to be by force of public opinion to mitigate and assuage it. A fire not to be quenched, it demands a uniform vigilance to prevent its bursting into a flame, lest, instead of warming, it should consume.

It is important, likewise, that the habits of thinking in a free country should inspire caution in those intrusted with its administration to confine themselves within their respective constitutional spheres, avoiding in the exercise of the powers of one department to encroach upon another. The spirit of encroachment tends to consolidate the powers of all the departments in one, and thus to create, whatever the form of government, a real despotism. . . . If in the opinion of the people the distribution or modification of the constitutional powers to be in any particular wrong, let it be corrected by an amendment in the way which the Constitution designates. But let there be no change by usurpation; for though this in one instance may be the instrument of good, it is the customary weapon by which free governments are destroyed. The precedent must always greatly over-balance in permanent evil any partial or transient benefit which the use can at any time yield.

Of all the dispositions and habits which lead to political prosperity, religion and morality are indispensable supports. In vain would that man claim the tribute of patriotism who should labor to subvert these great pillars of human happiness—these firmest groups of the duties of men and citizens. The mere politician, equally with the pious man, ought to respect and to cherish them. A volume could not trace all their connections with private and public felicity. Let it simply be asked, where is the security for property, for reputation, for life, if the sense of religious obligation desert the oaths which are the instruments of investigation in courts of justice? And let us with caution indulge the supposition that morality can be maintained without religion. Whatever may be conceded to the influence of refined education on minds of peculiar structure, reason and experience both forbid us to expect that national morality can prevail in exclusion of religious principle.

It is substantially true that virtue or morality is a necessary spring of popular government. The rule indeed extends with more or less force to every species of free government. Who that is a sincere friend to it can look with indifference upon attempts to shake the foundation of the fabric? Promote, then, as an object of primary importance, institutions for the general diffusion of knowledge. In proportion as the structure of a government gives forces to public opinion, it is essential that public opinion should be enlightened.

As a very important source of strength and security, cherish public credit. One method of preserving it is to use it as sparingly as possible, avoiding occasions of expense by cultivating peace, but remembering also that timely disbursements to prepare for danger frequently prevent much greater disbursements to repel it; avoiding likewise the accumulation of debt, not only by shunning occasions of expense, but by vigorous exertions in time of peace to discharge the debts which unavoidable wars have occasioned, not ungenerously throwing upon posterity the burden which we ourselves ought to bear.

Observe good faith and justice toward all nations. Cultivate peace and harmony with all. Religion and morality enjoin this conduct. And can it be that good policy does not equally enjoin it? It will be worthy of a free, enlightened, and at no distant period a great nation to give to mankind the magnanimous and too novel example of a people always guided by an exalted justice and benevolence. Who can doubt that in the course of time and things the fruits of such a plan would richly repay any temporary advantages which might be lost by a steady adherence to it? Can it be that Providence has not connected the permanent felicity of a nation with its virtue? The experiment, at least, is recommended by every sentiment which ennobles human nature. Alas! is it rendered impossible by its vices?

In the execution of such a plan nothing is more essential than that permanent, inveterate antipathies against particular nations and passionate attachments for others should be excluded, and that in place of them just and amicable feelings toward all should be cultivated. The nation which indulges toward another an habitual hatred or an habitual fondness is in some degrees a slave. It is a slave to its animosity or to its affection, either of which is sufficient to lead it astray from its duty and its interest. Antipathy in one nation against another disposes each more readily to offer insult and injury, to lay hold of slight causes of umbrage, and to be haughty and intractable when accidental or trifling occasions of dispute occur.

So likewise, a passionate attachment of one nation for another produces a variety of evils. Sympathy for the favorite nation, facilitating the illusion of an imagary common interest in cases where no ready common interest exists, and infusing into one body the favorite nation of privileges denied to others, which is apt doubly to injure the nation making the concessions by unnecessarily parting with what ought to have been retained, and by exciting jealousy, ill will, and a disposition to retaliate in the parties from whom equal privileges are withheld; and it gives to ambitious, corrupted, or deluded citizens (who devote themselves to the favorite nation) facility to betray or sacrifice the interests of their own country without odium, sometimes even with popularity, gilding with the appearances of a virtuous sense of obligation, a commendable deference for public opinion, or a laudable zeal for public good the base or foolish compliances of ambition, corruption, or infatuation.

Against the insidious wiles of foreign influence (I conjure you to believe me, fellow citizens) the jealousy of a free people ought to be constantly awake, since history and experience prove that foreign influence is one of the most baneful foes of republican government. But that jealousy, to be useful, most be impartial, else it becomes the instrument of the very influence to be avoided, instead of a defense against it. Excessive partiality for one foreign nation and excessive dislike of another cause those whom they actuate to see danger only on one side, and serve to veil and even second the arts of influence on the other. Real patriots who may resist the intrigues of the favorite are liable to become suspected and odious, while its tools and dupes usurp the applause and confidence of the people to surrender their interests.

The great rule of conduct for us in regard to foreign nations is, in extending our commercial relations to have with them as little political connection as possible. So far as we have already formed engagements let them be fulfilled with perfect good faith. Here let us stop.

Europe has a set of primary interests which to us have none or a very remote relation. Hence she must be engaged in frequent controversies, the causes of which are essentially foreign to our concerns. Hence, therefore, it must be unwise in us to implicate ourselves by artificial ties in the ordinary vicissitudes of her politics or the ordinary combinations and collisions of her friendships or enmities.

Our detached and distant situation invites and enables us to pursue a different course. If we remain one people, under an efficient government, the period is not far off when we may defy material injury for external annoyance; when we may take such an attitude as will cause the neutrality we may at any time resolve upon to be scrupulously respected; when belligerent nations, under the impossibility of making acquisitions upon us, will not lightly hazard the giving us provocation; when we may choose peace or war, as our interest, guided by justice, shall counsel.

Why forego the advantages of so peculiar a situation? Why quit our own to stand upon foreign ground? Why, by interweaving our destiny with that of any part of Europe, entangle our peace and prosperity in the toils of European ambition, rivalship, interest, humor, or caprice?

It is our true policy to steer clear of permanent alliances with any portion of the foreign world, so far, I mean, as we are now at liberty to do it; for let me not be understood as capable of patronizing infidelity to existing engagements. I hold the maxim no less applicable to public than to private affairs that honesty is always the best policy. I repeat, therefore, let those engagements be observed in their genuine sense. But in my opinion it is unnecessary and would be unwise to extend them.

Taking care always to keep ourselves by suitable establishments on a respectable defensive posture, we may safely trust to temporary alliances for extraordinary emergencies.

Harmony, liberal intercourse with all nations are recommended by policy, humanity, and interest. But even our commercial policy should hold an equal and impartial hand, neither seeking nor granting exclusive favors or preferences; consulting the natural course of things; diffusing and diversifying by gentle means the streams of commerce, but forcing nothing; establishing with powers so disposed, in order to give trade a stable course, to define the rights of our merchants, and to enable the Government to support them, conventional rules of intercourse, the best that present circumstances and mutual opinion will permit, but temporary and liable to be from time to time abandoned or varied as experience and circumstances shall dictate; constantly keeping in view that it is folly in one nation to look for disinterested favors from another; that it must pay with a portion of its independence for whatever it may accept under that character; that by such acceptance it may place itself in the condition of having given equivalents for nominal favors, and yet of being reproached with ingratitude for not giving more. There can be no greater error than to expect or calculate upon real favors from nation to nation. It is an illusion which experience must cure, which a just pride ought to discard.

Though in reviewing the incidents of my Administration I am unconscious of intentional error, I am nevertheless too sensible of my defects not to think it probably that I may have committed many errors. Whatever they may be, I fervently beseech the Almighty to avert to mitigate the evils to which they may tend. I shall also carry with me the hope that my country will never cease to view them with indulgence, and that, after forty-five years of my life dedicated to its service with an upright zeal, the faults of incompetent abilities will be consigned to oblivion, as myself must soon be to the mansions of rest.

Relying on its kindness in this as in other things, and actuated by that fervent love toward it which is so natural to a man who views in it the native soil of himself and his progenitors for several generations, I anticipate with pleasing expectation that retreat in which I promise myself to realize without alloy the sweet enjoyment of partaking in the midst of my fellow—citizens the benign influence of good laws under a free government—the ever-favorite object of my heart, and the happy reward, as I trust, of our mutual care, labors, and dangers.

Gº. WASHINGTON

Notes

Chapter 1. A Grim Awakening

1. John Fitzpatrick, ed., *The Writings of George Washington*, (1931), vol. 32., 370. Hereinafter abbreviated as 32 GW.

2. B. A. Botkin, *American Anecdotes* (1940), 140.

3. Philadelphia Dunlap's *American Daily Advertiser*, 5 March 1793.

4. William Maclay, *Sketches of Debates in the First Senate of the* United States (1888), 122–26; E. S. Corwin, *The President: Office and Powers* (1948), 205.

5. *Gazette of the United States*, 7 March 1793.

6. 32 GW, 374–75.

7. Washington Irving, *Life of George Washington*, (1855–59), 5, 163. Hereinafter abbreviated as Irving.

8. John A. Carroll and Mary Wells Ashworth, *George Washington*, (1957), 7, 27–28. Hereinafter abbreviated as C&A.

9. 32 GW, 386.

10. Ibid., 385–90.

11. C&A, 7, 135.

12. Lear to Washington, 29 March 1793, 259 *Papers of George Washington*, 57 Library of Congress. Hereinafter abbreviated as *Papers of GW*, LC.

13. C&A, 7, 40–41.

14. Lear to Washington, 29 March 1793, 259 *Papers of GW*, LC.

15. Washington to Knox, *Henry Knox Papers*, Massachusetts Historical Society. Hereinafter abbreviated as *Knox Papers*, MHS.

16. 32 GW, 398–99.

17. Forrest Mcdonald, *The Presidency of George Washington*, (1974), 127.

18. Edward N. Saveth, *Understanding the American Past*, (1965), 141.

19. Simon Schama, *Citizen: a Chronicle of the French Revolution*, (1989), 49.

20. James T. Flexner, *George Washington: Anguish and Farewell*, (1969), 34.

21. C&A, 7, 40.

Chapter 2. Washington—and Genet's Fiasco

1. McDonald, *The Presidency of George Washington*, 124.

2. Henry Ammon, *The Genet Mission*, (1973), 9; Chinard, Gilbert, *George Washington as the French Knew Him*, (1940), 164.

3. Lear to Washington, 71 *Papers of GW*, LC.

4. Archives, Etats-Unis, 5. 37, fo. 217.

5. Meade Minnigerode, *Jefferson Friend of France*, (1928), 195. Morison, S. E. and Commager, H. S., *Growth of the American Republic*, 1, 339.

6. Boston *Columbian Centinel*, 29 May 1793.

7. Philadelphia *Dunlap's American Advertiser,* 23 May 1793.

8. Minnigerode, 202–03.

9. *Adams Papers,* MHS, also quoted in Minnigerode, 184.

10. Chinard, 105; Archives des Affaires Etrangeres, 36, 473–74 vo.

11. *The Papers of Thomas Jefferson,* Princeton, N.J. (1952-) VI, 291. Hereinafter abbreviated as *Jefferson Papers.*

12. Jefferson to Madison, 19 May 1793, Ford, P. L. (ed.) *The Writings of Thomas Jefferson* (1892–99), 6, 260–61. Hereinafter abbreviated as Ford.

13. Knox to Washington, 5 August 1793, *Papers of GW,* LC; also quoted in Callahan, North, *Henry Knox: General Washington's General,* (1958) 294.

14. Jefferson to Washington, 31 July 1793, Ford, 6, 360–61.

15. Ibid., 23 May 1793, 6, 266; also Ammon, 65.

16. F. McDonald, 129.

17. *Independent Chronicle,* 8 November 1793.

18. John C. Miller, *The Federalist Era,* (1960), 137; Hereinafter abbreviated as Miller.

19. Henry Cabot Lodge, *The Works of Alexander Hamilton,* (1885), 6, 159; Ford, 6, 338.

20. Claude Bowers, *Jefferson and Hamilton,* (1926), 221.

21. 33 GW, 23.

22. *New Hampshire and Vermont Journal,* 12 July 1793.

23. *Jefferson Papers,* 9, 164; C&A, 391.

24. *New London Bee,* 11 July 1793; *American Daily Advertiser,* 11 July 1793.

25. Eugene Perry Link, *Democratic-Republican Societies, 1790–1800,* (1965), 196.

26. Delaligarre to Genet, 7 August 1795, Genet Papers, LC and NYHS.

27. Frederick Jackson Turner, "Genet's Projected Attack on Louisiana and Florida," *American Historical Review,* October, 1878, 650.

28. Ford, *Jefferson,* 236.

29. Archibald Henderson, "Isaac Shelby and the Genet Mission," *Mississippi Valley Historical Review* 6, no. 4, March, 1920, 451–69.

30. Genet to Cornelia Clinton, 24 February 1794, *Genet Papers,* New York Historical Society; Ammon, 171.

31. Ammon, 177.

Chapter 3. Diversion and Devotion

1. Don B. Wilreth, *Variety Entertainment and Indoor Amusements,* (1982), 50; Spreaght, George A., *A History of the Circus,* (1980), 111–15.

2. Henry Adams, *History of the United States of America,* (1889), 1, 190.

3. Russell B. Nye, *The Cultural Life of the New Nation,* (1960), 145.

4. Ibid., 291.

5. Henry Adams, 186.

6. *Salem Gazette,* 26 June 1793; GW Papers, LC.

7. Paul F. Boller, Jr., *Presidential Anecdotes,* (1981), 10.

8. Quoted in Fiske, John, *The Critical Period of American History* (Reprint 1962), 159.

9. *Maryland Gazette,* 1 January 1790; quoted in Karninski, John and Jill McCaughan, *A Great and Good Man* (1989), 142–43.

10. Brissot de Warville, J. P., *Noveau Voyage dans les Etats Unis d'Amerique* (Paris, 1791).

11. North Callahan, *The Tories of the American Revolution*, (1963).

12. Henry Adams, 1, 41–74.

13. Flexner, 113.

14. 14 GW, 267.

15. 27 GW, 424.

16. Ibid., 407.

17. Henry Harbaugh, *The Religious Character of Washington*, (1863), 7–23.

18. Jared Sparks, *The Writings of George Washington*, (1834–37), 2, 492.

19. Harbaugh, 15.

20. Richard Rush, *Washington in Domestic Life*, (1857), 494.

21. E. C. McGurge, *The Religious Opinions and Character of George Washington*, (1836), 158.

22. Sparks, 3, 91; George Trevelyan, *The American Revolution*, (1899–1914), 3, 304.

23. George H. Moore, *Libels on George Washington* quoted in Norton, John N., *Life of General Washington* (1870), 253.

24. H. W. Smith (ed.), *Orderly Book of the Siege of Yorktown*, (1865), 47; Baker, W. S., *Character Portraits of Washington*, (1887), 288. Sparks, 504–05.

25. Sparks, 8, 504–05; McGurge, 147.

26. John Marshall, *The Life of George Washington*, (1832), 2, 445.

27. William J. Johnson, *George Washington: the Christian*, (1919), 44.

28. Benjamin J. Lossing, *Field Book of the Revolution*, (1850–52), 2, 28, 29; McGurge, 130. Wylie, Theodore W. J. *Washington a Christian?* 130. 159.

29. Norma C. Camp, *George Washington*, (1977), 141–63.

30. C&A, 934.

31. Harold D. Eberlein, "190 High Street, the Home of Washington and Adams, 1790–1800," v. 43, Part 1, Transactions of the American Philosophical Society, (1953), 161–68.

Chapter 4. Yellow Fever

1. 37 GW, 661.

2. J. H. Powell, *Bring Out Your Dead*, Philadelphia, (1949), 1–11.

3. *National Gazette*, 10 September 1793.

4. Powell, 8.

5. C&A, 7, 121.

6. Samuel Breck, *Recollections*, (1877), 193–96.

7. Powell, 18–20.

8. L. H. Butterfield, *The Letters of Benjamin Rush*, (1951), 21–24.

9. 33 GW, 84, Letters from Martha Washington, Mount Vernon Ladies Association Library.

10. North Callahan, *Henry Knox: General Washington's General*, (1958), 295–97.

11. Butterfield, 2, 21–24.

12. Powell, 61–63.

13. Ibid., 70.

14. 33 GW, 86–87.

15. Powell, 111.

16. Richard Morris and H. Conyers, *Encyclopedia of American History*, (1965), 772.

Chapter 5. A Working Holiday

1. 33 GW, 125.
2. *Georgetown Times*, 21 September 1793.
3. Callahan, Knox, 297.
4. Rush to James Kidd, 25 November 1793; 2 Butterfield, 626.
5. P. F. Ford, (ed.), *Writings of Thomas Jefferson*, (1892–99), 6, 440.
6. 34 GW, 163.
7. C&A, 143.
8. Ford, 6, 485–88.
9. Dumas Malone, *Jefferson and the Rights of Man*, (1951), 467.
10. Ibid., 448–49.
11. Ford, 1, 168.
12. John Marshall, *George Washington*, (1804–07), 5, 251.
13. 34 GW, 325.
14. Ibid., 118–19.
15. C&A, 143n.
16. 33 GW, 110.
17. Ibid., 88.
18. *Papers of GW*, Library of Congress, 101.
19. Knox to Anthony Wayne, 25 November 1793, *Wayne Papers*, f. 17, Pennsylvania Historical Society.
20. *American State Papers*, 1. Foreign Relations, 240.
21. Callahan, Knox, 298.
22. G. A. Phelps, *George Washington: the Founding of the Presidency*, 353.
23. *American Historical Association Report for 1899*, 467.
24. 31 GW, 320; Miller, 146.
25. Marshall, 5, 537.
26. *Independent Chronicle*, 17 January 1794.
27. Bradford Perkins, *The First Rapprochement*, (1955), 27.
28. Miller, 150.
29. Lodge, *Hamilton*, 5, 66.
30. Jared Sparks, *Life of Gouverneur Morris* (1832), 2, 248.
31. John E. Ferling, *The First of Men*, (1988), 258–59.
32. 35 GW, 465.

Chapter 6. The Pursuit of Peace

1. Washington to the Senate, 26 February 1794, 33 GW, 382.
2. Ames to Christopher Gore, 23 February 1794, C&A, 158.
3. Ibid., 158.
4. 34 GW, 332.
5. Samuel Flagg Bemis, *Jay's Treaty; a Study in Commerce and Diplomacy*, (1923), 291.
6. Ibid., 175–76.
7. J. C. Hamilton, (ed.), *The Works of Alexander Hamilton*, (1851), 4, 561.
8. 33 GW, 386.
9. *Gazette of the United States*, 6 June 1794.
10. 33 GW, 402.
11. *Pennsylvania Magazine of History and Biography*, (1885), 9, 483.

12. 33 GW, 411.
13. Ibid., 318.
14. Ford, 6, 512.
15. J. C. Hamilton, *Works*, 4, 516.

Chapter 7. The Whiskey Rebellion

1. Thomas P. Slaughter, *The Whiskey Rebellion*, (1986), 11–12.
2. Hamilton, *Works*, 6, 441.
3. *General Advertiser*, 18 January 1794.
4. Ibid.
5. James Carnahan, *The Pennsylvania Insurrection of 1794*, New Jersey Historical Society, 122.
6. 30 GW, 506.
7. Washington to Knox, 30 June 1794, 34 GW, 418.
8. Carnahan, 122.
9. Slaughter, 152.
10. 33 GW, 465.
11. William Finley, *History of the Insurrection in the Four Western Counties of Pennsylvania in the Year M.DCC.XCIV*, (1796), 107–08.
12. 33 GW, 475–76.
13. 33 GW, 268.
14. 268 *Papers of GW*, LC.
15. 1 Statutes, 264–65.
16. 33 GW, 457–61.
17. Callahan, *Knox*, 308–10.
18. 33 GW, 500.
19. Irving, 5, 224–25; North Callahan, *Daniel Morgan: Ranger of the Revolution*, (1961), 274.
20. Halifax, *North Carolina Journal*, 27 October 1794.
21. F. J. Turner, "English Policy Toward America, 1790–91," *American Historical Review*, 7, (1901–02), 717–19; *London Chronicle*, 6 August 1785.
22. Slaughter, 3.
23. *National Gazette*, 29 November 1792.
24. 34 GW, 7.
25. Miller, 162.
26. Ford, *Jefferson*, 7, 95.
27. Dunlap's & Claypoole's *American Daily Advertiser*, 21 September 1794.
28. Quoted in Irving, 5, 231–32.

Chapter 8. Philadelphia à la Carte

1. 269 *Papers of GW*, LC; 34 GW, 17–18.
2. 34 GW, 28–35.
3. Ibid., 36–37.
4. Annals of 3d Congress, 901–02.
5. Albert Bowman, *Struggle for Neutrality*, (1974), 172, 179; C&A, 225n.
6. 269 *Papers of GW*, 32: Fiske, John, "The Critical Period of American History," in Wish, Harvey, (ed.) *American Historians, a Selection* (1962), 161.
7. C&A, 190.

8. 34 GW, 59n; Monroe, Paul, *Founding of the American Public School System,* (1940), 1, 208.

9. David Ramsay, *History of the American Revolution* (1789), 2, 315–24.

10. Callahan, *Knox,* 312; 34 GW, 22–23.

11. South Carolina *State Gazette,* 17 January 1795.

12. 34 GW, 9, 10.

13. 271 *Papers of GW,* LC, 63.

14. C&A, 235n.

15. 34 GW, 139–40.

16. Ibid., 183.

17. 5 Hamilton, 633.

Chapter 9. Jay's Treaty Mistreated

1. John Adolphus, *History of England,* (1843), 6, 25–33.

2. Sparks, 2, 2.

3. Bowman, 122; *Adams Papers,* MHS, 9 February 1793.

4. Jay to Washington, 19 November 1794, GW Papers, LC.

5. *Hamilton,* 5, 27.

6. 36 GW, 195.

7. Bowman, 172–74.

8. 5 *Hamilton* 75; 34 GW, 109–10.

9. Ibid., 120–21.

10. George Pellew, *Life of John Jay,* (1890), 304.

11. Samuel F. Bemis, *Jay's Treaty,* (1923), 212–17.

12. Miller, 166–67.

13. Ibid., 167.

14. Webster to Oliver Wolcott, 30 July 1795, Warfel, H. R. (ed.), *Letters of Noah Webster,* (1953), 129–30.

15. Bemis, *Jay's Treaty,* 246–48; C&A, 239n.

16. C&A, 2.

17. 34 GW, 226–28.

18. *Independent Gazette,* 4 July 1795.

19. 34 GW, 261.

20. William Masterson, *William Blount,* (1954), 339–41.

21. John Quincy Adams to John Adams, 10 February 1796, *Adams Papers,* 5, 381, MHS; Churchill, Winston, *History of the English-Speaking People* (1956), 3, 346.

22. 34 GW, 262.

23. Ibid., 266.

24. Ibid., 263.

25. Ibid., 270.

Chapter 10. An Old Friend Departs

1. *The George Washington Papers,* University of Virginia.

2. Irving, 5, 251.

3. John B. McMaster, *History of the People of the United States,* (1883–1913), 2, 234.

4. Miller, 165–70.

5. Hamilton, 6, 39; 34 GW, 315.
6. 34 GW, 277.
7. Ibid., 339.
8. 34 GW, 339.
9. Edmund Randolph, *Vindication*, (1795), 17–18.
10. 34 GW, 343–45.
11. *Vindication*, 37–39.
12. Ibid., 40–75.
13. C&A, 285; Irving Brant, "Edmund Randolph not Guilty," *William and Mary Quarterly*, 3d Series, 5, 7, (1950), 180–98.
14. Stephen G. Kurtz, *The Presidency of John Adams*, (1951), 264.
15. 34, GW, 315.
16. Ibid., 331–34.
17. *Independent Chronicle*, 7 September 1795; *Aurora*, 21 September 1795.
18. 34 GW, 343.
19. Plumer to Jeremiah Smith, 5 January 1796, *William Plumer Papers*, LC.
20. Esmund Wright, *Presidents of the United States, 1779–97*, 1965, 214.
21. *Aurora*, 27 October 1795.
22. 34 GW, 386–93.
23. Ibid., 397.
24. Ford, *Writings*, 7, 32.
25. Annals of the 4th Congress, 5, 1, 196–97.
26. Adams to Abigail, 8 February 1796, *Letters to Wife*, 195.

Chapter 11. Political Parties Appear

1. John C. Miller, 172.
2. S. G. Brown, *The First Republicans* (1954), 51–55; 31 GW, 28.
3. *Virginia Magazine of History and Biography*, 44, (1938), 288–89.
4. *Imperial Herald*, 21 May 1799.
5. M. J. Dauer, *The Adams Federalists*, (1953), 211.
6. Miller, 115.
7. H. C. Lodge, *Alexander Hamilton*, (1882), 10, 96.
8. Annals of Congress, 5, 28 April 1796, 1116.
9. Ibid., 1117–20.
10. Ibid., 1226; Barrett, J. S., *The Federalist System*, (1906), 100.
11. Ibid., 1255; Rossiter, Clinton, *Conservatism in America*, (1957), 112.
12. 35 GW, 36–37.
13. J. R. Pole, *Foundations of American Independence, 1763–1815*, (1972), 202.
14. Giles to Jeremiah Smith, 19 April 1796, *William Plumer Papers*, 146, LC; Giles to Jefferson, 6 April 1796, *Jefferson Papers*, LC.
15. Irving, 5, 270.
16. 35 GW, 38–41.
17. *Mercantile Evening Advertiser*, 17 May 1796.
18. Charles Beard, *Economic Origins of American Democracy*, (1915), 256.
19. Joseph Charles, *Origins of the American Party System*, (1946), 90.
20. Sparks, 2, 40.
21. North Callahan, *Henry Knox: General Washington's General*, (1958).
22. R. H. Hofstadter, *The American Political Tradition*, (1973), 26, 35.

23. Irving, 5, 271–73.
24. British State Papers, LC.
25. 34 GW, 252.
26. Mrs. Robert Liston, *Memoirs*, 1797, Mt. Vernon Ladies Association.
27. 34 GW, 401.

Chapter 12. Farewell to the Arena

1. 34 GW, 433–40.
2. Flexner, 311.
3. *Presidential Anecdotes*, 41.
4. Thomas Twining, *Travels in America*, (1902), 132–33.
5. 34 GW, 445.
6. Lodge, *Hamilton*, 7, 388–414; Miller, 205.
7. 35 GW, 38.
8. Ibid., 103.
9. Monroe to Logan, 24 June 1795, *Papers of GW*, 93 LC.
10. M. D. Conway, *The Writings of Thomas Paine*, (1892), 3, 213–52.
11. 35 GW, 355.
12. 35 GW, 229–30.
13. *London Times*, 11 November 1796.
14. H. C. Syrett (ed.), *The Papers of Alexander Hamilton*, (1974), 20, 311–12, 384–85.
15. T. A. Bailey, *The American Spirit*, (1963), 168.
16. Esmund Wright, *Presidents of the United States*, 215.
17. *American Advertiser*, 23 February 1797.
18. 35 GW, 318–20.
19. C&A, 436.
20. 35 GW, 408–10.
21. Irving, 278–82.
22. Callahan, *Knox*, 362.
23. Adams to Abigail, 5 March 1797, *Letters to Wife*, 244.
24. William A. Duer, quoted in Irving, 5, 288.
25. "Presidents," *American Heritage*, (1968), 28.
26. O. P. Chitwood, Patrick, R. W., and Owsley, F. L., *The American People*, (1962), 227.
27. North Callahan, *George Washington: Soldier and Man*, (1972), 278.
28. Letters from Martha Washington, Mount Vernon Ladies Association.

Select Bibliography

The original papers in the Library of Congress including the Pennsylvania Insurrection Papers, Papers of Edmund Genet, Papers of Alexander Hamilton, Thomas Jefferson, James Madison, James Monroe, William Plumer, George Washington, Henry Knox, and Timothy Pickering.

New York Historical Society: Papers of Edmund Genet, Albert Gallatin.

New York Public Library: Papers of Alexander Hamilton, James Madison, and James Monroe.

Historical Society of Pennsylvania: Papers of Anthony Wayne.

Virginia Historical Society: Edmund Randolph photostats.

Columbia University Library: Papers of Alexander Hamilton.

Connecticut Historical Society: Papers of Oliver Wolcott.

Essex Institute: Papers of Timothy Pickering.

Mount Vernon Library: Powel Family Papers.

Massachusetts Historical Society: The Papers of Henry Knox.

University of Virginia, the George Washington Papers.

Printed Sources: Official Documents

American State Papers. Washington, 1832–34.

Debates and Proceedings in the Congress of the United States, (1789–1824), 42 vols., Washington, 1834–56.

Journal of the House of Representatives of the United States, 9 vols., Philadelphia, 1826.

Journals of the Senate of the United States, 5 vols., Washington, 1820.

Mayo, Bernard, ed. "Instructions to the British Ministers to the United States, 1791–1812. *American Historical Association Annual Report for 1936*, vol. 3, Washington, 1941.

Miller, Hunter, ed. *Treaties and Other International Acts of the United States*, 8 vols., Washington, 1931.

Richardson, James D., ed. *A Compilation of the Messages and Public Papers of the Presidents, 1789–1927*. 20 vols., Washington, 1896–1927.

Turner, Frederick Jackson, ed. "Correspondence of the French Ministers to the United States, 1791–1797." *American Historical Association Annual Report for 1903*, vol. 2, Washington, 1904.

Printed Letters, Diaries, Memoirs

Adams, Charles Francis, ed. *Letters of John Adams Addressed to his Wife.* 2 vols., Boston, 1841.

——— *The Life of John Adams,* 2 vols., Boston, 1874.

Adams, Henry, ed. *The Writings of Albert Gallatin,* 3 vols., Philadelphia, 1879.

Ames, Seth, ed. *Works of Fisher Ames.* 2 vols., Boston, 1854.

Baker, William Spohn. *Washington After the Revolution, 1784–99.* Philadelphia, 1898.

Brackenridge, Hugh H. *Incidents of the Insurrection in the Western Parts of Pennsylvania in the year, 1794.* 3 vols., Philadelphia, 1795.

Butterfield, Lyman H. ed. *The Letters of Benjamin Rush.* 2 vols. Princeton, 1951.

Carey, Matthew. *A Short Account of the Malignant Fever Lately Prevalent in Philadelphia.* Philadelphia, 1793.

Carnahan, James. "The Pennsylvania Insurrection of 1794, Commonly Called the 'Whiskey Insurrection.'" *New Jersey Historical Society Proceedings.* 6, (1853), 115–52.

Chinard, Gilbert, ed. *George Washington as the French Knew Him.* Princeton, 1940.

Cobbett, William. *Porcupine's Works.* 12 vols., London, 1801.

Conway, Moncure, ed. *George Washington and Mount Vernon.* Brooklyn, 1889.

——— *The Writings of Thomas Paine.* 4 vols., New York, 1894.

Corner, George W. *Autobiography of Benjamin Rush.* Princeton, 1948.

Currie, William. *A Description of the Malignant, Infectious Fever Prevailing at Present in Philadelphia.* Philadelphia, 1793.

Custis, George Washington Parke. *Recollections and Private Memoirs of Washington by His Adopted Son.* New York, 1860.

Daniel, Peter V., ed. *A Vindication of Edmund Randolph, Written by Himself and Published in 1795.* Richmond, 1855.

Decatur, Stephen, Jr. *Private Affairs of George Washington, from the Records and Accounts of Tobias Lear, Esquire, His Secretary.* Boston, 1933.

Deveze, Jean. *An Inquiry Into and Observations upon the causes and Effects of the Epidemic Disease in Philadelphia.* Philadelphia, 1794.

Dodd, William E., ed. "Letters of John Taylor." *John P. Branch Historical Papers of Randolph-Macon College.* vol. 2, Richmond, 1903.

Drake, Francis S. *Life and Correspondence of Henry Knox.* Boston, 1873.

Fauchet, Joseph. *A Sketch of the Present State of Our Political Relations With the United States of America.* Philadelphia, 1797.

Findley, William. *History of the Insurrection of the Four Western Counties of Pennsylvania in the Year MDCCXCIV.* Philadelphia, 1796.

Fitzpatrick, John C., ed. *The Diaries of George Washington.* 4 volumes. Boston and New York, 1925.

———ed. *Writings of George Washington.* 39 vols., Washington, 1931–44.

Ford, David. "Journal of an Expedition Made in the Autumn of 1794 into Western Pennsylvania." *New Jersey Historical Proceedings.* 8 (1859), 76–88.

Ford, Paul Leicester, *Writings of Thomas Jefferson*. 10 vols., New York, 1892–99.

Ford, Worthington Chauncey, ed. "Edmund Randolph on the British Treaty" *American Historical Review*. 12 (1906–07), 590–99.

———ed. *The Writings of George Washington*. 14 vols. New York, 1889–93.

Gottschalk, Louis, ed. *The Letters of Layfayette to Washington, 1777–99*. New York, 1944.

Gould, William. "Journal by . . . during an Expedition into Pennsylvania in 1794." *New Jersey Historical Society Proceedings*. 3 (1848–49), 173–91.

Green, Ashbel. *Life of . . . Begun to be Written by Himself*. New York, 1849.

Griswold, Rufus. *The Republican Court or American Society in the Days of Washington*. New York, 1854.

Hamilton, John Church, ed. *Works of Alexander Hamilton*. 7 vols., New York, 1850–51.

Hunt, Gaillard, ed. *The Writings of James Madison*. 9 vols., New York, 1900–10.

Ingersoll, Charles Jared. *Recollections: Historical, Political, Biographical and Social*. Philadelphia, 1861.

Jameson, J. Franklin, ed. "Letters of Phineas Bond, British Consul at Philadelphia, to the Foreign Office of Great Britain, 1790–94." *American Historical Association Annual Report for 1897*, 454–568.

Jenkins, C. F., ed. *Jefferson's Germantown Letters*. Philadelphia, 1906.

Johnston, Henry P., ed. *The Correspondence and Public Papers of John Jay*. 4 vols., New York, 1890–93.

Letters and Recollections of George Washington . . . With a Diary of Washington's Last Days, kept by Mr. Lear. New York, 1906.

Lipscomb, Andrew A. and Albert E. Bergh, eds. *Writings of Thomas Jefferson*. 20 vols., Washington, 1903.

Lodge, Henry Cabot., ed. *The Works of Alexander Hamilton*. 12 vols., New York, 1904.

Marsh, Philip M. *The Prose of Philip Freneau*. New Brunswick, N. J., 1955.

Monroe, James. *A View of the Conduct of the Executive of the United States*. Philadelphia, 1797.

Morris, Anne C., ed. *Diary and Letters of Gouverneur Morris*. 2 vols., New York, 1888.

Moultrie, William, *Memoirs*, 2 vols., New York, 1802.

Mount Vernon Ladies Association Annual Report for 1950. Mount Vernon, 1951.

Pickering, Octavius and Charles W. Upham. *Life of Timothy Pickering*, 4 vols., Boston, 1867–73.

Randolph, Edmund, *Political Truth . . . or an Inquiry Into the Truth of the Charges Preferred Against Mr. Randolph*. Philadelphia, 1796.

Rush, Benjamin. *An Account of the Bilious Remitting Fever as it Appeared in the City of Philadelphia in the Year, 1793*. Philadelphia, 1794.

Sawvel, Franklin B., ed. *The Complete Anas of Thomas Jefferson*. New York, 1930.

Skeel, Emily E. F., comp. *Notes on the Life of Noah Webster*. 2 vols., New York, 1912.

Sparks, Jared, ed. *The Writings of George Washington*. 4 vols., Boston, 1853.

Steiner, Bernard C. *The Life and Correspondence of James McHenry*. Cleveland, 1907.

Trumbull, John. *Autobiography, Reminiscences and Letters*. New York, 1841.

Turner, Frederick Jackson, ed. "Documents on the Relations of France to Louisiana," *American Historical Review*. 3 (1898) 490–515.

——— ed. "The Mangourit Correspondence in Respect to Genet's Projected Attack on the Floridas, 1793–94." *American Historical Annual Report for 1897*, Washington, 1898, 569–679.

Twining, Thomas. *Travels in America 100 Years Ago*. New York, 1894.

Wansey, Henry. *An Excursion to the United States of North America in 1794*. London, 1798.

Washington, Henry A. *The Writings of Thomas Jefferson*. 9 vols., Washington, 1853–54.

Secondary Sources
Histories, Biographies, and Articles

Abernethy, Thomas P. *From Frontier to Plantation in Tennessee*. Chapel Hill, N.C. 1932.

Adams, Henry, *The Life of Albert Gallatin*. Philadelphia, 1879.

Adams, Henry C. *Taxation in the United States, 1776–1816*. Baltimore, 1884.

Adams, Herbert B. *Maryland's Influence Upon Land Cessions to the United States*, New York, no date.

Alden, John R. *George Washington: a Biography*. Baton Rouge, 1984.

Albert, George D. ed. *History of the County of Westmoreland, Pa. Philadelphia, 1882*.

Ambler, Charles H. *George Washington and the West*. New York, 1971.

Asonevich, Walter J. *George Washington's Speeches and Addresses: Origins of an American Presidential Rhetoric*. Dover, Del., 1987.

Baldwin, Leland D. *Whiskey Rebels: The Story of a Frontier Uprising*. Pittsburgh, 1939.

Barker, Creighton. "A Case Report." *Yale Journal of Biology and Medicine*. 9 (1936–37), 185–87.

Bassett, John Spencer. *The Federalist System, 1789–1801*. New York, 1906.

Beard, Charles A. *Economic Origins of Jeffersonian Democracy*. New York, 1915.

Bellamy, Francis R. *The Private Life of George Washington*. New York, 1951.

Bemis, Samuel Flagg. *A Diplomatic History of the United States*. New York, 1955.

——— *Jay's Treaty: A Study in Commerce and Diplomacy*. New York, 1923.

——— "The London Mission of Thomas Pinckney. 1792–96." *American Historical Review*. 28 (1923), 228–47.

——— "Payment of the French Loans to the United States, 1777–1795". *Current History*. 23 (1926), 824–31.

—— Pinckney's Treaty: a Study of America's Advantage from Europe's Distress, 1783–1800. Baltimore, 1926.

—— "Washington's Farewell Address: a Foreign Policy of Independence." American Historical Review. 39 (1934), 250–68.

Berry, Jane M. "The Indian Policy of Spain in the Southwest, 1783–1795." Mississippi Valley Historical Review. 3 (1917), 462–77.

Beveridge, Albert J. The Life of John Marshall. 4 vols., Boston, 1916–19.

Binney, Horace. An Inquiry Into the Formation of Washington's Farewell Address. New York, 1969.

Bond, Beverly W. "The Monroe Mission to France, 1794–1796." Johns Hopkins University Studies in Historical and Political Science. 25 (1907), 9–103.

Bourne, Miriam Anne; Hugh Rankin; and Daniel Blake Smith. First Family: George Washington and His Intimate Relations. New York, 1981.

Bowers, Claude G. Jefferson and Hamilton: the Struggle for Democracy in America. Boston, 1925.

Brackenridge, Henry M. History of the Western Insurrection in Western Pennsylvania, Commonly Called the Whiskey Insurrection. Pittsburgh, 1859.

Brant, Irving. "Edmund Randolph, Not Guilty!" William and Mary Quarterly. Third Series. 7 (1950), 180–98.

—— James Madison. 3 vols., Indianapolis, 1941– .

Bryan, W. B. A History of the National Capital. 2 vols., New York, 1914–16.

Burt, Alfred L. The United States, Great Britain and British North America, 1783–1812. New Haven, 1940.

Callahan, Charles M. Washington: the Man and the Mason. Washington, 1913.

Callahan, North. Henry Knox: General Washington's General. New York, 1958.

—— Daniel Morgan: Ranger of the Revolution. New York, 1961.

—— Royal Raiders: the Tories of the American Revolution. Indianapolis, New York, 1963.

—— Flight From the Republic: Vol. 2, The Tories of the American Revolution. Indianapolis, N.Y., 1967.

—— George Washington: Soldier and Man. New York, 1972.

Camp, Norma C. George Washington: Man of Courage and Prayer. Milford, Mich., 1977.

Carroll, John A. and Ashworth, Mary Wells, George Washington: First in Peace. New York, 1957. (Successors to Douglas Freeman)

Carroll, Thomas F. "Freedom of Speech and Press in the Federalist Period." Michigan Law Review. 18 (1920), 615–51.

Channing, Edward. History of the United States. 6 vols., New York, 1905–25.

—— "Washington and Parties, 1789–97." Massachusetts Historical Society Proceedings. 47 (1914), 35–44.

Chase, Philander D., ed. W. W. Abbott, series ed. Washington, George; North Callahan; and Charles Royster. The Papers of George Washington, Revolutionary War Series. Vol. 1, June–September 1775. Charlottesville, 1985.

Childs, Francis S. French Refugee Life in the United States, 1790–1800. Baltimore, 1940.

Chnard, Gilbert, ed. *George Washington as the French Knew Him.* Westport, Conn., n.d.

Clark, Mary E. *Peter Porcupine in America: The Career of William Cobbett, 1792–1800.* Philadelphia, 1939.

Clark, Victor S. *History of Manufactures in the United States.* 3 vols. Washington, 1916–28.

Clauder, Anna C. *American Commerce as Affected by the Wars of the French Revolution and Napoleon, 1793–1810.* Philadelphia, 1932.

Coulter, E. Merton. "The Efforts of the Democratic Societies of the West to Open the Navigation of the Mississippi." *Mississippi Valley Historical Review.* vol. 11 (1924), 376–89.

Craig, Neville B. *The History of Pittsburgh.* Pittsburgh, 1951.

Crandall, Reginia K. "Genet's Projected Attack on Louisiana and the Floridas, 1793–94." Doctoral Dissertation. University of Chicago, 1928.

Cresson, William Penn. *James Monroe.* Chapel Hill, N. C., 1946.

Cullen, Joseph P. "Washington at Mount Vernon," *American History Illustrated.* (May 1974), 4–11, 45–48.

Cunliffe, Marcus. *George Washington: Man and Monument.* New York, 1960.

Dangerfield, Royden J. *In Defense of the Senate: a Study in Treaty Making.* Norman, Okla., 1933.

Darling, Arthur Burr. *Our Rising Empire, 1763–1803.* New Haven, 1940.

Decatur, Stephen, *The Private Affairs of George Washington.* New York, 1969.

DeConde, Alexander, *Entangling Alliance: Politics and Diplomacy Under George Washington.* Durham, N.C., 1958.

Didier, Eugene L. "Le Citoyan Genet." *Revue de questions historiques.* 92 (1912), unpaged.

Downes, Randolph C. *Council Fires on the Upper Ohio: a Narrative of Indian Affairs in the Upper Ohio Valley until 1795.* Pittsburgh, 1940.

———— *Frontier Ohio, 1788–1803.* Columbus, 1935.

———— "Indian Affairs in the Southwest Territory, 1790–96." *Tennessee Historical Magazine.* 3d Series. vol. 2 (1937), 135–50.

Drinker, Cecil K. *Not So Long Ago: A Chronicle of Medicine and Doctors in Colonial Philadelphia.* New York, 1937.

Driver, Carl S. *John Sevier, Pioneer of the Old Southwest.* Chapel Hill, N. C., 1932.

Dunbar, Louis B. *A Study of Monarchical Tendencies in the United States from 1776 to 1801.* Urbana, Ill., 1922.

Dupre, Huntley. "The Kentucky Gazette Reports the French Revolution." *Mississippi Valley Historical Review.* 26 (1939): 163–80.

Emery, Noemi. *Washington: a Biography.* New York, 1976.

Eisenhart, Luther P., ed. *Historic Philadelphia from the Founding Until the Early Nineteenth Century.* vol. 43, Part 1, Transactions of the American Philosophical Society. Phildelphia, 1953.

Ellery, Elouise. *Brissot de Warville: a Study in the History of the French Revolution.* Boston, 1915.

Farrand, Max. "The Indian Boundary Line." *American Historical Review.* 10 (1905): 782–91.

Ferguson, Russell J. *Early Western Pennsylvania Politics.* Pittsburgh, 1938.

Ferling, John E. *The First of Men.* Knoxville, Tenn., 1988.

Fitzpatrick, John C. *The Last Will and Testament of George Washington.* Mount Vernon, n.d.

Fletcher, Mildred S. "The Policy of France Toward the Mississippi Valley in the Period of Washington and Adams." American *Historical Review.* 10 (1905): 249–79.

Flexner, James T. *Doctors on Horseback: Pioneers of American Medicine.* New York, 1937.

——— *George Washington: Anguish and Farewell.* Boston, 1972.

Flower, Lenore E. "Visit of President George Washington to Carlisle 1794." Carlise, Pa., 1932.

Ford, Paul L. *The True George Washington.* Salem, N.H., n.d.

——— *Washington and The Theater,* New York, 1970.

Ford, Worthington C. *Washington as an Employer and Importer of Labor.* New York, 1971.

Forman, Samuel E. *The Political Activities of Philip Freneau.* Baltimore, 1902.

Freeman, Douglas Southall. *George Washington: A Biography.* 6 vols., New York, 1948–54.

Gaintner, J. Richard. "The 250th Birthday Anniversary: George Washington, 1732–99." *Journal, Lancaster County Historical Society.* 85, no. 2 (1981): 50–52.

Ganoe, William A. *History of the United States Army.* New York, 1924.

Gibbs, George. *Memoirs of the Administrations of Washington and John Adams.* New York, 1971.

Graham, Gerald S. *Sea Power and British North America, 1783–1820.* Cambridge, 1941.

Hall, F. R. "Genet's Western Intrigue, 1793–94." *Illinois State Historical Society Journal.* 21 (1928): 355–81.

Harmon, George D. *Sixty Years of Indian Affairs, 1789–1850.* Chapel Hill, N. C., 1941.

Harrison, James A. *George Washington: Patriot, Soldier, Statesman, First President.* New York, n.d.

Hart, James. *The American Presidency in Action.* New York, 1948.

Hayden, Ralston. *The Senate and Treaties, 1789–1817.* New York, 1920.

Hazen, Charles Downer. *Contemporary American Opinion of the French Revolution.* Baltimore, 1897.

——— *The French Revolution.* vols. 1–2, New York, 1932.

Helderman, Leonard C. *George Washington: Patron of Learning.* New York, 1932.

Henderson, Archibald, "Isaac Shelby and the Genet Mission." *Mississippi Valley Historical Review.* 6 (1920): 451–69.

Hildreth, Richard. *The History of the United States.* 6 vols., New York, 1849–56.

Hidy, Ralph W. "The House of Baring in American Trade and Finance." *Harvard Studies in Business History.* 14 (1950): 63.

Hunsicker, Frank R. "What Kind of Leader Was George Washington?" *West Georgia College Review.* 15 (1983): 29–36.

Hutchins, J. G. B. *American Maritime Industries and Public Policy, 1789–1914.* Cambridge, 1941.

Hyneman, Charles S. *The First American Neutrality: A Study of the American Understanding of Neutral Obligations during the Years 1792 to 1815.* Urbana, Ill., 1934.

Irving, Washington. *Life of George Washington.* Tarrytown, N.Y., 1975.

Jackson, Donald and Dorothy Twohig, eds. *The Diaries of George Washington.* vol. 6, January 1790–December 1799. Charlottesville, 1979.

James, James Alton. "French Diplomacy and American Politics, 1783–1812." *American Historical Association Annual Report for 1911.* vol. 1, 151–63.

—— *The Life of George Rogers Clark.* Chicago, 1928.

Jones, Howard Mumford. *America and French Culture, 1750–1848.* Chapel Hill, N. C. 1927.

Jones, Robert F. "George Washington and the Politics of the Presidency." *Presidential Studies Quarterly.* 10: 1 (1980): 28–35.

—— *George Washington.* New York, 1986.

Kavinski, John P., ed. *A Great and Good Man.* Madison, Wis., 1989.

Ketchum, Richard M. *The World of George Washington.* New York, 1984.

Klapthor, Margaret B. *George Washington: A Figure Upon the Stage.* Washington, 1982.

Knox, J. H. Mason. "The Medical History of George Washington: His Physicians, Friends and Advisers." *Bulletin of the Institute of Medical History.* (1933): 174–91.

Koch, Adrienne. *Jefferson and Madison: the Great Collaboration.* New York, 1950.

Krout, John A. and Dixon Ryan Fox. *The Completion of Independence, 1790–1830.* New York, 1944.

LaFollette, R. R. "The American Revolutionary Foreign Debt and its Liquidation." Doctoral Dissertation, George Washington University, 1931.

Lambertson, James M. *Washington as a Freemason.* Philadelphia, 1902.

LaRoche, René. *Yellow Fever Considered in its Historical, Pathological, Etiological and Therapeutical Relations.* 3 vols., Philadelphia, 1855.

Leary, Lewis. *That Rascal Freneau.* New Brunswick, N. J., 1941.

Levitt, Orpha E. "British Policy on the Canadian Frontier, 1789–92." *Wisconsin Historical Society Proceedings for 1915,* 151–85.

Letters of George Washington in the Library of the Connecticut Historical Society. Hartford, 1932.

Libby, Oran G. "Political Factions in Washington's Administrations". *University of North Dakota Quarterly Journal.* 2 (1913): 293–318.

Link, Eugene P. *Democrat-Republican Societies, 1790–1800.* New York, 1942.

Lodge, Henry Cabot. *George Washington.* 2 vols. Boston, 1889.

Lossing, Benson J. *Mount Vernon and Its Associations.* New York, 1859.

Longmore, Paul K. "The Enigma of George Washington: How did the Man Become the Myth?" *Reviews in American History.* 13; no. 2 (1985): 184–90.

Lyon, E. Wilson. "The Directory and the United States." *American Historical Review.* 43 (1938): 514–32.

————— *Louisiana in French Diplomacy, 1759–1804.* Norman, Okla., 1934.

McLaughlin, Andrew C. "The Western Posts and the British Debts." *American Historical Association Annual Report for 1894.* (1894): 413–44.

McMaster, John Bach. *History of the People of the United States.* 8 vols., New York, 1886–1913.

McMurry, Donald L. "The Indian Policy of the Federal Government and the Economic Development of the Southwest, 1789–1801." *Tennessee Historical Magazine.* 1 (1915–16): 21–39, 106–19.

Mahan, Alfred Thayer. *The Influence of Sea Power Upon the French Revolution and Empire, 1793–1812.* 2 vols., Boston, 1892.

Malone, Dumas. *Jefferson and His Time.* 4 vols., New York, 1948–62.

Mantoux, Paul. "Le comité de salut public et la mission de Genet aux Etats-Unis." *Revue d'Histoire moderne et contemporaine.* 13 (Paris, 1909–10), 5–35.

Marshall, John. *Life of George Washington.* New York, 1804–7.

McDonald, Forrest. *The Presidency of George Washington.* Lawrence, Kan., 1974.

Marx, Rudolph. "A Medical Profile of George Washington." *American Heritage.* 6, no. 5 (August 1955), 43–47, 106–107.

Masterson, William H. *William Blount.* Baton Rouge, 1954.

Miller, William. "Democratic Societies and the Whiskey Rebellion." *Pennsylvania Magazine of History and Biography.* 62 (1938), 324–49.

Minnigerode, Meade. *Jefferson, Friend of France, 1793: The Career of Edmund Charles Genet as Revealed by his Private Papers, 1763–1834.* New York, 1928.

Monaghan, Frank. *John Jay, Defender of Liberty.* Indianapolis, 1935.

Moore, John Bassett. *International Adjudications, Ancient and Modern: History and Documents.* 6 vols., New York, 1929–34.

Morgan, Edmund S. *The Meaning of Independence.* Charlottesville, 1979.

————— *The Genius of George Washington.* New York, 1987.

Morgan, John Hill, and Fielding, Mantle. *The Life Portraits of Washington and Their Replicas.* Philadelphia, 1931.

Morison, Samuel Eliot. *The Maritime History of Massachusetts.* Boston, 1921.

————— *History of the American People.* New York, 1965.

Morris, Richard. *John Jay: the Nation and the Court.* Boston, 1967.

Morse, Anson E. *The Federalist Party in Massachusetts.* Princeton, 1909.

Mumford, James G. *A Narrative of Medicine in America.* Philadelphia, 1903.

Murdock, R. K. "The Genesis of the Genet Schemes." *Franco-American Review.* 2 (1938): 81–97.

Newcomb, Josiah T. "New Light on Jay's Treaty." *American Journal of International Law.* 28 (1934): 81–97.

Niles, Blair. *Martha's Husband.* New York, 1951.

Nordham, John. "George Washington: A Remembrance on the 25th Anniversary of His Birth." *Daughters of the American Revolution Magazine.* 116: 2 (1982): 84–88.

Oberholtzer, Ellis P. Philadelphia: *A History of the City and Its People.* 4 vols., Philadelphia, 1912.

Ogg, Frederick Austin. *The Opening of the Mississippi: a Struggle for Supremacy in the American Interior.* New York, 1904.

Osgood, Herbert L. "The British Evacuation of the United States." *Rochester Historical Society Publications.* 6 (1927), 55–63.

Packard, Francis R. *History of Medicine in the United States.* 2 vols., New York, 1931.

Padover, Saul., ed. *The Washington Papers: Basic Selections.* New York, 1955.

Paltsits, Victor H. *Washington's Farewell Address.* New York, 1935.

Parkes, Henry Bamford, *The United States of America: A History.* New York, 1959.

Pellew, George. *Life of John Jay.* New York, 1890.

Perkins, Bradford. *The First Rapprochement: England and the United States, 1795–1805.* Philadelphia, 1955.

———— "Lord Hawkesbury and the Jay-Grenville Negotiations". *Mississippi Valley Historical Review.* 40 (1953): 291–304.

Pessen, Edward. "George Washington's Farewell Address, The Cold War and the Timeless National Interest." *Journal of the Early Republic.* 7, no. 1 (1987): 1–27.

———— "George Washington and the Building of the Constitution: Presidential Interpretation and Constitutional Development." *Congress and the Presidency, 1985.* 12, no. 2 (1985): 95–109.

Phelps, Glenn A. "George Washington and the Founding of the Presidency." *Presidential Studies Quarterly.* New York, 17, no. 2 (1987): 345–63.

Phillips, Edward H. "The Public Career of Timothy Pickering." Doctoral Dissertation, Harvard University, Cambridge, Mass., 1950.

Powell, John H. *Bring Out Your Dead: the Great Plague of Yellow Fever in Philadelphia in 1793.* Philadelphia, 1949.

Pryor, W. J. "The Closed Bite Relations of the Jaws of George Washington, with Comments on his Tooth Troubles and General Health." *Journal of American Dental Association.* 20 (1933): 567–79.

Randall, James G. "George Washington and 'Entangling Alliances'." *South Atlantic Quarterly.* 30 (1931): 222–29.

Reuter, Frank T. and Johnson, Richard R. *Trials and Triumph: George Washington's Foreign Policy.* Fort Worth, 1983.

Rich, Bennett M. *The Presidents and Civil Disorder.* Washington, 1941.

Riddell, William R. *Life of John Simcoe, First Lieutenant Governor of Upper Canada, 1792–96.* Toronto, 1926.

Rippy, J. Fred and Angie Debo. "The Historical Background of the American Policy of Isolation." *Smith College Studies in History.* 9 (1924): 71–165.

Roberts, Allen E. *George Washington: Master Mason.* Oklahoma City, 1976.

Rose, J. Holland. *The Revolutionary and Napoleonic Era, 1789–1815.* Cambridge, England, 1901.

Royce, Charles C. "Indian Land Cessions." *American Bureau of Ethnology. Eighteenth Annual Report.* Part 2 (1896–97): 521–997.

Russell, Nelson V. *The British Regime in Michigan and the Old Northwest, 1760–1796.* Northfield, Minn., 1939.

Savage, Kirk. "The Self-Made Movement: George Washington and the Fight to Erect a National Memorial." Winterthur, Del., 22, no. 4 (1987): 225–242.

Schama, Simon. *Citizen: a Chronicle of the French Revolution.* New York, 1989.

Schwartz, Barry. *George Washington: The Making of an American Symbol.* New York, 1987.

Schachner, Nathan. *Alexander Hamilton.* New York, 1946.

—— *The Founding Fathers.* New York, 1954.

—— *Thomas Jefferson: A Biography.* 2 vols., New York, 1951.

Scharf, J. Thomas, and Wescott Thompson. *History of Philadelphia, 1609–1884.* 3 vols., Philadelphia, 1884.

Schminke, Frederick A. *Genet: the Origins of his Mission to America.* Toulouse, 1939.

Schouler, James. *History of the United States Under the Constitution.* 6 vols., New York, 1880–99.

Shepherd, William R. "Wilkinson and the Beginnings of the Spanish Conspiracy." *American Historical Review.* 9 (1904): 400–506.

Schulz, Constance B. "The Papers of George Washington: A Review." *Virginia Magazine of History and Biography.* 96, no. 1 (1988): 95–104.

Sears, Louis M. *George Washington and the French Revolution.* Westport, Conn. 1973.

Sioussat, St. George L. "The Farewell Address in the Twentieth Century." *Genealogical and Historical Chronicle of the University of Pennsylvania.* 34 (1932): 319–30.

Sipe, Chester Hale. *Mount Vernon and the Washington Family.* Butler, Pa., 1925.

Slocum, Charles E. *The Ohio Country, 1783–1815.* New York, 1910.

Smith, James M. *George Washington: a Profile.* New York, 1969.

Spaulding, E. Wilder. *His Excellency George Clinton.* New York, 1938.

Stetson, Charles W. *Washington and His Neighbors.* Richmond, 1956.

Stevens, Wayne E. *The Northwest Fur Trade, 1763–1800.* Urbana, Ill., 1928.

Tansill, Charles C. "The Treaty-Making Powers of the Senate." *American Journal of International Law.* 18 (1924): 459–82.

Tachau, Mary K. Bonsteel. "George Washington and the Reputation of Edmund Randolph." *Journal of American History.* 73, no. 1 (1986): 15–34.

Tatsch, J. Hugo. *The Facts About Washington as a Freemason.* New York, 1931.

Tebbel, John; Sara Miles Watts; Robert G. Blanchard; and Kernell. *The Press and the Presidency: from George Washington to Ronald Reagan.* N.Y. 1985.

Thomas, Charles M. *American Neutrality in 1793: a Study in Cabinet Government.* New York, 1931.

Thomas, Earl Bruce. *Political Tendencies in Pennsylvania, 1783–94.* Philadelphia, 1939.

Thompson, Isabel. "The Blount Conspiracy," *East Tennessee Historical Society Publications.* 2 (1930): 3–21.

Tinkcom, Harry M. *The Republicans and Federalists in Pennsylvania, 1790–1801: a Study in National Stimulus and Local Response.* Philadelphia, 1950.

Trescot, William H. *The Diplomatic History of the Administrations of Washington and Adams, 1789–1801.* Boston, 1857.

Tucker, Glenn. *Mad Anthony Wayne and the New Nation.* Harrisburg, Pa., 1973.

Turner, Frederick Jackson. "The Diplomatic Contest for the Mississippi Valley," *Atlantic.* 93 (1904): 676–91, 807–17.

——— "The Origin of Genet's Projected Attack on Louisiana and the Floridas." *American Historical Review.* (1898): 650–71.

Usher, R. G. "Washington and Entangling Alliances." *North American Review.* 204 (1916): 29–38.

Veech, James. *The Monongahela of Old: Historical Sketches of Southwestern Pennsylvania to the Year 1800.* Pittsburgh, 1858–92.

Wallace, Paul A. W. *The Muhlenbergs of Pennsylvania.* Philadelphia, 1950.

Walther, Daniel. *Gouverneur Morris, temoin de deux revolutions.* Lausanne, 1932.

Ward, Townsend. "The Insurrection of the Year 1794 in the Western Counties of Pennsylvania." *Pennsylvania Historical Society Memoirs.* 6 (1858): 117–203.

Weems, Mason L. *Life of Washington,* Cambridge, Mass., 1962.

Weinberg, Albert K. "Washington's 'Great Rule' in its Historical Evolution." *Historiography and Urbanization: Essays in American History in Honor of W. Stull Holt.* Baltimore, 1941, 263–85.

Whitaker, Arthur P. "Godoy's Knowledge of the Terms of Jay's Treaty." *American Historical Review.* 35 (1930): 804–10.

——— "New Light on the Treaty of San Lorenzo." *Mississippi Valley Historical Review.* 15 (1929): 435–54.

White, Leonard. *The Federalists: A Study in Administrative History.* New York, 1948.

Wick, Wendy C.; Lloyd, Phoebe. *George Washington, an American Icon: The Eighteenth-Century Graphic Portraits.* Charlottesville, 1982.

Wildes, Harry E. *Anthony Wayne.* New York, 1941.

Wiley, Richard T. *The Whiskey Insurrection: A General View.* Elizabeth, Pa., 1912.

Willis, Garry; Ward, John William; Colbourn, Trevor; Banning, Lance; Thomas E. Templin; Paul K. Longmore; and Charles Royster. *Cincinnatus: George Washington and the Enlightenment.* Garden City, N.Y., 1984.

Willson, Beckles, *Friendly Relations: A Narrative of Britain's Ministers and Ambassadors to America, 1791–1930.* Boston, 1934.

Wilson, Frazier E. *The Peace of Mad Anthony.* Greenville, Ohio, 1909.

Wilson, Woodrow, *George Washington.* New York, 1969.

Wilstach, Paul. *Mount Vernon.* Indianapolis, 1930.

Woodbury, Margaret. *Public Opinion in Philadelphia, 1789–1801.* Durham, N.C., 1919.

Woodfin, Maude Howlett. "Citizen Genet and His Mission." Doctoral Dissertation, University of Chicago, Chicago, Ill., 1928.

Lecture on Tape

Hobsbawm, Eric, Emeritus Professor, University of London: *The French Revolution and Its Modern Legacy: A Bicentennial Reappraisal at New York University*. 1990.

About the Author

Dr. North Callahan is Professor Emeritus of History at New York University, where he specialized in early American history. He is the author of fifteen books on American history and biography. Born in Tennessee, he was graduated from the University of Tennessee with honors. He holds the Master's Degree in American History from Columbia University and the Ph.D. in American Civilization from New York University, where he was Class Representative and a Penfield Fellow. In an honorary degree from the University of Chattanooga, the citation said in part, "Professor Callahan has found teaching and writing exciting."

The author was a newspaper reporter, editor, and columnist in Tennessee, Texas, and New York, eventually writing a syndicated column. In World War II, he was a Lieutenant Colonel in the U.S. Army, serving as editor of "Army Life Magazine" and supervisor of the national radio program, "The Voice of the Army," which received an Ohio State University award. Entering the field of higher education, Dr. Callahan became chairman of the history department at Finch College, then joined the faculty of New York University, where he taught American History at Washington Square College and the Graduate School of Arts and Science until his retirement in 1973. During this time, he was a visiting lecturer at several British universities and a visiting professor at the University of Tennessee. He is a member of national historical societies, was president of the Civil War Round Table of New York and founder of the American Revolution Round Table, member of the New York City Bicentennial Commission, and has appeared on national radio and television. North Callahan has contributed to the Encyclopedia Britannica, Colliers Encyclopedia, and others, and has contributed articles and reviewed books for newspapers and scholarly journals. He has been historical consultant to American Express, Twentieth Century-Fox, and National Cash Register. In 1983 he was given the Distinguished Alumnus Award of the University of Tennessee at Chattanooga.

Books by North Callahan include a biography of George Washington that was adopted by a national book club; a biography of

Henry Knox, selected by the *New York Times* as an outstanding biography of the publication year; a biography of Daniel Morgan, similarly selected by the *New York Herald-Tribune;* two volumes on the Tories of the American Revolution; a biography of Carl Sandburg; a history of the Tennessee Valley Authority; a historical novel on the wife of Benedict Arnold; an autobiographical novel; and he was editor of the Leaders of the American Revolution series. He is married and has a son and daughter.

Index